KAHLIL GIBRAN
CLASSICS COLLECTION

*The Prophet, The Madman, Sand and Foam,
The Broken Wings, A Tear and a Smile, Twenty Drawings,
The Forerunner & Spirits Rebellious*

by
KAHLIL GIBRAN

CLASSY
PUBLISHING

KAHLIL GIBRAN CLASSICS COLLECTION
by Kahlil Gibran
Published by Classy Publishing, 2023

www.classypublishing.com
info@classypublishing.com

ISBN: 978-93-5522-545-0

No part of this publication may be reproduced, stored in a retrieval system, or transmitted, in any form or by any means, electronic, mechanical, photocopying, recording or otherwise, without the prior permission of the publisher.

Cover Design by Classy Publishing

CONTENTS

THE PROPHET	1
The Coming of the Ship	3
On Love	8
On Marriage	11
On Children	13
On Giving	14
On Eating and Drinking	18
On Work	19
On Joy and Sorrow	21
On Houses	22
On Clothes	24
On Buying and Selling	25
On Crime and Punishment	26
On Laws	30
On Freedom	32
On Reason and Passion	34
On Pain	35
On Self-Knowledge	36
On Teaching	38
On Friendship	39
On Talking	40
On Time	41
On Good and Evil	42
On Prayer	44
On Pleasure	46
On Beauty	48
On Religion	50
On Death	52
The Farewell	53

THE MADMAN 63

God 66
My Friend 67
The Scarecrow 69
The Sleep-Walkers 70
The Wise Dog 71
The Two Hermits 72
On Giving and Taking 73
The Seven Selves 74
War 76
The Fox 77
The Wise King 78
Ambition 79
The New Pleasure 80
The Other Language 81
The Pomegranate 83
The Two Cages 84
The Three Ants 85
The Grave-Digger 86
On the Steps of the Temple 87
The Blessed City 88
The Good God and the Evil God 90
Defeat 91
Night and the Madman 92
Faces 94
The Greater Sea 95
Crucified 97
The Astronomer 98
The Great Longing 99
Said a Blade of Grass 100
The Eye 101
The Two Learned Men 102
When My Sorrow Was Born 103
And When My Joy Was Born 104
"The Perfect World" 105

SAND AND FOAM	107
THE BROKEN WINGS	163
Silent Sorrow	167
The Hand of Destiny	169
Entrance to the Shrine	172
The White Torch	175
The Tempest	177
The Lake of Fire	184
Before the Throne of Death	194
Between Christ and Ishtar	203
The Sacrifice	207
The Rescuer	213
A TEAR AND A SMILE	217
The Creation	219
Two Infants	220
The House of Fortune	222
A Poet's Death Is his Life	223
The Criminal	225
Song of Fortune	227
Song of the Rain	229
The Poet	231
Laughter and Tears	233
Vision	235
Two Wishes	237
Yesterday and Today	239
Leave Me, My Blamer	242
The Beauty of Death	244
A Poet's Voice	247
The Life of Love	252
Song of the Wave	255
Peace	257
The Playground of Life	259

The City of the Dead	261
The Widow and her Son	263
Song of the Soul	265
Song of the Flower	267
Song of Love	268
Song of Man	270
Before the Throne of Beauty	272
A Lover's Call	274
The Palace and the Hut	276
TWENTY DRAWINGS	277
On the Art of Kahlil Gibran	280
PLATES	
Towards the Infinite	279
The Greater Self	292
The Blind	293
The Mountain	294
Flight	295
Centaur and Child	296
Uplifted	297
The Rock	298
The Waterfall	299
The Burden	300
The Great Longing	301
Veiled Face	302
Crucified	303
Compassion	304
The Triangle	305
The Struggle	306
The Great Aloneness	307
Woman with Garment	308
Mother and Child	309
The Innermost	310

THE FORERUNNER	311
God's Fool	314
Love	317
The King-Hermit	318
The Lion's Daughter	320
Tyranny	323
The Saint	324
The Plutocrat	325
The Greater Self	326
War and the Small Nations	327
Critics	329
Poets	330
The Weather-cock	331
The King of Aradus	332
Out of My Deeper Heart	333
Dynasties	335
Knowledge and Half-Knowledge	337
"Said a Sheet of Snow-White Paper...."	338
The Scholar and the Poet	339
Values	341
Other Seas	342
Repentance	343
The Dying Man and the Vulture	344
Beyond My Solitude	346
The Last Watch	347
SPIRITS REBELLIOUS	351
Madame Rose Hanie	353
The Cry of the Graves	365
Khalil the Heretic	373

THE PROPHET

The Coming of the Ship

Almustafa, the chosen and the beloved, who was a dawn unto his own day, had waited twelve years in the city of Orphalese for his ship that was to return and bear him back to the isle of his birth.

And in the twelfth year, on the seventh day of Ielool, the month of reaping, he climbed the hill without the city walls and looked seaward; and he beheld his ship coming with the mist.

Then the gates of his heart were flung open, and his joy flew far over the sea. And he closed his eyes and prayed in the silences of his soul.

But as he descended the hill, a sadness came upon him, and he thought in his heart:

How shall I go in peace and without sorrow? Nay, not without a wound in the spirit shall I leave this city. Long were the days of pain I have spent within its walls, and long were the nights of aloneness; and who can depart from his pain and his aloneness without regret?

Too many fragments of the spirit have I scattered in these streets, and too many are the children of my longing that walk naked among these hills, and I cannot withdraw from them without a burden and an ache.

It is not a garment I cast off this day, but a skin that I tear with my own hands.

Nor is it a thought I leave behind me, but a heart made sweet with hunger and with thirst.

Yet I cannot tarry longer.

The sea that calls all things unto her calls me, and I must embark.

For to stay, though the hours burn in the night, is to freeze and crystallize and be bound in a mould.

Fain would I take with me all that is here. But how shall I?

A voice cannot carry the tongue and the lips that gave it wings. Alone must it seek the ether.

And alone and without his nest shall the eagle fly across the sun.

Now when he reached the foot of the hill, he turned again towards the sea, and he saw his ship approaching the harbour, and upon her prow the mariners, the men of his own land.

And his soul cried out to them, and he said:

Sons of my ancient mother, you riders of the tides,

How often have you sailed in my dreams. And now you come in my awakening, which is my deeper dream.

Ready am I to go, and my eagerness with sails full set awaits the wind.

Only another breath will I breathe in this still air, only another loving look cast backward,

And then I shall stand among you, a seafarer among seafarers. And you, vast sea, sleepless mother,

Who alone are peace and freedom to the river and the stream,

Only another winding will this stream make, only another murmur in this glade,

And then shall I come to you, a boundless drop to a boundless ocean.

And as he walked he saw from afar men and women leaving their fields and their vineyards and hastening towards the city gates.

And he heard their voices calling his name, and shouting from field to field telling one another of the coming of his ship.

And he said to himself:

Shall the day of parting be the day of gathering?

And shall it be said that my eve was in truth my dawn?

And what shall I give unto him who has left his plough in midfurrow, or to him who has stopped the wheel of his winepress? Shall my heart become a tree heavy-laden with fruit that I may gather and give unto them?

And shall my desires flow like a fountain that I may fill their cups?

Am I a harp that the hand of the mighty may touch me, or a flute that his breath may pass through me?

A seeker of silences am I, and what treasure have I found in silences that I may dispense with confidence?

If this is my day of harvest, in what fields have I sowed the seed, and in what unremembered seasons?

If this indeed be the hour in which I lift up my lantern, it is not my flame that shall burn therein.

Empty and dark shall I raise my lantern,

And the guardian of the night shall fill it with oil and he shall light it also.

These things he said in words. But much in his heart remained unsaid. For he himself could not speak his deeper secret.

And when he entered into the city all the people came to meet him, and they were crying out to him as with one voice.

And the elders of the city stood forth and said:

Go not yet away from us.

A noontide have you been in our twilight, and your youth has given us dreams to dream.

No stranger are you among us, nor a guest, but our son and our dearly beloved.

Suffer not yet our eyes to hunger for your face.

And the priests and the priestesses said unto him:

Let not the waves of the sea separate us now, and the years you have spent in our midst become a memory.

You have walked among us a spirit, and your shadow has been a light upon our faces.

Much have we loved you. But speechless was our love, and with veils has it been veiled.

Yet now it cries aloud unto you, and would stand revealed before you.

And ever has it been that love knows not its own depth until the hour of separation.

And others came also and entreated him. But he answered them not. He only bent his head; and those who stood near saw his tears falling upon his breast.

And he and the people proceeded towards the great square before the temple.

And there came out of the sanctuary a woman whose name was Almitra. And she was a seeress.

And he looked upon her with exceeding tenderness, for it was she who had first sought and believed in him when he had been but a day in their city. And she hailed him, saying:

Prophet of God, in quest of the uttermost, long have you searched the distances for your ship.

And now your ship has come, and you must needs go.

Deep is your longing for the land of your memories and the dwelling place of your greater desires; and our love would not bind you nor our needs hold you.

Yet this we ask ere you leave us, that you speak to us and give us of your truth.

And we will give it unto our children, and they unto their children, and it shall not perish.

In your aloneness you have watched with our days, and in your wakefulness you have listened to the weeping and the laughter of our sleep.

Now therefore disclose us to ourselves, and tell us all that has been shown you of that which is between birth and death.

And he answered,

People of Orphalese, of what can I speak save of that which is even now moving within your souls?

On Love

Then said Almitra, Speak to us of *Love*.

And he raised his head and looked upon the people, and there fell a stillness upon them. And with a great voice he said:

When love beckons to you, follow him,
Though his ways are hard and steep.
And when his wings enfold you yield to him,
Though the sword hidden among his pinions may wound you.
And when he speaks to you believe in him,
Though his voice may shatter your dreams as the north wind lays waste the garden.

For even as love crowns you so shall he crucify you. Even as he is for your growth so is he for your pruning.

Even as he ascends to your height and caresses your tenderest branches that quiver in the sun,

So shall he descend to your roots and shake them in their clinging to the earth.

Like sheaves of corn he gathers you unto himself.
He threshes you to make you naked.
He sifts you to free you from your husks.
He grinds you to whiteness.
He kneads you until you are pliant;
And then he assigns you to his sacred fire, that you may become sacred bread for God's sacred feast.

All these things shall love do unto you that you may know the secrets of your heart, and in that knowledge become a fragment of Life's heart.

But if in your fear you would seek only love's peace and love's pleasure,

Then it is better for you that you cover your nakedness and pass out of love's threshing-floor,

Into the seasonless world where you shall laugh, but not all of your laughter, and weep, but not all of your tears.

Love gives naught but itself and takes naught but from itself.

Love possesses not nor would it be possessed;

For love is sufficient unto love.

When you love you should not say, "God is in my heart," but rather, "I am in the heart of God."

And think not you can direct the course of love, for love, if it finds you worthy, directs your course.

Love has no other desire but to fulfil itself.

But if you love and must needs have desires, let these be your desires:

To melt and be like a running brook that sings its melody to the night.

To know the pain of too much tenderness.

To be wounded by your own understanding of love;

And to bleed willingly and joyfully.

To wake at dawn with a winged heart and give thanks for another day of loving;

To rest at the noon hour and meditate love's ecstacy;

To return home at eventide with gratitude;

And then to sleep with a prayer for the beloved in your heart and a song of praise upon your lips.

On Marriage

Then Almitra spoke again and said, And what of *Marriage* master?
And he answered saying:
You were born together, and together you shall be forevermore.
You shall be together when the white wings of death scatter your days.
Aye, you shall be together even in the silent memory of God.
But let there be spaces in your togetherness,
And let the winds of the heavens dance between you.

Love one another, but make not a bond of love:
Let it rather be a moving sea between the shores of your souls.
Fill each other's cup but drink not from one cup.
Give one another of your bread but eat not from the same loaf. Sing and dance together and be joyous, but let each one of you be alone,
Even as the strings of a lute are alone though they quiver with the same music.

Give your hearts, but not into each other's keeping.
For only the hand of Life can contain your hearts.
And stand together yet not too near together:
For the pillars of the temple stand apart,
And the oak tree and the cypress grow not in each other's shadow.

On Children

And a woman who held a babe against her bosom said, Speak to us of *Children*.

And he said:

Your children are not your children.

They are the sons and daughters of Life's longing for itself.

They come through you but not from you,

And though they are with you yet they belong not to you.

You may give them your love but not your thoughts,

For they have their own thoughts.

You may house their bodies but not their souls,

For their souls dwell in the house of tomorrow, which you cannot visit, not even in your dreams.

You may strive to be like them, but seek not to make them like you. For life goes not backward nor tarries with yesterday.

You are the bows from which your children as living arrows are sent forth.

The archer sees the mark upon the path of the infinite, and He bends you with His might that His arrows may go swift and far.

Let your bending in the Archer's hand be for gladness;

For even as he loves the arrow that flies, so He loves also the bow that is stable.

On Giving

Then said a rich man, Speak to us of *Giving*.

And he answered:

You give but little when you give of your possessions.

It is when you give of yourself that you truly give.

For what are your possessions but things you keep and guard for fear you may need them tomorrow?

And tomorrow, what shall tomorrow bring to the overprudent dog burying bones in the trackless sand as he follows the pilgrims to the holy city?

And what is fear of need but need itself?

Is not dread of thirst when your well is full, the thirst that is unquenchable?

There are those who give little of the much which they have—and they give it for recognition and their hidden desire makes their gifts unwholesome.

And there are those who have little and give it all.

These are the believers in life and the bounty of life, and their coffer is never empty.

There are those who give with joy, and that joy is their reward.

And there are those who give with pain, and that pain is their baptism.

And there are those who give and know not pain in giving, nor do they seek joy, nor give with mindfulness of virtue;

They give as in yonder valley the myrtle breathes its fragrance into space.

Through the hands of such as these God speaks, and from behind their eyes He smiles upon the earth.

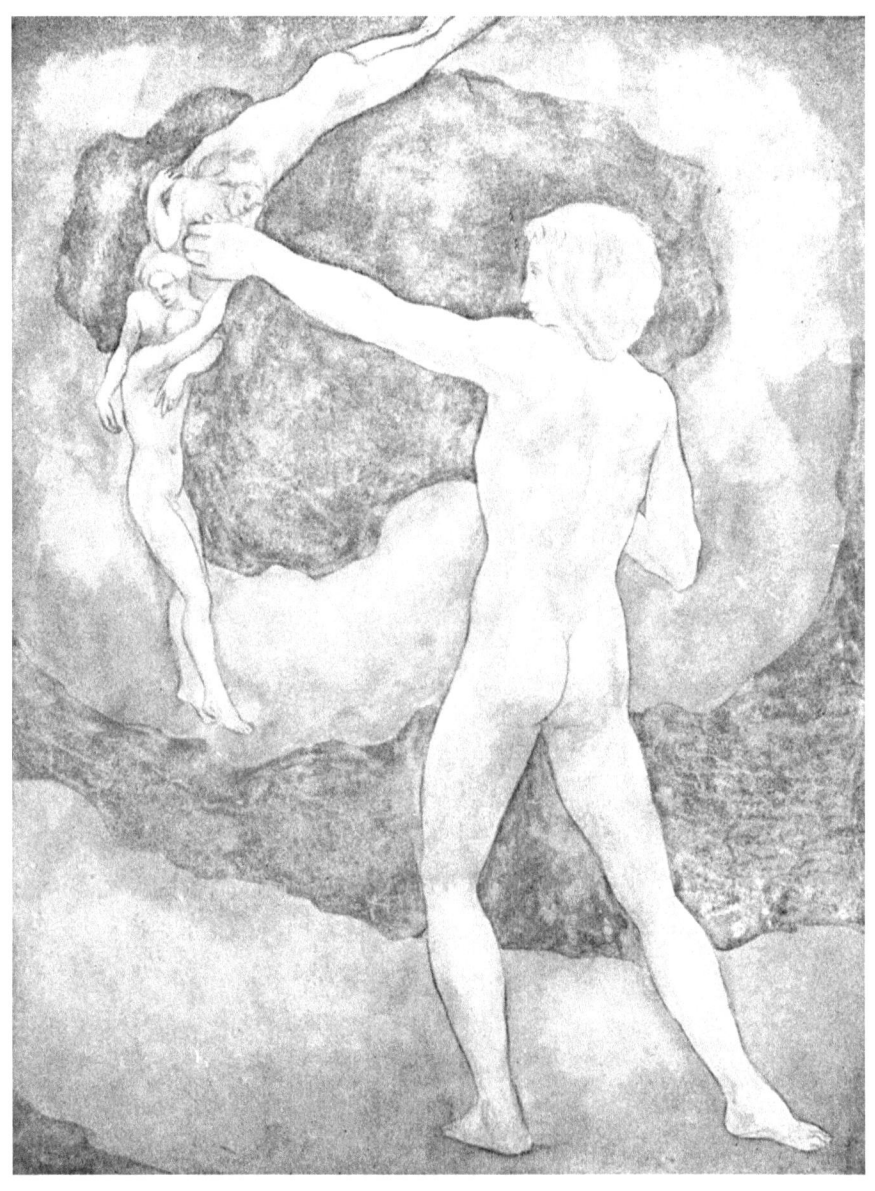

It is well to give when asked, but it is better to give unasked, through understanding;

And to the open-handed the search for one who shall receive is joy greater than giving.

And is there aught you would withhold?

All you have shall some day be given;

Therefore give now, that the season of giving may be yours and not your inheritors'.

You often say, "I would give, but only to the deserving."

The trees in your orchard say not so, nor the flocks in your pasture.

They give that they may live, for to withhold is to perish.

Surely he who is worthy to receive his days and his nights, is worthy of all else from you.

And he who has deserved to drink from the ocean of life deserves to fill his cup from your little stream.

And what desert greater shall there be, than that which lies in the courage and the confidence, nay the charity, of receiving?

And who are you that men should rend their bosom and unveil their pride, that you may see their worth naked and their pride unabashed?

See first that you yourself deserve to be a giver, and an instrument of giving.

For in truth it is life that gives unto life—while you, who deem yourself a giver, are but a witness.

And you receivers—and you are all receivers—assume no weight of gratitude, lest you lay a yoke upon yourself and upon him who gives.

Rather rise together with the giver on his gifts as on wings;

For to be overmindful of your debt, is ito doubt his generosity who has the freehearted earth for mother, and God for father.

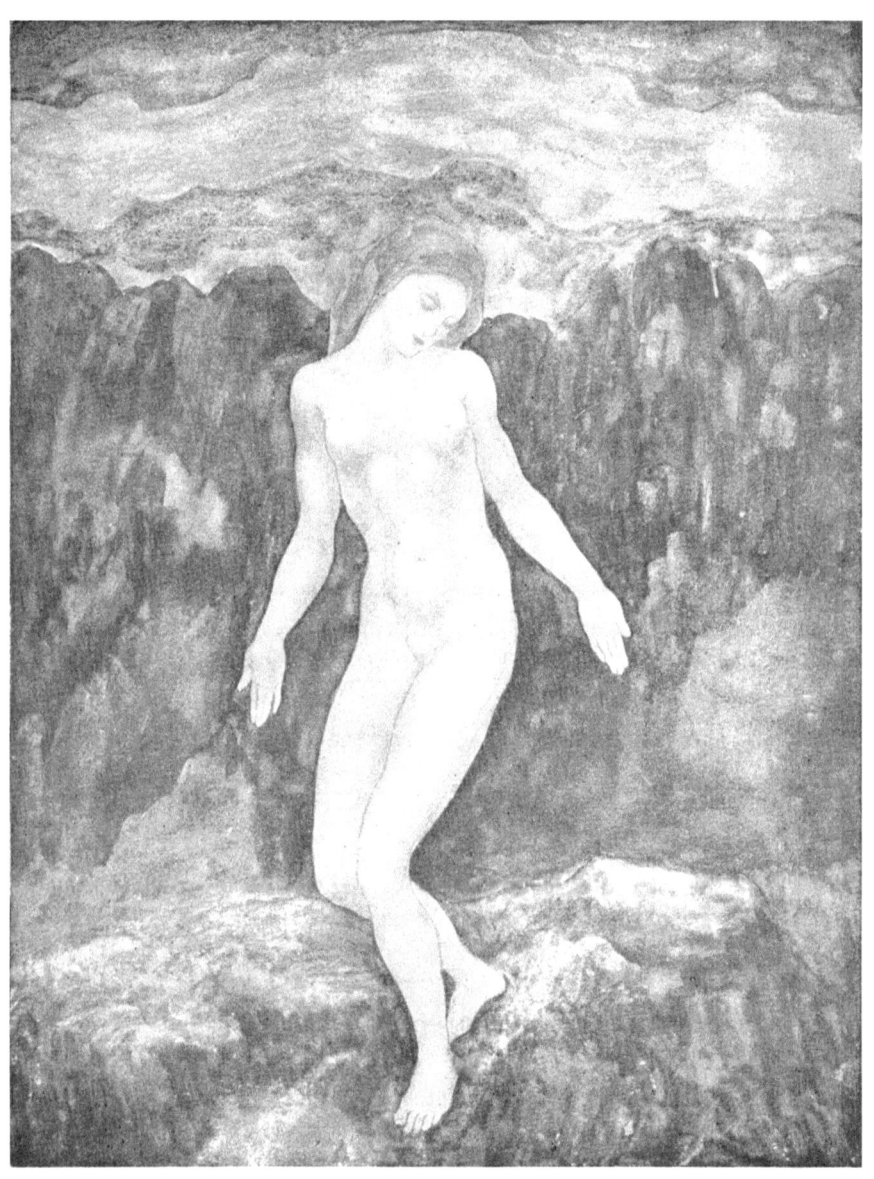

On Eating and Drinking

Then an old man, a keeper of an inn, said, Speak to us of *Eating and Drinking*.

And he said:

Would that you could live on the fragrance of the earth, and like an air plant be sustained by the light.

But since you must kill to eat, and rob the newly born of its mother's milk to quench your thirst, let it then be an act of worship,

And let your board stand an altar on which the pure and the innocent of forest and plain are sacrificed for that which is purer and still more innocent in man.

When you kill a beast say to him in your heart,

"By the same power that slays you, I too am slain; and I too shall be consumed. For the law that delivered you into my hand shall deliver me into a mightier hand.

Your blood and my blood is naught but the sap that feeds the tree of heaven."

And when you crush an apple with your teeth, say to it in your heart,

"Your seeds shall live in my body,

And the buds of your tomorrow shall blossom in my heart,

And your fragrance shall be my breath, And together we shall rejoice through all the seasons."

And in the autumn, when you gather the grapes of your vineyards for the winepress, say in your heart,

"I too am a vineyard, and my fruit shall be gathered for the winepress,

And like new wine I shall be kept in eternal vessels."

And in winter, when you draw the wine, let there be in your heart a song for each cup;

And let there be in the song a remembrance for the autumn days, and for the vineyard, and for the winepress.

On Work

Then a ploughman said, Speak to us of *Work*.

And he answered, saying:

You work that you may keep pace with the earth and the soul of the earth.

For to be idle is to become a stranger unto the seasons, and to step out of life's procession, that marches in majesty and proud submission towards the infinite.

When you work you are a flute through whose heart the whispering of the hours turns to music.

Which of you would be a reed, dumb and silent, when all else sings together in unison?

Always you have been told that work is a curse and labour a misfortune.

But I say to you that when you work you fulfil a part of earth's furthest dream, assigned to you when that dream was born,

And in keeping yourself with labour you are in truth loving life,

And to love life through labour is to be intimate with life's inmost secret.

But if you in your pain call birth an affliction and the support of the flesh a curse written upon your brow, then I answer that naught but the sweat of your brow shall wash away that which is written.

You have been told also that life is darkness, and in your weariness you echo what was said by the weary.

And I say that life is indeed darkness 'save when there is urge,

And all urge is blind save when there is knowledge,

And all knowledge is vain save when there is work,

And all work is empty save when there is love;

And when you work with love you bind yourself to yourself, and to one another, and to God.

And what is it to work with love?

It is to weave the cloth with threads drawn from your heart, even as if your beloved were to wear that cloth.

It is to build a house with affection, even as if your beloved were to dwell in that house.

It is to sow seeds with tenderness and reap the harvest with joy, even as if your beloved were to eat the fruit.

It is to charge all things you fashion with a breath of your own spirit,

And to know that all the blessed dead are standing about you and watching.

Often have I heard you say, as if speaking in sleep, "He who works in marble, and finds the shape of his own soul in the stone, is nobler than he who ploughs the soil. And he who seizes the rainbow to lay it on a cloth in the likeness of man, is more than he who makes the sandals for our feet."

But I say, not in sleep but in the overwakefulness of noontide, that the wind speaks not more sweetly to the giant oaks than to the least of all the blades of grass;

And he alone is great who turns the voice of the wind into a song made sweeter by his own loving.

Work is love made visible.

And if you cannot work with love but only with distaste, it is better that you should leave your work and sit at the gate of the temple and take alms of those who work with joy.

For if you bake bread with indifference, you bake a bitter bread that feeds but half man's hunger.

And if you grudge the crushing of the grapes, your grudge distils a poison in the wine. And if you sing though as angels, and love not the singing, you muffle man's ears to the voices of the day and the voices of the night.

On Joy and Sorrow

Then a woman said, Speak to us of *Joy and Sorrow*.

And he answered:

Your joy is your sorrow unmasked.

And the selfsame well from which your laughter rises was oftentimes filled with your tears.

And how else can it be?

The deeper that sorrow carves into your being, the more joy you can contain.

Is not the cup that holds your wine the very cup that was burned in the potter's oven?

And is not the lute that soothes your spirit, the very wood that was hollowed with knives?

When you are joyous, look deep into your heart and you shall find it is only that which has given you sorrow that is giving you joy.

When you are sorrowful look again in your heart, and you shall see that in truth you are weeping for that which has been your delight.

Some of you say, "Joy is greater than sorrow," and others say, "Nay, sorrow is the greater."

But I say unto you, they are inseparable.

Together they come, and when one sits alone with you at your board, remember that the other is asleep upon your bed.

Verily you are suspended like scales between your sorrow and your joy.

Only when you are empty are you at standstill and balanced.

When the treasure-keeper lifts you to weigh his gold and his silver, needs must your joy or your sorrow rise or fall.

On Houses

Then a mason came forth and said, Speak to us of *Houses*.

And he answered and said:

Build of your imaginings a bower in the wilderness ere you build a house within the city walls.

For even as you have home-comings in your twilight, so has the wanderer in you, the ever distant and alone.

Your house is your larger body.

It grows in the sun and sleeps in the stillness of the night; and it is not dreamless. Does not your house dream? and dreaming, leave the city for grove or hilltop?

Would that I could gather your houses into my hand, and like a sower scatter them in forest and meadow.

Would the valleys were your streets, and the green paths your alleys, that you might seek one another through vineyards, and come with the fragrance of the earth in your garments.

But these things are not yet to be.

In their fear your forefathers gathered you too near together. And that fear shall endure a little longer. A little longer shall your city walls separate your hearths from your fields.

And tell me, people of Orphalese, what have you in these houses? And what is it you guard with fastened doors?

Have you peace, the quiet urge that reveals your power?

Have you remembrances, the glimmering arches that span the summits of the mind?

Have you beauty, that leads the heart from things fashioned of wood and stone to the holy mountain?

Tell me, have you these in your houses?

Or have you only comfort, and the lust for comfort, that stealthy thing that enters the house a guest, and then becomes a host, and then a master?

Ay, and it becomes a tamer, and with hook and scourge makes puppets of your larger desires.

Though its hands are silken, its heart is of iron.

It lulls you to sleep only to stand by your bed and jeer at the dignity of the flesh.

It makes mock of your sound senses, and lays them in thistledown like fragile vessels.

Verily the lust for comfort murders the passion of the soul, and then walks grinning in the funeral.

But you, children of space, you restless in rest, you shall not be trapped nor tamed.

Your house shall be not an anchor but a mast.

It shall not be a glistening film that covers a wound, but an eyelid that guards the eye.

You shall not fold your wings that you may pass through doors, nor bend your heads that they strike not against a ceiling, nor fear to breathe lest walls should crack and fall down.

You shall not dwell in tombs made by the dead for the living.

And though of magnificence and splendour, your house shall not hold your secret nor shelter your longing.

For that which is boundless in you abides in the mansion of the sky, whose door is the morning mist, and whose windows are the songs and the silences of night.

On Clothes

And the weaver said, Speak to us of *Clothes*.

And he answered:

Your clothes conceal much of your beauty, yet they hide not the unbeautiful.

And though you seek in garments the freedom of privacy you may find in them a harness and a chain.

Would that you could meet the sun and the wind with more of your skin and less of your raiment,

For the breath of life is in the sunlight and the hand of life is in the wind.

Some of you say, "It is the north wind who has woven the clothes we wear."

And I say, Ay, it was the north wind,

But shame was his loom, and the softening of the sinews was his thread.

And when his work was done he laughed in the forest. Forget not that modesty is for a shield against the eye of the unclean.

And when the unclean shall be no more, what were modesty but a fetter and a fouling of the mind?

And forget not that the earth delights to feel your bare feet and the winds long to play with your hair.

On Buying and Selling

And a merchant said, Speak to us of *Buying and Selling*.

And he answered and said:

To you the earth yields her fruit, and you shall not want if you but know how to fill your hands.

It is in exchanging the gifts of the earth that you shall find abundance and be satisfied.

Yet unless the exchange be in love and kindly justice, it will but lead some to greed and others to hunger.

When in the market place you toilers of the sea and fields and vineyards meet the weavers and the potters and the gatherers of spices,—

Invoke then the master spirit of the earth, to come into your midst and sanctify the scales and the reckoning that weighs value against value. And suffer not the barren-handed to take part in your transactions, who would sell their words for your labour.

To such men you should say,

"Come with us to the field, or go with our brothers to the sea and cast your net;

For the land and the sea shall be bountiful to you even as to us."

And if there come the singers and the dancers and the flute players,— buy of their gifts also.

For they too are gatherers of fruit and frankincense, and that which they bring, though fashioned of dreams, is raiment and food for your soul.

And before you leave the market place, see that no one has gone his way with empty hands.

For the master spirit of the earth shall not sleep peacefully upon the wind till the needs of the least of you are satisfied.

On Crime and Punishment

Then one of the judges of the city stood forth and said, Speak to us of *Crime and Punishment*.

And he answered, saying:

It is when your spirit goes wandering upon the wind,

That you, alone and unguarded, commit a wrong unto others and therefore unto yourself.

And for that wrong committed must you knock and wait a while unheeded at the gate of the blessed.

Like the ocean is your god-self;

It remains for ever undefiled.

And like the ether it lifts but the winged.

Even like the sun is your god-self;

It knows not the ways of the mole nor seeks it the holes of the serpent. But your god-self dwells not alone in your being.

Much in you is still man, and much in you is not yet man,

But a shapeless pigmy that walks asleep in the mist searching for its own awakening.

And of the man in you would I now speak.

For it is he and not your god-self nor the pigmy in the mist, that knows crime and the punishment of crime.

Oftentimes have I heard you speak of one who commits a wrong as though he were not one of you, but a stranger unto you and an intruder upon your world.

But I say that even as the holy and the righteous cannot rise beyond the highest which is in each one of you,

So the wicked and the weak cannot fall lower than the lowest which is in you also.

And as a single leaf turns not yellow but with the silent knowledge of the whole tree, So the wrong-doer cannot do wrong without the hidden will of you all.

Like a procession you walk together towards your god-self.

You are the way and the wayfarers.

And when one of you falls down he falls for those behind him, a caution against the stumbling stone.

Ay, and he falls for those ahead of him, who though faster and surer of foot, yet removed not the stumbling stone.

And this also, though the word lie heavy upon your hearts:

The murdered is not unaccountable for his own murder,

And the robbed is not blameless in being robbed.

The righteous is not innocent of the deeds of the wicked,

And the white-handed is not clean in the doings of the felon.

Yea, the guilty is oftentimes the victim of the injured,

And still more often the condemned is the burden bearer for the guiltless and unblamed.

You cannot separate the just from the unjust and the good from the wicked;

For they stand together before the face of the sun even as the black thread and the white are woven together.

And when the black thread breaks, the weaver shall look into the whole cloth, and he shall examine the loom also.

If any of you would bring to judgment the unfaithful wife,

Let him also weigh the heart of her husband in scales, and measure his soul with measurements.

And let him who would lash the offender look unto the spirit of the offended.

And if any of you would punish in the name of righteousness and lay the ax unto the evil tree, let him see to its roots;

And verily he will find the roots of the good and the bad, the fruitful and the fruitless, all entwined together in the silent heart of the earth.

And you judges who would be just,

What judgment pronounce you upon him who though honest in the flesh yet is a thief in spirit?

What penalty lay you upon him who slays in the flesh yet is himself slain in the spirit?

And how prosecute you him who in action is a deceiver and an oppressor,

Yet who also is aggrieved and outraged?

And how shall you punish those whose remorse is already greater than their misdeeds?

Is not remorse the justice which is administered by that very law which you would fain serve?

Yet you cannot lay remorse upon the innocent nor lift it from the heart of the guilty.

Unbidden shall it call in the night, that men may wake and gaze upon themselves. And you who would understand justice, how shall you unless you look upon all deeds in the fullness of light?

Only then shall you know that the erect and the fallen are but one man standing in twilight between the night of his pigmy-self and the day of his god-self, And that the corner-stone of the temple is not higher than the lowest stone in its foundation.

On Laws

Then a lawyer said, But what of our *Laws*, master?
And he answered:
You delight in laying down laws,
Yet you delight more in breaking them.
Like children playing by the ocean who build sand-towers with constancy and then destroy them with laughter.
But while you build your sand-towers the ocean brings more sand to the shore,
And when you destroy them the ocean laughs with you.
Verily the ocean laughs always with the innocent.
But what of those to whom life is not an ocean, and man-made laws are not sand-towers,
But to whom life is a rock, and the law a chisel with which they would carve it in their own likeness? What of the cripple who hates dancers?
What of the ox who loves his yoke and deems the elk and deer of the forest stray and vagrant things?
What of the old serpent who cannot shed his skin, and calls all others naked and shameless?
And of him who comes early to the wedding-feast, and when over-fed and tired goes his way saying that all feasts are violation and all feasters lawbreakers?

What shall I say of these save that they too stand in the sunlight, but with their backs to the sun?
They see only their shadows, and their shadows are their laws.
And what is the sun to them but a caster of shadows?
And what is it to acknowledge the laws but to stoop down and trace their shadows upon the earth?
But you who walk facing the sun, what images drawn on the earth can hold you?

You who travel with the wind, what weather-vane shall direct your course?

What man's law shall bind you if you break your yoke but upon no man's prison door?

What laws shall you fear if you dance but stumble against no man's iron chains?

And who is he that shall bring you to judgment if you tear off your garment yet leave it in no man's path?

People of Orphalese, you can muffle the drum, and you can loosen the strings of the lyre, but who shall command the skylark not to sing?

On Freedom

And an orator said, Speak to us of *Freedom*.

And he answered:

At the city gate and by your fireside I have seen you prostrate yourself and worship your own freedom,

Even as slaves humble themselves before a tyrant and praise him though he slays them.

Ay, in the grove of the temple and in the shadow of the citadel I have seen the freest among you wear their freedom as a yoke and a handcuff.

And my heart bled within me; for you can only be free when even the desire of seeking freedom becomes a harness to you, and when you cease to speak of freedom as a goal and a fulfilment.

You shall be free indeed when your days are not without a care nor your nights without a want and a grief,

But rather when these things girdle your life and yet you rise above them naked and unbound.

And how shall you rise beyond your days and nights unless you break the chains which you at the dawn of your understanding have fastened around your noon hour?

In truth that which you call freedom is the strongest of these chains, though its links glitter in the sun and dazzle your eyes.

And what is it but fragments of your own self you would discard that you may become free?

If it is an unjust law you would abolish, that law was written with your own hand upon your own forehead.

You cannot erase it by burning your law books nor by washing the foreheads of your judges, though you pour the sea upon them.

And if it is a despot you would dethrone, see first that his throne erected within you is destroyed.

For how can a tyrant rule the free and the proud, but for a tyranny in their own freedom and a shame in their own pride?

And if it is a care you would cast off, that cart has been chosen by you rather than imposed upon you.

And if it is a fear you would dispel, the seat of that fear is in your heart and not in the hand of the feared.

Verily all things move within your being in constant half embrace, the desired and the dreaded, the repugnant and the cherished, the pursued and that which you would escape.

These things move within you as lights and shadows in pairs that cling.

And when the shadow fades and is no more, the light that lingers becomes a shadow to another light.

And thus your freedom when it loses its fetters becomes itself the fetter of a greater freedom.

On Reason and Passion

And the priestess spoke again and said: Speak to us of *Reason and Passion*.

And he answered, saying:

Your soul is oftentimes a battlefield, upon which your reason and your judgment wage war against your passion and your appetite.

Would that I could be the peacemaker in your soul, that I might turn the discord and the rivalry of your elements into oneness and melody.

But how shall I, unless you yourselves be also the peacemakers, nay, the lovers of all your elements?

Your reason and your passion are the rudder and the sails of your seafaring soul.

If either your sails or your rudder be broken, you can but toss and drift, or else be held at a standstill in mid-seas. For reason, ruling alone, is a force confining; and passion, unattended, is a flame that burns to its own destruction.

Therefore let your soul exalt your reason to the height of passion, that it may sing;

And let it direct your passion with reason, that your passion may live through its own daily resurrection, and like the phoenix rise above its own ashes.

I would have you consider your judgment and your appetite even as you would two loved guests in your house.

Surely you would not honour one guest above the other; for he who is more mindful of one loses the love and the faith of both

Among the hills, when you sit in the cool shade of the white poplars, sharing the peace and serenity of distant fields and meadows—then let your heart say in silence, "God rests in reason."

And when the storm comes, and the mighty wind shakes the forest, and thunder and lightning proclaim the majesty of the sky,—then let your heart say in awe, "God moves in passion."

And since you are a breath in God's sphere, and a leaf in God's forest, you too should rest in reason and move in passion.

On Pain

And a woman spoke, saying, Tell us of *Pain*.

And he said:

Your pain is the breaking of the shell that encloses your understanding.

Even as the stone of the fruit must break, that its heart may stand in the sun, so must you know pain.

And could you keep your heart in wonder at the daily miracles of your life, your pain would not seem less wondrous than your joy;

And you would accept the seasons of your heart, even as you have always accepted the seasons that pass over your fields.

And you would watch with serenity through the winters of your grief.

Much of your pain is self-chosen.

It is the bitter potion by which the physician within you heals your sick self.

Therefore trust the physician, and drink his remedy in silence and tranquillity: For his hand, though heavy and hard, is guided by the tender hand of the Unseen, And the cup he brings, though it burn your lips, has been fashioned of the clay which the Potter has moistened with His own sacred tears.

On Self-Knowledge

And a man said, Speak to us of *Self-Knowledge.*
And he answered, saying:
Your hearts know in silence the secrets of the days and the nights.
But your ears thirst for the sound of your heart's knowledge.
You would know in words that which you have always known in thought.
You would touch with your fingers the naked body of your dreams.
And it is well you should.
The hidden well-spring of your soul must needs rise and run murmuring to the sea;
And the treasure of your infinite depths would be revealed to your eyes.
But let there be no scales to weigh your unknown treasure;
And seek not the depths of your knowledge with staff or sounding line.
For self is a sea boundless and measureless.

Say not, "I have found the truth," but rather, "I have found a truth."
Say not, "I have found the path of the soul." Say rather, "I have met the soul walking upon my path."
For the soul walks upon all paths.
The soul walks not upon a line, neither does it grow like a reed.
The soul unfolds itself, like a lotus of countless petals.

On Teaching

Then said a teacher, Speak to us of *Teaching*.

And he said:

"No man can reveal to you aught but that which already lies half asleep in the dawning of your knowledge.

The teacher who walks in the shadow of the temple, among his followers, gives not of his wisdom but rather of his faith and his lovingness.

If he is indeed wise he does not bid you enter the house of his wisdom, but rather leads you to the threshold of your own mind.

The astronomer may speak to you of his understanding of space, but he cannot give you his understanding.

The musician may sing to you of the rhythm which is in all space, but he cannot give you the ear which arrests the rhythm nor the voice that echoes it. And he who is versed in the science of numbers can tell of the regions of weight and measure, but he cannot conduct you thither.

For the vision of one man lends not its wings to another man.

And even as each one of you stands alone in God's knowledge, so must each one of you be alone in his knowledge of God and in his understanding of the earth.

On Friendship

And a youth said, Speak to us of *Friendship*.
And he answered, saying:
Your friend is your needs answered.
He is your field which you sow with love and reap with thanksgiving.
And he is your board and your fireside.
For you come to him with your hunger, and you seek him for peace.
When your friend speaks his mind you fear not the "nay" in your own mind, nor do you withhold the "ay."
And when he is silent your heart ceases not to listen to his heart;
For without words, in friendship, all thoughts, all desires, all expectations are born and shared, with joy that is unacclaimed.
When you part from your friend, you grieve not;
For that which you love most in him may be clearer in his absence, as the mountain to the climber is clearer from the plain. And let there be no purpose in friendship save the deepening of the spirit.
For love that seeks aught but the disclosure of its own mystery is not love but a net cast forth: and only the unprofitable is caught.

And let your best be for your friend.
If he must know the ebb of your tide, let him know its flood also.
For what is your friend that you should seek him with hours to kill?
Seek him always with hours to live.
For it is his to fill your need, but not your emptiness.
And in the sweetness of friendship let there be laughter, and sharing of pleasures.
For in the dew of little things the heart finds its morning and is refreshed.

On Talking

And then a scholar said, Speak of *Talking*.
And he answered, saying:
You talk when you cease to be at peace with your thoughts;
And when you can no longer dwell in the solitude of your heart you live in your lips, and sound is a diversion and a pastime.
And in much of your talking, thinking is half murdered.
For thought is a bird of space, that in a cage of words may indeed unfold its wings but cannot fly.
There are those among you who seek the talkative through fear of being alone.
The silence of aloneness reveals to their eyes their naked selves and they would escape.
And there are those who talk, and without knowledge or forethought reveal a truth which they themselves do not understand.
And there are those who have the truth within them, but they tell it not in words.
In the bosom of such as these the spirit dwells in rhythmic silence.

When you meet your friend on the roadside or in the market place, let the spirit in you move your lips and direct your tongue.
Let the voice within your voice speak to the ear of his ear;
For his soul will keep the truth of your heart as the taste of the wine is remembered
When the colour is forgotten and the vessel is no more.

On Time

And an astronomer said, Master, what of *Time*?

And he answered:

You would measure time the measureless and the immeasurable.

You would adjust your conduct and even direct the course of your spirit according to hours and seasons.

Of time you would make a stream upon whose bank you would sit and watch its flowing.

Yet the timeless in you is aware of life's timelessness,

And knows that yesterday is but today's memory and tomorrow is today's dream.

And that that which sings and contemplates in you is still dwelling within the bounds of that first moment which scattered the stars into space. Who among you does not feel that his power to love is boundless?

And yet who does not feel that very love, though boundless, encompassed within the centre of his being, and moving not from love thought to love thought, nor from love deeds to other love deeds?

And is not time even as love is, undivided and paceless?

But if in your thought you must measure time into seasons, let each season encircle all the other seasons,

And let today embrace the past with remembrance and the future with longing.

On Good and Evil

And one of the elders of the city said, Speak to us of *Good and Evil*.

And he answered:

Of the good in you I can speak, but not of the evil.

For what is evil but good tortured by its own hunger and thirst?

Verily when good is hungry it seeks food even in dark caves, and when it thirsts it drinks even of dead waters.

You are good when you are one with yourself.

Yet when you are not one with yourself you are not evil.

For a divided house is not a den of thieves; it is only a divided house.

And a ship without rudder may wander aimlessly among perilous isles yet sink not to the bottom. You are good when you strive to give of yourself.

Yet you are not evil when you seek gain for yourself.

For when you strive for gain you are but a root that clings to the earth and sucks at her breast.

Surely the fruit cannot say to the root, "Be like me, ripe and full and ever giving of your abundance."

For to the fruit giving is a need, as receiving is a need to the root.

You are good when you are fully awake in your speech,

Yet you are not evil when you sleep while your tongue staggers without purpose.

And even stumbling speech may strengthen a weak tongue.

You are good when you walk to your goal firmly and with bold steps.

Yet you are not evil when you go thither limping. Even those who limp go not backward.

But you who are strong and swift, see that you do not limp before the lame, deeming it kindness.

You are good in countless ways, and you are not evil when you are not good,

You are only loitering and sluggard.

Pity that the stags cannot teach swiftness to the turtles.

In your longing for your giant self lies your goodness: and that longing is in all of you.

But in some of you that longing is a torrent rushing with might to the sea, carrying the secrets of the hillsides and the songs of the forest.

And in others it is a flat stream that loses itself in angles and bends and lingers before it reaches the shore.

But let not him who longs much say to him who longs little, "Wherefore are you slow and halting?"

For the truly good ask not the naked, "Where is your garment?" nor the houseless, "What has befallen your house?"

On Prayer

Then a priestess said, Speak to us of *Prayer*.

And he answered, saying:

You pray in your distress and in your need; would that you might pray also in the fullness of your joy and in your days of abundance.

For what is prayer but the expansion of yourself into the living ether?

And if it is for your comfort to pour your darkness into space, it is also for your delight to pour forth the dawning of your heart.

And if you cannot but weep when your soul summons you to prayer, she should spur you again and yet again, though weeping, until you shall come laughing.

When you pray you rise to meet in the air those who are praying at that very hour, and whom save in prayer you may not meet.

Therefore let your visit to that temple invisible be for naught but ecstasy and sweet communion.

For if you should enter the temple for no other purpose than asking you shall not receive:

And if you should enter into it to humble yourself you shall not be lifted:

Or even if you should enter into it to beg for the good of others you shall not be heard.

It is enough that you enter the temple invisible.

I cannot teach you how to pray in words.

God listens not to your words save when He Himself utters them through your lips.

And I cannot teach you the prayer of the seas and the forests and the mountains. But you who are born of the mountains and the forests and the seas can find their prayer in your heart,

And if you but listen in the stillness of the night you shall hear them saying in silence,

"Our God, who art our winged self, it is thy will in us that willeth.

It is thy desire in us that desireth.

It is thy urge in us that would turn our nights, which are thine, into days which are thine also.

We cannot ask thee for aught, for thou knowest our needs before they are born in us:

Thou art our need; and in giving us more of thyself thou givest us all."

On Pleasure

Then a hermit, who visited the city once a year, came forth and said, Speak to us of *Pleasure*.

And he answered, saying:

Pleasure is a freedom-song,

But it is not freedom.

It is the blossoming of your desires,

But it is not their fruit.

It is a depth calling unto a height,

But it is not the deep nor the high.

It is the caged taking wing,

But it is not space encompassed.

Ay, in very truth, pleasure is a freedom-song.

And I fain would have you sing it with fullness of heart; yet I would not have you lose your hearts in the singing.

Some of your youth seek pleasure as if it were all, and they are judged and rebuked. I would not judge nor rebuke them. I would have them seek.

For they shall find pleasure, but not her alone;

Seven are her sisters, and the least of them is more beautiful than pleasure.

Have you not heard of the man who was digging in the earth for roots and found a treasure?

And some of your elders remember pleasures with regret like wrongs committed in drunkenness.

But regret is the beclouding of the mind and not its chastisement.

They should remember their pleasures with gratitude, as they would the harvest of a summer.

Yet if it comforts them to regret, let them be comforted.

And there are among you those who are neither young to seek nor old to remember;

And in their fear of seeking and remembering they shun all pleasures, lest they neglect the spirit or offend against it.

But even in their foregoing is their pleasure.

And thus they too find a treasure though they dig for roots with quivering hands.

But tell me, who is he that can offend the spirit?

Shall the nightingale offend the stillness of the night, or the firefly the stars?

And shall your flame or your smoke burden the wind?

Think you the spirit is a still pool which you can trouble with a staff?

Oftentimes in denying yourself pleasure you do but store the desire in the recesses of your being.

Who knows but that which seems omitted today, waits for tomorrow?

Even your body knows its heritage and its rightful need and will not be deceived.

And your body is the harp of your soul,

And it is yours to bring forth sweet music from it or confused sounds.

And now you ask in your heart, "How shall we distinguish that which is good in pleasure from that which is not good?"

Go to your fields and your gardens, and you shall learn that it is the pleasure of the bee to gather honey of the flower,

But it is also the pleasure of the flower to yield its honey to the bee.

For to the bee a flower is a fountain of life,

And to the flower a bee is a messenger of love,

And to both, bee and flower, the giving and the receiving of pleasure is a need and an ecstasy.

People of Orphalese, be in your pleasures like the flowers and the bees.

On Beauty

And a poet said, Speak to us of *Beauty*.

And he answered:

Where shall you seek beauty, and how shall you find her unless she herself be your way and your guide?

And how shall you speak of her except she be the weaver of your speech?

The aggrieved and the injured say, "Beauty is kind and gentle.

Like a young mother half-shy of her own glory she walks among us."

And the passionate say, "Nay, beauty is a thing of might and dread.

Like the tempest she shakes the earth beneath us and the sky above us."

The tired and the weary say, "Beauty is of soft whisperings. She speaks in our spirit. Her voice yields to our silences like a faint light that quivers in fear of the shadow."

But the restless say, "We have heard her shouting among the mountains,

And with her cries came the sound of hoofs, and the beating of wings and the roaring of lions."

At night the watchmen of the city say, "Beauty shall rise with the dawn from the east."

And at noontide the toilers and the wayfarers say, "We have seen her leaning over the earth from the windows of the sunset."

In winter say the snow-bound, "She shall come with the spring leaping upon the hills."

And in the summer heat the reapers say, "We have seen her dancing with the autumn leaves, and we saw a drift of snow in her hair." All these things have you said of beauty,

Yet in truth you spoke not of her but of needs unsatisfied,

And beauty is not a need but an ecstasy.

It is not a mouth thirsting nor an empty hand stretched forth,

But rather a heart enflamed and a soul enchanted.

It is not the image you would see nor the song you would hear,

But rather an image you see though you close your eyes and a song you hear though you shut your ears.

It is not the sap within the furrowed bark, nor a wing attached to a claw,

But rather a garden for ever in bloom and a flock of angels for ever in flight.

People of Orphalese, beauty is life when life unveils her holy face.

But you are life and you are the veil. Beauty is eternity gazing at itself in a mirror.

But you are eternity and you are the mirror.

On Religion

And an old priest said, Speak to us of *Religion*.
And he said:
Have I spoken this day of aught else?
Is not religion all deeds and all reflection,
And that which is neither deed nor reflection, but a wonder and a surprise ever springing in the soul, even while the hands hew the stone or tend the loom?
Who can separate his faith from his actions, or his belief from his occupations?
Who can spread his hours before him, saying, "This for God and this for myself; This for my soul, and this other for my body?"
All your hours are wings that beat through space from self to self. He who wears his morality but as his best garment were better naked.
The wind and the sun will tear no holes in his skin.
And he who defines his conduct by ethics imprisons his song-bird in a cage.
The freest song comes not through bars and wires.
And he to whom worshipping is a window, to open but also to shut, has not yet visited the house of his soul whose windows are from dawn to dawn.

Your daily life is your temple and your religion.
Whenever you enter into it take with you your all.
Take the plough and the forge and the mallet and the lute,
The things you have fashioned in necessity or for delight.
For in revery you cannot rise above your achievements nor fall lower than your failures.
And take with you all men: For in adoration you cannot fly higher than their hopes nor humble yourself lower than their despair.

And if you would know God be not therefore a solver of riddles.

Rather look about you and you shall see Him playing with your children.

And look into space; you shall see Him walking in the cloud, outstretching His arms in the lightning and descending in rain.

You shall see Him smiling in flowers, then rising and waving His hands in trees.

On Death

Then Almitra spoke, saying, We would ask now of *Death*.
And he said:
You would know the secret of death.
But how shall you find it unless you seek it in the heart of life?
The owl whose night-bound eyes are blind unto the day cannot unveil the mystery of light.
If you would indeed behold the spirit of death, open your heart wide unto the body of life.
For life and death are one, even as the river and the sea are one.
In the depth of your hopes and desires lies your silent knowledge of the beyond;
And like seeds dreaming beneath the snow your heart dreams of spring.
Trust the dreams, for in them is hidden the gate to eternity. Your fear of death is but the trembling of the shepherd when he stands before the king whose hand is to be laid upon him in honour.
Is the shepherd not joyful beneath his trembling, that he shall wear the mark of the king?
Yet is he not more mindful of his trembling?

For what is it to die but to stand naked in the wind and to melt into the sun?
And what is it to cease breathing, but to free the breath from its restless tides, that it may rise and expand and seek God unencumbered?
Only when you drink from the river of silence shall you indeed sing.
And when you have reached the mountain top, then you shall begin to climb.
And when the earth shall claim your limbs, then shall you truly dance.

The Farewell

And now it was evening.
And Almitra the seeress said, Blessed be this day and this place and your spirit that has spoken.
And he answered, Was it I who spoke? Was I not also a listener?

Then he descended the steps of the Temple and all the people followed him. And he reached his ship and stood upon the deck.
And facing the people again, he raised his voice and said:
People of Orphalese, the wind bids me leave you.
Less hasty am I than the wind, yet I must go.
We wanderers, ever seeking the lonelier way, begin no day where we have ended another day; and no sunrise finds us where sunset left us. Even while the earth sleeps we travel.
We are the seeds of the tenacious plant, and it is in our ripeness and our fullness of heart that we are given to the wind and are scattered.

Brief were my days among you, and briefer still the words I have spoken.
But should my voice fade in your ears, and my love vanish in your memory, then I will come again,
And with a richer heart and lips more yielding to the spirit will I speak.
Yea, I shall return with the tide,
And though death may hide me, and the greater silence enfold me, yet again will I seek your understanding.
And not in vain will I seek.
If aught I have said is truth, that truth shall reveal itself in a clearer voice, and in words more kin to your thoughts.
I go with the wind, people of Orphalese, but not down into emptiness; And if this day is not a fulfilment of your needs and my love, then let it be a promise till another day.
Man's needs change, but not his love, nor his desire that his love should satisfy his needs.

Know therefore, that from the greater silence I shall return.

The mist that drifts away at dawn, leaving but dew in the fields, shall rise and gather into a cloud and then fall down in rain.

And not unlike the mist have I been.

In the stillness of the night I have walked in your streets, and my spirit has entered your houses,

And your heart-beats were in my heart, and your breath was upon my face, and I knew you all.

Ay, I knew your joy and your pain, and in your sleep your dreams were my dreams.

And oftentimes I was among you a lake among the mountains.

I mirrored the summits in you and the bending slopes, and even the passing flocks of your thoughts and your desires.

And to my silence came the laughter of your children in streams, and the longing of your youths in rivers.

And when they reached my depth the streams and the rivers ceased not yet to sing.

But sweeter still than laughter and greater than longing came to me.
It was the boundless in you;
The vast man in whom you are all but cells and sinews;
He in whose chant all your singing is but a soundless throbbing.
It is in the vast man that you are vast,
And in beholding him that I beheld you and loved you.
For what distances can love reach that are not in that vast sphere?
What visions, what expectations and what presumptions can outsoar that flight?
Like a giant oak tree covered with apple blossoms is the vast man in you. His might binds you to the earth, his fragrance lifts you into space, and in his durability you are deathless.

You have been told that, even like a chain, you are as weak as your weakest link.

This is but half the truth. You are also as strong as your strongest link.

To measure you by your smallest deed is to reckon the power of ocean by the frailty of its foam.

To judge you by your failures is to cast blame upon the seasons for their inconstancy.

Ay, you are like an ocean,
And though heavy-grounded ships await the tide upon your shores, yet, even like an ocean, you cannot hasten your tides.
And like the seasons you are also,
And though in your winter you deny your spring,

Yet spring, reposing within you, smiles in her drowsiness and is not offended. Think not I say these things in order that you may say the one to the other, "He praised us well. He saw but the good in us."

I only speak to you in words of that which you yourselves know in thought.

And what is word knowledge but a shadow of wordless knowledge?

Your thoughts and my words are waves from a sealed memory that keeps records of our yesterdays,

And of the ancient days when the earth knew not us nor herself,

And of nights when earth was up-wrought with confusion.

Wise men have come to you to give you of their wisdom. I came to take of your wisdom:

And behold I have found that which is greater than wisdom.

It is a flame spirit in you ever gathering more of itself,

While you, heedless of its expansion, bewail the withering of your days. It is life in quest of life in bodies that fear the grave.

There are no graves here.

These mountains and plains are a cradle and a stepping-stone.

Whenever you pass by the field where you have laid your ancestors look well thereupon, and you shall see yourselves and your children dancing hand in hand.

Verily you often make merry without knowing.

Others have come to you to whom for golden promises made unto your faith you have given but riches and power and glory.

Less than a promise have I given, and yet more generous have you been to me.

You have given me my deeper thirsting after life.

Surely there is no greater gift to a man than that which turns all his aims into parching lips and all life into a fountain.

And in this lies my honour and my reward,—
That whenever I come to the fountain to drink I find the living water itself thirsty;
And it drinks me while I drink it.

Some of you have deemed me proud and over-shy to receive gifts.

Too proud indeed am I to receive wages, but not gifts.

And though I have eaten berries among the hills when you would have had me sit at your board,

And slept in the portico of the temple when you would gladly have sheltered me,

Yet was it not your loving mindfulness of my days and my nights that made food sweet to my mouth and girdled my sleep with visions?

For this I bless you most:

You give much and know not that you give at all. Verily the kindness that gazes upon itself in a mirror turns to stone,

And a good deed that calls itself by tender names becomes the parent to a curse.

And some of you have called me aloof, and drunk with my own aloneness,

And you have said, "He holds council with the trees of the forest, but not with men.

He sits alone on hill-tops and looks down upon our city."

True it is that I have climbed the hills and walked in remote places.

How could I have seen you save from a great height or a great distance?

How can one be indeed near unless he be far?

And others among you called unto me, not in words, and they said,

"Stranger, stranger, lover of unreachable heights, why dwell you among the summits where eagles build their nests? Why seek you the unattainable?

What storms would you trap in your net,

And what vaporous birds do you hunt in the sky?

Come and be one of us.

Descend and appease your hunger with our bread and quench your thirst with our wine."

In the solitude of their souls they said these things;

But were their solitude deeper they would have known that I sought but the secret of your joy and your pain,

And I hunted only your larger selves that walk the sky.

But the hunter was also the hunted;
For many of my arrows left my bow only to seek my own breast.
And the flier was also the creeper;
For when my wings were spread in the sun their shadow upon the earth was a turtle.
And I the believer was also the doubter; For often have I put my finger in my own wound that I might have the greater belief in you and the greater knowledge of you.

And it is with this belief and this knowledge that I say,
You are not enclosed within your bodies, nor confined to houses or fields.
That which is you dwells above the mountain and roves with the wind.
It is not a thing that crawls into the sun for warmth or digs holes into darkness for safety,
But a thing free, a spirit that envelops the earth and moves in the ether.
If these be vague words, then seek not to clear them.
Vague and nebulous is the beginning of all things, but not their end,
And I fain would have you remember me as a beginning.
Life, and all that lives, is conceived in the mist and not in the crystal. And who knows but a crystal is mist in decay?

This would I have you remember in remembering me:
That which seems most feeble and bewildered in you is the strongest and most determined.
Is it not your breath that has erected and hardened the structure of your bones?
And is it not a dream which none of you remember having dreamt, that built your city and fashioned all there is in it?
Could you but see the tides of that breath you would cease to see all else,
And if you could hear the whispering of the dream you would hear no other sound.
But you do not see, nor do you hear, and it is well.
The veil that clouds your eyes shall be lifted by the hands that wove it,
And the clay that fills your ears shall be pierced by those fingers that kneaded it. And you shall see.
And you shall hear.

Yet you shall not deplore having known blindness, nor regret having been deaf.

For in that day you shall know the hidden purposes in all things,

And you shall bless darkness as you would bless light.

After saying these things he looked about him, and he saw the pilot of his ship standing by the helm and gazing now at the full sails and now at the distance.

And he said:

Patient, over patient, is the captain of my ship.

The wind blows, and restless are the sails;

Even the rudder begs direction;

Yet quietly my captain awaits my silence.

And these my mariners, who have heard the choir of the greater sea, they too have heard me patiently. Now they shall wait no longer.

I am ready.

The stream has reached the sea, and once more the great mother holds her son against her breast.

Fare you well, people of Orphalese.

This day has ended.

It is closing upon us even as the water-lily upon its own tomorrow.

What was given us here we shall keep,

And if it suffices not, then again must we come together and together stretch our hands unto the giver.

Forget not that I shall come back to you.

A little while, and my longing shall gather dust and foam for another body.

A little while, a moment of rest upon the wind, and another woman shall bear me.

Farewell to you and the youth I have spent with you.

It was but yesterday we met in a dream. You have sung to me in my aloneness, and I of your longings have built a tower in the sky.

But now our sleep has fled and our dream is over, and it is no longer dawn.

The noontide is upon us and our half waking has turned to fuller day, and we must part.

If in the twilight of memory we should meet once more, we shall speak again together and you shall sing to me a deeper song.

And if our hands should meet in another dream we shall build another tower in the sky.

So saying he made a signal to the seamen, and straightway they weighed anchor and cast the ship loose from its moorings, and they moved eastward.

And a cry came from the people as from a single heart, and it rose into the dusk and was carried out over the sea like a great trumpeting.

Only Almitra was silent, gazing after the ship until it had vanished into the mist.

And when all the people were dispersed she still stood alone upon the sea-wall, remembering in her heart his saying,

"A little while, a moment of rest upon the wind, and another woman shall bear me."

THE MADMAN

His Parables and Poems

You ask me how I became a madman. It happened thus: One day, long before many gods were born, I woke from a deep sleep and found all my masks were stolen,—the seven masks I have fashioned and worn in seven lives,—I ran maskless through the crowded streets shouting, "Thieves, thieves, the cursed thieves."

Men and women laughed at me and some ran to their houses in fear of me.

And when I reached the market place, a youth standing on a house-top cried, "He is a madman." I looked up to behold him; the sun kissed my own naked face for the first time. For the first time the sun kissed my own naked face and my soul was inflamed with love for the sun, and I wanted my masks no more. And as if in a trance I cried, "Blessed, blessed are the thieves who stole my masks."

Thus I became a madman.

And I have found both freedom and safety in my madness; the freedom of loneliness and the safety from being understood, for those who understand us enslave something in us.

But let me not be too proud of my safety. Even a Thief in a jail is safe from another thief.

God

In the ancient days, when the first quiver of speech came to my lips, I ascended the holy mountain and spoke unto God, saying, "Master, I am thy slave. Thy hidden will is my law and I shall obey thee for ever more."

But God made no answer, and like a mighty tempest passed away.

And after a thousand years I ascended the holy mountain and again spoke unto God, saying, "Creator, I am thy creation. Out of clay hast thou fashioned me and to thee I owe mine all."

And God made no answer, but like a thousand swift wings passed away.

And after a thousand years I climbed the holy mountain and spoke unto God again, saying, "Father, I am thy son. In pity and love thou hast given me birth, and through love and worship I shall inherit thy kingdom."

And God made no answer, and like the mist that veils the distant hills he passed away.

And after a thousand years I climbed the sacred mountain and again spoke unto God, saying, "My God, my aim and my fulfillment; I am thy yesterday and thou are my tomorrow. I am thy root in the earth and thou art my flower in the sky, and together we grow before the face of the sun."

Then God leaned over me, and in my ears whispered words of sweetness, and even as the sea that enfoldeth a brook that runneth down to her, he enfolded me.

And when I descended to the valleys and the plains God was there also.

My Friend

My friend, I am not what I seem. Seeming is but a garment I wear—a care-woven garment that protects me from thy questionings and thee from my negligence.

The "I" in me, my friend, dwells in the house of silence, and therein it shall remain for ever more, unperceived, unapproachable.

I would not have thee believe in what I say nor trust in what I do—for my words are naught but thy own thoughts in sound and my deeds thy own hopes in action.

When thou sayest, "The wind bloweth eastward," I say, "Aye it doth blow eastward"; for I would not have thee know that my mind doth not dwell upon the wind but upon the sea.

Thou canst not understand my seafaring thoughts, nor would I have thee understand. I would be at sea alone.

When it is day with thee, my friend, it is night with me; yet even then I speak of the noontide that dances upon the hills and of the purple shadow that steals its way across the valley; for thou canst not hear the songs of my darkness nor see my wings beating against the stars—and I fain would not have thee hear or see. I would be with night alone.

When thou ascendest to thy Heaven I descend to my Hell—even then thou callest to me across the unbridgeable gulf, "My companion, my comrade," and I call back to thee, "My comrade, my companion"—for I would not have thee see my Hell. The flame would burn thy eyesight and the smoke would crowd thy nostrils. And I love my Hell too well to have thee visit it. I would be in Hell alone.

Thou lovest Truth and Beauty and Righteousness; and I for thy sake say it is well and seemly to love these things. But in my heart I laugh at thy love. Yet I would not have thee see my laughter. I would laugh alone.

My friend, thou art good and cautious and wise; nay, thou art perfect—and I, too, speak with thee wisely and cautiously. And yet I am mad. But I mask my madness. I would be mad alone.

My friend, thou art not my friend, but how shall I make thee understand? My path is not thy path, yet together we walk, hand in hand.

The Scarecrow

Once I said to a scarecrow, "You must be tired of standing in this lonely field."

And he said, "The joy of scaring is a deep and lasting one, and I never tire of it."

Said I, after a minute of thought, "It is true; for I too have known that joy."

Said he, "Only those who are stuffed with straw can know it."

Then I left him, not knowing whether he had complimented or belittled me.

A year passed, during which the scarecrow turned philosopher.

And when I passed by him again I saw two crows building a nest under his hat.

The Sleep-Walkers

In the town where I was born lived a woman and her daughter, who walked in their sleep.

One night, while silence enfolded the world, the woman and her daughter, walking, yet asleep, met in their mist-veiled garden.

And the mother spoke, and she said: "At last, at last, my enemy! You by whom my youth was destroyed—who have built up your life upon the ruins of mine! Would I could kill you!"

And the daughter spoke, and she said: "O hateful woman, selfish and old! Who stand between my freer self and me! Who would have my life an echo of your own faded life! Would you were dead!"

At that moment a cock crew, and both women awoke. The mother said gently, "Is that you, darling?" And the daughter answered gently, "Yes, dear."

The Wise Dog

One day there passed by a company of cats a wise dog.

And as he came near and saw that they were very intent and heeded him not, he stopped.

Then there arose in the midst of the company a large, grave cat and looked upon them and said, "Brethren, pray ye; and when ye have prayed again and yet again, nothing doubting, verily then it shall rain mice."

And when the dog heard this he laughed in his heart and turned from them saying, "O blind and foolish cats, has it not been written and have I not known and my fathers before me, that that which raineth for prayer and faith and supplication is not mice but bones."

The Two Hermits

Upon a lonely mountain, there lived two hermits who worshipped God and loved one another.

Now these two hermits had one earthen bowl, and this was their only possession.

One day an evil spirit entered into the heart of the older hermit and he came to the younger and said, "It is long that we have lived together. The time has come for us to part. Let us divide our possessions."

Then the younger hermit was saddened and he said, "It grieves me, Brother, that thou shouldst leave me. But if thou must needs go, so be it," and he brought the earthen bowl and gave it to him saying, "We cannot divide it, Brother, let it be thine."

Then the older hermit said, "Charity I will not accept. I will take nothing but mine own. It must be divided."

And the younger one said, "If the bowl be broken, of what use would it be to thee or to me? If it be thy pleasure let us rather cast a lot."

But the older hermit said again, "I will have but justice and mine own, and I will not trust justice and mine own to vain chance. The bowl must be divided."

Then the younger hermit could reason no further and he said, "If it be indeed thy will, and if even so thou wouldst have it let us now break the bowl."

But the face of the older hermit grew exceedingly dark, and he cried, "O thou cursed coward, thou wouldst not fight."

On Giving and Taking

Once there lived a man who had a valley-full of needles. And one day the mother of Jesus came to him and said: "Friend, my son's garment is torn and I must needs mend it before he goeth to the temple. Wouldst thou not give me a needle?"

And he gave her not a needle, but he gave her a learned discourse on Giving and Taking to carry to her son before he should go to the temple.

The Seven Selves

In the stillest hour of the night, as I lay half asleep, my seven selves sat together and thus conversed in whisper:

First Self: Here, in this madman, I have dwelt all these years, with naught to do but renew his pain by day and recreate his sorrow by night. I can bear my fate no longer, and now I rebel.

Second Self: Yours is a better lot than mine, brother, for it is given to me to be this madman's joyous self. I laugh his laughter and sing his happy hours, and with thrice winged feet I dance his brighter thoughts. It is I that would rebel against my weary existence.

Third Self: And what of me, the love-ridden self, the flaming brand of wild passion and fantastic desires? It is I the love-sick self who would rebel against this madman.

Fourth Self: I, amongst you all, am the most miserable, for naught was given me but odious hatred and destructive loathing. It is I, the tempest-like self, the one born in the black caves of Hell, who would protest against serving this madman.

Fifth Self: Nay, it is I, the thinking self, the fanciful self, the self of hunger and thirst, the one doomed to wander without rest in search of unknown things and things not yet created; it is I, not you, who would rebel.

Sixth Self: And I, the working self, the pitiful labourer, who, with patient hands, and longing eyes, fashion the days into images and give the formless elements new and eternal forms—it is I, the solitary one, who would rebel against this restless madman.

Seventh Self: How strange that you all would rebel against this man, because each and every one of you has a preordained fate to fulfill. Ah! could I but be like one of you, a self with a determined lot! But I have none, I am the do-nothing self, the one who sits in the dumb, empty nowhere and nowhen, while you are busy re-creating life. Is it you or I, neighbours, who should rebel?

When the seventh self thus spake the other six selves looked with pity upon him but said nothing more; and as the night grew deeper one after the other went to sleep enfolded with a new and happy submission.

But the seventh self remained watching and gazing at nothingness, which is behind all things.

War

One night a feast was held in the palace, and there came a man and prostrated himself before the prince, and all the feasters looked upon him; and they saw that one of his eyes was out and that the empty socket bled. And the prince inquired of him, "What has befallen you?" And the man replied, "O prince, I am by profession a thief, and this night, because there was no moon, I went to rob the money-changer's shop, and as I climbed in through the window I made a mistake and entered the weaver's shop, and in the dark I ran into the weaver's loom and my eye was plucked out. And now, O prince, I ask for justice upon the weaver."

Then the prince sent for the weaver and he came, and it was decreed that one of his eyes should be plucked out.

"O prince," said the weaver, "the decree is just. It is right that one of my eyes be taken. And yet, alas! both are necessary to me in order that I may see the two sides of the cloth that I weave. But I have a neighbour, a cobbler, who has also two eyes, and in his trade both eyes are not necessary."

Then the prince sent for the cobbler. And he came. And they took out one of the cobbler's two eyes.

And justice was satisfied.

The Fox

A fox looked at his shadow at sunrise and said, "I will have a camel for lunch today." And all morning he went about looking for camels. But at noon he saw his shadow again—and he said, "A mouse will do."

The Wise King

Once there ruled in the distant city of Wirani a king who was both mighty and wise. And he was feared for his might and loved for his wisdom.

Now, in the heart of that city was a well, whose water was cool and crystalline, from which all the inhabitants drank, even the king and his courtiers; for there was no other well.

One night when all were asleep, a witch entered the city, and poured seven drops of strange liquid into the well, and said, "From this hour he who drinks this water shall become mad."

Next morning all the inhabitants, save the king and his lord chamberlain, drank from the well and became mad, even as the witch had foretold.

And during that day the people in the narrow streets and in the market places did naught but whisper to one another, "The king is mad. Our king and his lord chamberlain have lost their reason. Surely we cannot be ruled by a mad king. We must dethrone him."

That evening the king ordered a golden goblet to be filled from the well. And when it was brought to him he drank deeply, and gave it to his lord chamberlain to drink.

And there was great rejoicing in that distant city of Wirani, because its king and its lord chamberlain had regained their reason.

Ambition

Three men met at a tavern table. One was a weaver, another a carpenter and the third a ploughman.

Said the weaver, "I sold a fine linen shroud today for two pieces of gold. Let us have all the wine we want."

"And I," said the carpenter, "I sold my best coffin. We will have a great roast with the wine."

"I only dug a grave," said the ploughman, "but my patron paid me double. Let us have honey cakes too."

And all that evening the tavern was busy, for they called often for wine and meat and cakes. And they were merry.

And the host rubbed his hands and smiled at his wife; for his guests were spending freely.

When they left the moon was high, and they walked along the road singing and shouting together.

The host and his wife stood in the tavern door and looked after them.

"Ah!" said the wife, "these gentlemen! So freehanded and so gay! If only they could bring us such luck every day! Then our son need not be a tavern-keeper and work so hard. We could educate him, and he could become a priest."

The New Pleasure

Last night I invented a new pleasure, and as I was giving it the first trial an angel and a devil came rushing toward my house. They met at my door and fought with each other over my newly created pleasure; the one crying, "It is a sin!"—the other, "It is a virtue!"

The Other Language

Three days after I was born, as I lay in my silken cradle, gazing with astonished dismay on the new world round about me, my mother spoke to the wet-nurse, saying, "How does my child?"

And the wet-nurse answered, "He does well, Madame, I have fed him three times; and never before have I seen a babe so young yet so gay."

And I was indignant; and I cried, "It is not true, mother; for my bed is hard, and the milk I have sucked is bitter to my mouth, and the odour of the breast is foul in my nostrils, and I am most miserable."

But my mother did not understand, nor did the nurse; for the language I spoke was that of the world from which I came.

And on the twenty-first day of my life, as I was being christened, the priest said to my mother, "You should indeed by happy, Madame, that your son was born a Christian."

And I was surprised,—and I said to the priest, "Then your mother in Heaven should be unhappy, for you were not born a Christian."

But the priest too did not understand my language.

And after seven moons, one day a soothsayer looked at me, and he said to my mother, "Your son will be a statesman and a great leader of men."

But I cried out,—"That is a false prophet; for I shall be a musician, and naught but a musician shall I be."

But even at that age my language was not understood—and great was my astonishment.

And after three and thirty years, during which my mother, and the nurse, and the priest have all died, (the shadow of God be upon their spirits) the soothsayer still lives. And yesterday I met him near the gates of the temple;

and while we were talking together he said, "I have always known you would become a great musician. Even in your infancy I prophesied and foretold your future."

And I believed him—for now I too have forgotten the language of that other world.

The Pomegranate

Once when I was living in the heart of a pomegranate, I heard a seed saying, "Someday I shall become a tree, and the wind will sing in my branches, and the sun will dance on my leaves, and I shall be strong and beautiful through all the seasons."

Then another seed spoke and said, "When I was as young as you, I too held such views; but now that I can weigh and measure things, I see that my hopes were vain."

And a third seed spoke also, "I see in us nothing that promises so great a future."

And a fourth said, "But what a mockery our life would be, without a greater future!"

Said a fifth, "Why dispute what we shall be, when we know not even what we are."

But a sixth replied, "Whatever we are, that we shall continue to be."

And a seventh said, "I have such a clear idea how everything will be, but I cannot put it into words."

Then an eight spoke—and a ninth—and a tenth—and then many—until all were speaking, and I could distinguish nothing for the many voices.

And so I moved that very day into the heart of a quince, where the seeds are few and almost silent.

The Two Cages

In my father's garden there are two cages. In one is a lion, which my father's slaves brought from the desert of Ninavah; in the other is a songless sparrow.

Every day at dawn the sparrow calls to the lion, "Good morrow to thee, brother prisoner."

The Three Ants

Three ants met on the nose of a man who was asleep in the sun. And after they had saluted one another, each according to the custom of his tribe, they stood there conversing.

The first ant said, "These hills and plains are the most barren I have known. I have searched all day for a grain of some sort, and there is none to be found."

Said the second ant, "I too have found nothing, though I have visited every nook and glade. This is, I believe, what my people call the soft, moving land where nothing grows."

Then the third ant raised his head and said, "My friends, we are standing now on the nose of the Supreme Ant, the mighty and infinite Ant, whose body is so great that we cannot see it, whose shadow is so vast that we cannot trace it, whose voice is so loud that we cannot hear it; and He is omnipresent."

When the third ant spoke thus the other ants looked at each other and laughed.

At that moment the man moved and in his sleep raised his hand and scratched his nose, and the three ants were crushed.

The Grave-Digger

Once, as I was burying one of my dead selves, the grave-digger came by and said to me, "Of all those who come here to bury, you alone I like."

Said I, "You please me exceedingly, but why do you like me?"

"Because," said he, "They come weeping and go weeping—you only come laughing and go laughing."

On the Steps of the Temple

Yestereve, on the marble steps of the Temple, I saw a woman sitting between two men. One side of her face was pale, the other was blushing.

The Blessed City

In my youth I was told that in a certain city every one lived according to the Scriptures.

And I said, "I will seek that city and the blessedness thereof." And it was far. And I made great provision for my journey. And after forty days I beheld the city and on the forty-first day I entered into it.

And lo! the whole company of the inhabitants had each but a single eye and but one hand. And I was astonished and said to myself, "Shall they of this so holy city have but one eye and one hand?"

Then I saw that they too were astonished, for they were marveling greatly at my two hands and my two eyes. And as they were speaking together I inquired of them saying, "Is this indeed the Blessed City, where each man lives according to the Scriptures?" And they said, "Yes, this is that city."

"And what," said I, "hath befallen you, and where are your right eyes and your right hands?"

And all the people were moved. And they said, "Come thou and see."

And they took me to the temple in the midst of the city. And in the temple I saw a heap of hands and eyes. All withered. Then said I, "Alas! what conqueror hath committed this cruelty upon you?"

And there went a murmur amongst them. And one of their elders stood forth and said, "This doing is of ourselves. God hath made us conquerors over the evil that was in us."

And he led me to a high altar, and all the people followed. And he showed me above the altar an inscription graven, and I read:

"If thy right eye offend thee, pluck it out and cast it from thee; for it is profitable for thee that one of thy members should perish, and not that the whole body should be cast into hell. And if thy right hand offend thee, cut it off and cast it from thee; for it is profitable for thee that one of thy members should perish, and not that thy whole body should be cast into hell."

Then I understood. And I turned about to all the people and cried, "Hath no man or woman among you two eyes or two hands?"

And they answered me saying, "No, not one. There is none whole save such as are yet too young to read the Scripture and to understand its commandment."

And when we had come out of the temple, I straightway left that Blessed City; for I was not too young, and I could read the scripture.

The Good God and the Evil God

The Good God and the Evil God met on the mountain top.

The Good God said, "Good day to you, brother."

The Evil God did not answer.

And the Good God said, "You are in a bad humour today."

"Yes," said the Evil God, "for of late I have been often mistaken for you, called by your name, and treated as if I were you, and it ill-pleases me."

And the Good God said, "But I too have been mistaken for you and called by your name."

The Evil God walked away cursing the stupidity of man.

Defeat

Defeat, my Defeat, my solitude and my aloofness;
You are dearer to me than a thousand triumphs,
And sweeter to my heart than all world-glory.

Defeat, my Defeat, my self-knowledge and my defiance,
Through you I know that I am yet young and swift of foot
And not to be trapped by withering laurels.
And in you I have found aloneness
And the joy of being shunned and scorned.

Defeat, my Defeat, my shining sword and shield,
In your eyes I have read
That to be enthroned is to be enslaved,
And to be understood is to be leveled down,
And to be grasped is but to reach one's fullness
And like a ripe fruit to fall and be consumed.

Defeat, my Defeat, my bold companion,
You shall hear my songs and my cries and my silences,
And none but you shall speak to me of the beating of wings,
And urging of seas,
And of mountains that burn in the night,
And you alone shall climb my steep and rocky soul.

Defeat, my Defeat, my deathless courage,
You and I shall laugh together with the storm,
And together we shall dig graves for all that die in us,
And we shall stand in the sun with a will,
And we shall be dangerous.

Night and the Madman

"I am like thee, O, Night, dark and naked; I walk on the flaming path which is above my day-dreams, and whenever my foot touches earth a giant oak tree comes forth."

"Nay, thou art not like me, O, Madman, for thou still lookest backward to see how large a foot-print thou leavest on the sand."

"I am like thee, O, Night, silent and deep; and in the heart of my loneliness lies a Goddess in child-bed; and in him who is being born Heaven touches Hell."

"Nay, thou art not like me, O, Madman, for thou shudderest yet before pain, and the song of the abyss terrifies thee."

"I am like thee, O, Night, wild and terrible; for my ears are crowded with cries of conquered nations and sighs for forgotten lands."

"Nay, thou art not like me, O, Madman, for thou still takest thy little-self for a comrade, and with thy monster-self thou canst not be friend."

"I am like thee, O, Night, cruel and awful; for my bosom is lit by burning ships at sea, and my lips are wet with blood of slain warriors."

"Nay, thou art not like me, O, Madman; for the desire for a sister-spirit is yet upon thee, and thou has not become alone unto thyself."

"I am like thee, O, Night, joyous and glad; for he who dwells in my shadow is now drunk with virgin wine, and she who follows me is sinning mirthfully."

"Nay, thou art not like me, O, Madman, for thy soul is wrapped in the veil of seven folds and thou holdest not thy heart in thine hand."

"I am like thee, O, Night, patient and passionate; for in my breast a thousand dead lovers are buried in shrouds of withered kisses."

"Yea, Madman, art thou like me? Art thou like me? And canst thou ride the tempest as a steed, and grasp the lightning as a sword?"

"Like thee, O, Night, like thee, mighty and high, and my throne is built upon heaps of fallen Gods; and before me too pass the days to kiss the hem of my garment but never to gaze at my face."

"Art thou like me, child of my darkest heart? And dost thou think my untamed thoughts and speak my vast language?"

"Yea, we are twin brothers, O, Night; for thou revealest space and I reveal my soul."

Faces

I have seen a face with a thousand countenances, and a face that was but a single countenance as if held in a mould.

I have seen a face whose sheen I could look through to the ugliness beneath, and a face whose sheen I had to lift to see how beautiful it was.

I have seen an old face much lined with nothing, and a smooth face in which all things were graven.

I know faces, because I look through the fabric my own eye weaves, and behold the reality beneath.

The Greater Sea

My soul and I went to the great sea to bathe. And when we reached the shore, we went about looking for a hidden and lonely place.

But as we walked, we saw a man sitting on a grey rock taking pinches of salt from a bag and throwing them into the sea.

"This is the pessimist," said my soul, "Let us leave this place. We cannot bathe here."

We walked on until we reached an inlet. There we saw, standing on a white rock, a man holding a bejeweled box, from which he took sugar and threw it into the sea.

"And this is the optimist," said my soul, "And he too must not see our naked bodies."

Further on we walked. And on a beach we saw a man picking up dead fish and tenderly putting them back into the water.

"And we cannot bathe before him," said my soul. "He is the humane philanthropist."

And we passed on.

Then we came where we saw a man tracing his shadow on the sand. Great waves came and erased it. But he went on tracing it again and again.

"He is the mystic," said my soul, "Let us leave him."

And we walked on, till in a quiet cover we saw a man scooping up the foam and putting it into an alabaster bowl.

"He is the idealist," said my soul, "Surely he must not see our nudity."

And on we walked. Suddenly we heard a voice crying, "This is the sea. This is the deep sea. This is the vast and mighty sea." And when we reached the voice it was a man whose back was turned to the sea, and at his ear he held a shell, listening to its murmur.

And my soul said, "Let us pass on. He is the realist, who turns his back on the whole he cannot grasp, and busies himself with a fragment."

So we passed on. And in a weedy place among the rocks was a man with his head buried in the sand. And I said to my soul, "We can bath here, for he cannot see us."

"Nay," said my soul, "For he is the most deadly of them all. He is the puritan."

Then a great sadness came over the face of my soul, and into her voice.

"Let us go hence," she said, "For there is no lonely, hidden place where we can bathe. I would not have this wind lift my golden hair, or bare my white bosom in this air, or let the light disclose my sacred nakedness."

Then we left that sea to seek the Greater Sea.

Crucified

I cried to men, "I would be crucified!"

And they said, "Why should your blood be upon our heads?"

And I answered, "How else shall you be exalted except by crucifying madmen?"

And they heeded and I was crucified. And the crucifixion appeased me.

And when I was hanged between earth and heaven they lifted up their heads to see me. And they were exalted, for their heads had never before been lifted.

But as they stood looking up at me one called out, "For what art thou seeking to atone?"

And another cried, "In what cause dost thou sacrifice thyself?"

And a third said, "Thinkest thou with this price to buy world glory?"

Then said a fourth, "Behold, how he smiles! Can such pain be forgiven?"

And I answered them all, and said:

"Remember only that I smiled. I do not atone—nor sacrifice—nor wish for glory; and I have nothing to forgive. I thirsted—and I besought you to give me my blood to drink. For what is there can quench a madman's thirst but his own blood? I was dumb—and I asked wounds of you for mouths. I was imprisoned in your days and nights—and I sought a door into larger days and nights.

And now I go—as others already crucified have gone. And think not we are weary of crucifixion. For we must be crucified by larger and yet larger men, between greater earths and greater heavens."

The Astronomer

In the shadow of the temple my friend and I saw a blind man sitting alone. And my friend said, "Behold the wisest man of our land."

Then I left my friend and approached the blind man and greeted him. And we conversed.

After a while I said, "Forgive my question; but since when has thou been blind?"

"From my birth," he answered.

Said I, "And what path of wisdom followest thou?"

Said he, "I am an astronomer."

Then he placed his hand upon his breast saying, "I watch all these suns and moons and stars."

The Great Longing

Here I sit between my brother the mountain and my sister the sea.

We three are one in loneliness, and the love that binds us together is deep and strong and strange. Nay, it is deeper than my sister's depth and stronger than my brother's strength, and stranger than the strangeness of my madness.

Aeons upon aeons have passed since the first grey dawn made us visible to one another; and though we have seen the birth and the fullness and the death of many worlds, we are still eager and young.

We are young and eager and yet we are mateless and unvisited, and though we lie in unbroken half embrace, we are uncomforted. And what comfort is there for controlled desire and unspent passion? Whence shall come the flaming god to warm my sister's bed? And what she-torrent shall quench my brother's fire? And who is the woman that shall command my heart?

In the stillness of the night my sister murmurs in her sleep the fire-god's unknown name, and my brother calls afar upon the cool and distant goddess. But upon whom I call in my sleep I know not.

Here I sit between my brother the mountain and my sister the sea. We three are one in loneliness, and the love that binds us together is deep and strong and strange.

Said a Blade of Grass

Said a blade of grass to an autumn leaf, "You make such a noise falling! You scatter all my winter dreams."

Said the leaf indignant, "Low-born and low-dwelling! Songless, peevish thing! You live not in the upper air and you cannot tell the sound of singing."

Then the autumn leaf lay down upon the earth and slept. And when spring came she waked again—and she was a blade of grass.

And when it was autumn and her winter sleep was upon her, and above her through all the air the leaves were falling, she muttered to herself, "O these autumn leaves! They make such noise! They scatter all my winter dreams."

The Eye

Said the Eye one day, "I see beyond these valleys a mountain veiled with blue mist. Is it not beautiful?"

The Ear listened, and after listening intently awhile, said, "But where is any mountain? I do not hear it."

Then the Hand spoke and said, "I am trying in vain to feel it or touch it, and I can find no mountain."

And the Nose said, "There is no mountain, I cannot smell it."

Then the Eye turned the other way, and they all began to talk together about the Eye's strange delusion. And they said, "Something must be the matter with the Eye."

The Two Learned Men

Once there lived in the ancient city of Afkar two learned men who hated and belittled each other's learning. For one of them denied the existence of the gods and the other was a believer.

One day the two met in the marketplace, and amidst their followers they began to dispute and to argue about the existence or the non-existence of the gods. And after hours of contention they parted.

That evening the unbeliever went to the temple and prostrated himself before the altar and prayed the gods to forgive his wayward past.

And the same hour the other learned man, he who had upheld the gods, burned his sacred books. For he had become an unbeliever.

When My Sorrow Was Born

When my Sorrow was born I nursed it with care, and watched over it with loving tenderness.

And my Sorrow grew like all living things, strong and beautiful and full of wondrous delights.

And we loved one another, my Sorrow and I, and we loved the world about us; for Sorrow had a kindly heart and mine was kindly with Sorrow.

And when we conversed, my Sorrow and I, our days were winged and our nights were girdled with dreams; for Sorrow had an eloquent tongue, and mine was eloquent with Sorrow.

And when we sang together, my Sorrow and I, our neighbors sat at their windows and listened; for our songs were deep as the sea and our melodies were full of strange memories.

And when we walked together, my Sorrow and I, people gazed at us with gentle eyes and whispered in words of exceeding sweetness. And there were those who looked with envy upon us, for Sorrow was a noble thing and I was proud with Sorrow.

But my Sorrow died, like all living things, and alone I am left to muse and ponder.

And now when I speak my words fall heavily upon my ears.

And when I sing my songs my neighbours come not to listen.

And when I walk the streets no one looks at me.

Only in my sleep I hear voices saying in pity, "See, there lies the man whose Sorrow is dead."

And When My Joy Was Born

And when my Joy was born, I held it in my arms and stood on the house-top shouting, "Come ye, my neighbours, come and see, for Joy this day is born unto me. Come and behold this gladsome thing that laugheth in the sun."

But none of my neighbours came to look upon my Joy, and great was my astonishment.

And every day for seven moons I proclaimed my Joy from the house-top—and yet no one heeded me. And my Joy and I were alone, unsought and unvisited.

Then my Joy grew pale and weary because no other heart but mine held its loveliness and no other lips kissed its lips.

Then my Joy died of isolation.

And now I only remember my dead Joy in remembering my dead Sorrow. But memory is an autumn leaf that murmurs a while in the wind and then is heard no more.

"The Perfect World"

God of lost souls, thou who are lost amongst the gods, hear me:

Gentle Destiny that watchest over us, mad, wandering spirits, hear me:

I dwell in the midst of a perfect race, I the most imperfect.

I, a human chaos, a nebula of confused elements, I move amongst finished worlds—peoples of complete laws and pure order, whose thoughts are assorted, whose dreams are arranged, and whose visions are enrolled and registered.

Their virtues, O God, are measured, their sins are weighed, and even the countless things that pass in the dim twilight of neither sin nor virtue are recorded and catalogued.

Here days and night are divided into seasons of conduct and governed by rules of blameless accuracy.

To eat, to drink, to sleep, to cover one's nudity, and then to be weary in due time.

To work, to play, to sing, to dance, and then to lie still when the clock strikes the hour.

To think thus, to feel thus much, and then to cease thinking and feeling when a certain star rises above yonder horizon.

To rob a neighbour with a smile, to bestow gifts with a graceful wave of the hand, to praise prudently, to blame cautiously, to destroy a sound with a word, to burn a body with a breath, and then to wash the hands when the day's work is done.

To love according to an established order, to entertain one's best self in a preconceived manner, to worship the gods becomingly, to intrigue the devils artfully—and then to forget all as though memory were dead.

To fancy with a motive, to contemplate with consideration, to be happy sweetly, to suffer nobly—and then to empty the cup so that tomorrow may fill it again.

All these things, O God, are conceived with forethought, born with determination, nursed with exactness, governed by rules, directed by reason, and then slain and buried after a prescribed method. And even their silent graves that lie within the human soul are marked and numbered.

It is a perfect world, a world of consummate excellence, a world of supreme wonders, the ripest fruit in God's garden, the master-thought of the universe.

But why should I be here, O God, I a green seed of unfulfilled passion, a mad tempest that seeketh neither east nor west, a bewildered fragment from a burnt planet?

Why am I here, O God of lost souls, thou who art lost amongst the gods?

SAND AND FOAM

I am forever walking upon these shores,
Betwixt the sand and the foam,
The high tide will erase my foot-prints,
And the wind will blow away the foam.
But the sea and the shore will remain
Forever.

Once I filled my hand with mist.
Then I opened it and lo, the mist was a worm.
And I closed and opened my hand again, and behold there was a bird.
And again I closed and opened my hand, and in its hollow stood a man with a sad face, turned upward.
And again I closed my hand, and when I opened it there was naught but mist.
But I heard a song of exceeding sweetness.

It was but yesterday I thought myself a fragment quivering without rhythm in the sphere of life.
Now I know that I am the sphere, and all life in rhythmic fragments moves within me.

They say to me in their awakening, "You and the world you live in are but a grain of sand upon the infinite shore of an infinite sea."

And in my dream I say to them, "I am the infinite sea, and all worlds are but grains of sand upon my shore."

Only once have I been made mute. It was when a man asked me, "Who are you?"

The first thought of God was an angel.
The first word of God was a man.

We were fluttering, wandering, longing creatures a thousand thousand years before the sea and the wind in the forest gave us words.

Now how can we express the ancient of days in us with only the sounds of our yesterdays?

The Sphinx spoke only once, and the Sphinx said, "A grain of sand is a desert, and a desert is a grain of sand; and now let us all be silent again."
I heard the Sphinx, but I did not understand.

Long did I lie in the dust of Egypt, silent and unaware of the seasons.
Then the sun gave me birth, and I rose and walked upon the banks of the Nile,
Singing with the days and dreaming with the nights.
And now the sun threads upon me with a thousand feet that I may lie again in the dust of Egypt.
But behold a marvel and a riddle!
The very sun that gathered me cannot scatter me.
Still erect am I, and sure of foot do I walk upon the banks of the Nile.

Remembrance is a form of meeting.

Forgetfulness is a form of freedom.

We measure time according to the movement of countless suns; and they measure time by little machines in their little pockets.
Now tell me, how could we ever meet at the same place and the same time?

Space is not space between the earth and the sun to one who looks down from the windows of the Milky Way.

Humanity is a river of light running from the ex-eternity to eternity.

Do not the spirits who dwell in the ether envy man his pain?

On my way to the Holy City I met another pilgrim and I asked him, "Is this indeed the way to the Holy City?"

And he said, "Follow me, and you will reach the Holy City in a day and a night."

And I followed him. And we walked many days and many nights, yet we did not reach the Holy City.

And what was to my surprise he became angry with me because he had misled me.

Make me, oh God, the prey of the lion, ere You make the rabbit my prey.

One may not reach the dawn save by the path of the night.

My house says to me, "Do not leave me, for here dwells your past."

And the road says to me, "Come and follow me, for I am your future."

And I say to both my house and the road, "I have no past, nor have I a future. If I stay here, there is a going in my staying; and if I go there is a staying in my going. Only love and death will change all things."

How can I lose faith in the justice of life, when the dreams of those who sleep upon feathers are not more beautiful than the dreams of those who sleep upon the earth?

Strange, the desire for certain pleasures is a part of my pain.

Seven times have I despised my soul:
The first time when I saw her being meek that she might attain height.
The second time when I saw her limping before the crippled.
The third time when she was given to choose between the hard and the easy, and she chose the easy.
The fourth time when she committed a wrong, and comforted herself that others also commit wrong.
The fifth time when she forbore for weakness, and attributed her patience to strength.
The sixth time when she despised the ugliness of a face, and knew not that it was one of her own masks.
And the seventh time when she sang a song of praise, and deemed it a virtue.

I am ignorant of absolute truth. But I am humble before my ignorance and therein lies my honor and my reward.

There is a space between man's imagination and man's attainment that may only be traversed by his longing.

Paradise is there, behind that door, in the next room; but I have lost the key.

Perhaps I have only mislaid it.

You are blind and I am deaf and dumb, so let us touch hands and understand.

The significance of man is not in what he attains, but rather in what he longs to attain.

Some of us are like ink and some like paper.

And if it were not for the blackness of some of us, some of us would be dumb;

And if it were not for the whiteness of some of us, some of us would be blind.

Give me an ear and I will give you a voice.

Our mind is a sponge; our heart is a stream.

Is it not strange that most of us choose sucking rather than running?

When you long for blessings that you may not name, and when you grieve knowing not the cause, then indeed you are growing with all things that grow, and rising toward your greater self.

When one is drunk with a vision, he deems his faint expression of it the very wine.

You drink wine that you may be intoxicated; and I drink that it may sober me from that other wine.

When my cup is empty I resign myself to its emptiness; but when it is half full I resent its half-fulness.

The reality of the other person is not in what he reveals to you, but in what he cannot reveal to you.
Therefore, if you would understand him, listen not to what he says but rather to what he does not say.

Half of what I say is meaningless; but I say it so that the other half may reach you.

A sense of humour is a sense of proportion.

❦

My loneliness was born when men praised my talkative faults and blamed my silent virtues.

❦

When Life does not find a singer to sing her heart she produces a philosopher to speak her mind.

❦

A truth is to be known always, to be uttered sometimes.

❦

The real in us is silent; the acquired is talkative.

❦

The voice of life in me cannot reach the ear of life in you; but let us talk that we may not feel lonely.

❦

When two women talk they say nothing; when one woman speaks she reveals all of life.

❦

Frogs may bellow louder than bulls, but they cannot drag the plough in the field not turn the wheel of the winepress, and of their skins you cannot make shoes.

Only the dumb envy the talkative.

If winter should say, "Spring is in my heart," who would believe winter?

Every seed is a longing.

Should you really open your eyes and see, you would behold your image in all images.
And should you open your ears and listen, you would hear your own voice in all voices.

It takes two of us to discover truth: one to utter it and one to understand it.

Though the wave of words is forever upon us, yet our depth is forever silent.

Many a doctrine is like a window pane. We see truth through it but it divides us from truth.

Now let us play hide and seek. Should you hide in my heart it would not be difficult to find you. But should you hide behind your own shell, then it would be useless for anyone to seek you.

A woman may veil her face with a smile.

How noble is the sad heart who would sing a joyous song with joyous hearts.

He who would understand a woman, or dissect genius, or solve the mystery of silence is the very man who would wake from a beautiful dream to sit at a breakfast table.

I would walk with all those who walk. I would not stand still to watch the procession passing by.

You owe more than gold to him who serves you. Give him of your heart or serve him.

Nay, we have not lived in vain. Have they not built towers of our bones?

Let us not be particular and sectional. The poet's mind and the scorpion's tail rise in glory from the same earth.

Every dragon gives birth to a St. George who slays it.

Trees are poems that the earth writes upon the sky. We fell them down and turn them into paper that we may record our emptiness.

Should you care to write (and only the saints know why you should) you must needs have knowledge and art and music – the knowledge of the music of words, the art of being artless, and the magic of loving your readers.

They dip their pens in our hearts and think they are inspired.

Should a tree write its autobiography it would not be unlike the history of a race.

If I were to choose between the power of writing a poem and the ecstasy of a poem unwritten, I would choose the ecstasy. It is better poetry. But you and all my neighbors agree that I always choose badly.

Poetry is not an opinion expressed. It is a song that rises from a bleeding wound or a smiling mouth.

Words are timeless. You should utter them or write them with a knowledge of their timelessness.

A poet is a dethroned king sitting among the ashes of his palace trying to fashion an image out of the ashes.

Poetry is a deal of joy and pain and wonder, with a dash of the dictionary.

In vain shall a poet seek the mother of the songs of his heart.

Once I said to a poet, "We shall not know your worth until you die."
And he answered saying, "Yes, death is always the revealer. And if indeed you would know my worth it is that I have more in my heart than upon my tongue, and more in my desire than in my hand."

If you sing of beauty though alone in the heart of the desert you will have an audience.

Poetry is wisdom that enchants the heart.
Wisdom is poetry that sings in the mind.
If we could enchant man's heart and at the same time sing in his mind,
Then in truth he would live in the shadow of God.

Inspiration will always sing; inspiration will never explain.

We often sing lullabies to our children that we ourselves may sleep.

All our words are but crumbs that fall down from the feast of the mind.

Thinking is always the stumbling stone to poetry.

A great singer is he who sings our silences.

How can you sing if your mouth be filled with food?
How shall your hand be raised in blessing if it is filled with gold?

They say the nightingale pierces his bosom with a thorn when he sings his love song.
So do we all. How else should we sing?

Genius is but a robin's song at the beginning of a slow spring.

Even the most winged spirit cannot escape physical necessity.

A madman is not less a musician than you or myself; only the instrument on which he plays is a little out of tune.

The song that lies silent in the heart of a mother sings upon the lips of her child.

No longing remains unfulfilled.

I have never agreed with my other self wholly. The truth of the matter seems to lie between us.

Your other self is always sorry for you. But your other self grows on sorrow; so all is well.

There is no struggle of soul and body save in the minds of those whose souls are asleep and whose bodies are out of tune.

When you reach the heart of life you shall find beauty in all things, even in the eyes that are blind to beauty.

We live only to discover beauty. All else is a form of waiting.

Sow a seed and the earth will yield you a flower. Dream your dream to the sky and it will bring you your beloved.

The devil died the very day you were born.
Now you do not have to go through hell to meet an angel.

Many a woman borrows a man's heart; very few could possess it.

If you would possess you must not claim.

When a man's hand touches the hand of a woman they both touch the heart of eternity.

Love is the veil between lover and lover.

Every man loves two women; the one is the creation of his imagination, and the other is not yet born.

Men who do not forgive women their little faults will never enjoy their great virtues.

Love that does not renew itself every day becomes a habit and in turn a slavery.

Lovers embrace that which is between them rather than each other.

Love and doubt have never been on speaking terms.

Love is a word of light, written by a hand of light, upon a page of light.

Friendship is always a sweet responsibility, never an opportunity.

If you do not understand your friend under all conditions you will never understand him.

Your most radiant garment is of the other person's weaving;
You most savory meal is that which you eat at the other person's table;
Your most comfortable bed is in the other person's house.
Now tell me, how can you separate yourself from the other person?

Your mind and my heart will never agree until your mind ceases to live in numbers and my heart in the mist.

We shall never understand one another until we reduce the language to seven words.

How shall my heart be unsealed unless it be broken?

Only great sorrow or great joy can reveal your truth.
If you would be revealed you must either dance naked in the sun, or carry your cross.

Should nature heed what we say of contentment no river would seek the sea, and no winter would turn to Spring. Should she heed all we say of thrift, how many of us would be breathing this air?

You see but your shadow when you turn your back to the sun.

You are free before the sun of the day, and free before the stars of the night;
And you are free when there is no sun and no moon and no star.
You are even free when you close your eyes upon all there is.
But you are a slave to him whom you love because you love him,
And a slave to him who loves you because he loves you.

We are all beggars at the gate of the temple, and each one of us receives his share of the bounty of the King when he enters the temple, and when he goes out.

But we are all jealous of one another, which is another way of belittling the King.

You cannot consume beyond your appetite. The other half of the loaf belongs to the other person, and there should remain a little bread for the chance guest.

If it were not for your guests all houses would be graves.

Said a gracious wolf to a simple sheep, "Will you not honor our house with a visit?"

And the sheep answered, "We would have been honored to visit your house if it were not in your stomach."

I stopped my guest on the threshold and said, "Nay, wipe not your feet as you enter, but as you go out."

Generosity is not in giving me that which I need more than you do, but it is in giving me that which you need more than I do.

You are indeed charitable when you give, and while giving, turn your face away so that you may not see the shyness of the receiver.

The difference between the richest man and the poorest is but a day of hunger and an hour of thirst.

We often borrow from our tomorrows to pay our debts to our yesterdays.

I too am visited by angels and devils, but I get rid of them.
When it is an angel I pray an old prayer, and he is bored;
When it is a devil I commit an old sin, and he passes me by.

After all this is not a bad prison; but I do not like this wall between my cell and the next prisoner's cell;
Yet I assure you that I do not wish to reproach the warder not the Builder of the prison.

Those who give you a serpent when you ask for a fish, may have nothing but serpents to give. It is then generosity on their part.

Trickery succeeds sometimes, but it always commits suicide.

You are truly a forgiver when you forgive murderers who never spill blood, thieves who never steal, and liars who utter no falsehood.

He who can put his finger upon that which divides good from evil is he who can touch the very hem of the garment of God.

If your heart is a volcano how shall you expect flowers to bloom in your hands?

A strange form of self-indulgence! There are times when I would be wronged and cheated, that I may laugh at the expense of those who think I do not know I am being wronged and cheated.

What shall I say of him who is the pursuer playing the part of the pursued?

Let him who wipes his soiled hands with your garment take your garment. He may need it again; surely you would not.

It is a pity that money-changers cannot be good gardeners.

Please do not whitewash your inherent faults with your acquired virtues. I would have the faults; they are like mine own.

How often have I attributed to myself crimes I have never committed, so that the other person may feel comfortable in my presence.

Even the masks of life are masks of deeper mystery.

You may judge others only according to your knowledge of yourself. Tell me now, who among us is guilty and who is unguilty?

The truly just is he who feels half guilty of your misdeeds.

Only an idiot and a genius break man-made laws; and they are the nearest to the heart of God.

It is only when you are pursued that you become swift.

I have no enemies, O God, but if I am to have an enemy
Let his strength be equal to mine,
That truth alone may be the victor.

You will be quite friendly with your enemy when you both die.

Perhaps a man may commit suicide in self-defense.

Long ago there lived a Man who was crucified for being too loving and too lovable.

And strange to relate I met him thrice yesterday.

The first time He was asking a policeman not to take a prostitute to prison; the second time He was drinking wine with an outcast; and the third time He was having a fist-fight with a promoter inside a church.

If all they say of good and evil were true, then my life is but one long crime.

Pity is but half justice.

The only one who has been unjust to me is the one to whose brother I have been unjust.

When you see a man led to prison say in your heart, "Mayhap he is escaping from a narrower prison."

And when you see a man drunken say in your heart, "Mayhap he sought escape from something still more unbeautiful."

Oftentimes I have hated in self-defense; but if I were stronger I would not have used such a weapon.

How stupid is he who would patch the hatred in his eyes with the smile of his lips.

Only those beneath me can envy or hate me.
I have never been envied nor hated; I am above no one.
Only those above me can praise or belittle me.
I have never been praised nor belittled; I am below no one.

Your saying to me, "I do not understand you," is praise beyond my worth, and an insult you do not deserve.

How mean am I when life gives me gold and I give you silver, and yet I deem myself generous.

When you reach the heart of life you will find yourself not higher than the felon, and not lower than the prophet.

Strange that you should pity the slow-footed and not the slow-minded,
And the blind-eyed rather than the blind-hearted.

It is wiser for the lame not to break his crutches upon the head of his enemy.

How blind is he who gives you out of his pocket that he may take out of your heart.

Life is a procession. The slow of foot finds it too swift and he steps out;
And the swift of foot finds it too slow and he too steps out.

If there is such a thing as sin some of us commit it backward following our forefathers' footsteps;
And some of us commit it forward by overruling our children.

The truly good is he who is one with all those who are deemed bad.

We are all prisoners but some of us are in cells with windows and some without.

Strange that we all defend our wrongs with more vigor than we do our rights.

Should we all confess our sins to one another we would all laugh at one another for our lack of originality.
Should we all reveal our virtues we would also laugh for the same cause.

An individual is above man-made laws until he commits a crime against man-made conventions; After that he is neither above anyone nor lower than anyone.

Government is an agreement between you and myself. You and myself are often wrong.

Crime is either another name of need or an aspect of a disease.

Is there a greater fault than being conscious of the other person's faults?

If the other person laughs at you, you can pity him; but if you laugh at him you may never forgive yourself.

If the other person injures you, you may forget the injury; but if you injure him you will always remember.

In truth the other person is your most sensitive self given another body.

How heedless you are when you would have men fly with your wings and you cannot even give them a feather.

Once a man sat at my board and ate my bread and drank my wine and went away laughing at me.

Then he came again for bread and wine, and I spurned him;

And the angels laughed at me.

Hate is a dead thing. Who of you would be a tomb?

It is the honor of the murdered that he is not the murderer.

The tribune of humanity is in its silent heart, never its talkative mind.

They deem me mad because I will not sell my days for gold;
And I deem them mad because they think my days have a price.

They spread before us their riches of gold and silver, of ivory and ebony, and we spread before them our hearts and our spirits.;
And yet they deem themselves the hosts and us the guests.

I would not be the least among men with dreams and the desire to fulfill them, rather than the greatest with no dreams and no desires.

The most pitiful among men is he who turns his dreams into silver and gold.

We are all climbing toward the summit of our hearts' desire. Should the other climber steal your sack and your purse and wax fat on the one and heavy on the other, you should pity him;
The climbing will be harder for his flesh, and the burden will make his way longer.
And should you in your leanness see his flesh puffing upward, help him a step; it will add to your swiftness.

You cannot judge any man beyond your knowledge of him, and how small is your knowledge.

I would not listen to a conqueror preaching to the conquered.

The truly free man is he who bears the load of the bond slave patiently.

A thousand years ago my neighbor said to me, "I hate life, for it is naught but a thing of pain."
And yesterday I passed by a cemetery and saw life dancing upon his grave.

Strife in nature is but disorder longing for order.

Solitude is a silent storm that breaks down all our dead branches;
Yet it sends our living roots deeper into the living heart of the living earth.

Once I spoke of the sea to a brook, and the brook thought me but an imaginative exaggerator;
And once I spoke of a brook to the sea, and the sea thought me but a depreciative defamer.

How narrow is the vision that exalts the busyness of the ant above the singing of the grasshopper.

The highest virtue here may be the least in another world.

The deep and the high go to the depth or to the height in a straight line; only the spacious can move in circles.

If it were not for our conception of weights and measures we would stand in awe of the firefly as we do before the sun.

A scientist without imagination is a butcher with dull knives and outworn scales.
But what would you, since we are not all vegetarians?

When you sing the hungry hears you with his stomach.

Death is not nearer to the aged than to the new-born; neither is life.

If indeed you must be candid, be candid beautifully; otherwise keep silent, for there is a man in our neighborhood who is dying.

Mayhap a funeral among men is a wedding feast among the angels.

A forgotten reality may die and leave in its will seven thousand actualities and facts to be spent in its funeral and the building of a tomb.

In truth we talk only to ourselves, but sometimes we talk loud enough that others may hear us.

The obvious is that which is never seen until someone expresses it simply.

If the Milky Way were not within me how should I have seen it or known it?

Unless I am a physician among physicians they would not believe that I am an astronomer.

Perhaps the sea's definition of a shell is the pearl.
Perhaps time's definition of coal is the diamond.

Fame is the shadow of passion standing in the light.

A root is a flower that disdains fame.

There is neither religion nor science beyond beauty.

Every great man I have known had something small in his make-up; and it was that small something which prevented inactivity or madness or suicide.

The truly great man is he who would master no one, and who would be mastered by none.

I would not believe that a man is mediocre simply because he kills the criminals and the prophets.

Tolerance is love sick with the sickness of haughtiness.

Worms will turn; but is it not strange that even elephants will yield?

A disagreement may be the shortest cut between two minds.

I am the flame and I am the dry bush, and one part of me consumes the other part.

We are all seeking the summit of the holy moutain; but shall not our road be shorter if we consider the past a chart and not a guide?

Wisdom ceases to be wisdom when it becomes too proud to weep, too grave to laugh, and too self-ful to seek other than itself.

Had I filled myself with all that you know what room should I have for all that you do not know?

I have learned silence from the talkative, toleration from the intolerant, and kindness from the unkind; yet strange, I am ungrateful to these teachers.

A bigot is a stone-leaf orator.

The silence of the envious is too noisy.

When you reach the end of what you should know, you will be at the beginning of what you should sense.

An exaggeration is a truth that has lost its temper.

If you can see only what light reveals and hear only what sound announces,
Then in truth you do not see nor do you hear.

A fact is a truth unsexed.

You cannot laugh and be unkind at the same time.

The nearest to my heart are a king without a kingdom and a poor man who does not know how to beg.

A shy failure is nobler than an immodest success.

Dig anywhere in the earth and you will find a treasure, only you must dig with the faith of a peasant.

Said a hunted fox followed by twenty horsemen and a pack of twenty hounds, "Of course they will kill me. But how poor and how stupid they must be. Surely it would not be worth while for twenty foxes riding on twenty asses and accompanied by twenty wolves to chase and kill one man."

It is the mind in us that yields to the laws made by us, but never the spirit in us.

A traveler am I and a navigator, and every day I discover a new region within my soul.

A woman protested saying, "Of course it was a righteous war. My son fell in it."

I said to Life, "I would hear Death speak."
And Life raised her voice a little higher and said, "You hear him now."

When you have solved all the mysteries of life you long for death, for it is but another mystery of life.

Birth and death are the two noblest expressions of bravery.

My friend, you and I shall remain strangers unto life,
And unto one another, and each unto himself,
Until the day when you shall speak and I shall listen
Deeming your voice my own voice;
And when I shall stand before you
Thinking myself standing before a mirror.

They say to me, "Should you know yourself you would know all men."
And I say, "Only when I seek all men shall I know myself."

Man is two men; one is awake in darkness, the other is asleep in light.

A hermit is one who renounces the world of fragments that he may enjoy the world wholly and without interruption.

There lies a green field between the scholar and the poet; should the scholar cross it he becomes a wise man; should the poet cross it, he becomes a prophet.

Yestereve I saw philosophers in the market-place carrying their heads in baskets, and crying aloud, "Wisdom! Wisdom for sale!"

Poor philosophers! They must needs sell their heads to feed their hearts.

Said a philosopher to a street sweeper, "I pity you. Yours is a hard and dirty task."

And the street sweeper said, "Thank you, sir. But tell me what is your task?"

And the philosopher answered saying, "I study man's mind, his deeds and his desires."

Then the street sweeper went on with his sweeping and said with a smile, "I pity you too."

He who listens to truth is not less than he who utters truth.

No man can draw the line between necessities and luxuries. Only the angels can do that, and the angels are wise and wistful.

Perhaps the angels are our better thought in space.

He is the true prince who finds his throne in the heart of the dervish.

Generosity is giving more than you can, and pride is taking less than you need.

In truth you owe naught to any man. You owe all to all men.

All those who have lived in the past live with us now. Surely none of us would be an ungracious host.

He who longs the most lives the longest.

They say to me, "A bird in the hand is worth ten in the bush."
But I say, "A bird and a feather in the bush is worth more than ten birds in the hand."
Your seeking after *that feather* is life with winged feet; nay, it is life itself.

There are only two elements here, beauty and truth; beauty in the hearts of lovers, and truth in the arms of the tillers of the soil.

Great beauty captures me, but a beauty still greater frees me even from itself.

Beauty shines brighter in the heart of him who longs for it than in the eyes of him who sees it.

I admire him who reveals his mind to me; I honor him who unveils his dreams. But why am I shy, and even a little ashamed before him who serves me?

The gifted were once proud in serving princes.
Now they claim honor in serving paupers.

The angels know that too many practical men eat their bread with the sweat of the dreamer's brow.

Wit is often a mask. If you could tear it you would find either a genius irritated or cleverness juggling.

The understanding attributes to me understanding and the dull, dullness. I think they are both right.

Only those with secrets in their hearts could divine the secrets in our hearts.

He who would share your pleasure but not your pain shall lose the key to one of the seven gates of Paradise.

Yes, there is a Nirvanah; it is in leading your sheep to a green pasture, and in putting your child to sleep, and in writing the last line of your poem.

We choose our joys and our sorrows long before we experience them.

Sadness is but a wall between two gardens.

When either your joy or your sorrow becomes great the world becomes small.

Desire is half of life; idifference is half of death.

The bitterest thing in our today's sorrow is the memory of our yesterday's joy.

They say to me, "You must needs choose between the pleasures of this world and the peace of the next world."
And I say to them, "I have chosen both the delights of this world and the peace of the next. For I know in my heart that the Supreme Poet wrote but one poem, and it scans perfectly, and it also rhymes perfectly."

Faith is an oasis in the heart which will never be reached by the caravan of thinking.

When you reach your height you shall desire but only for desire; and you shall hunger, for hunger; and you shall thirst for greater thirst.

If you reveal your secrets to the wind you should not blame the wind for revealing them to the trees.

The flowers of spring are winter's dreams related at the breakfast table of the angels.

Said a skunk to a tube-rose, "See how swiftly I run, while you cannot walk nor even creep."
Said the tube-rose to the skunk, "Oh, most noble swift runner, please run swiftly!"

Turtles can tell more about roads than hares.

Strange that creatures without backbones have the hardest shells.

The most talkative is the least intelligent, and there is hardly a difference between an orator and an auctioneer.

Be grateful that you do not have to live down the renown of a father nor the wealth of an uncle.
But above all be grateful that no one will have to live down either your renown or your wealth.

Only when a juggler misses catching his ball does he appeal to me.

The envious praises me unknowingly.

Long were you a dream in your mother's sleep, and then she woke to give you birth.

The germ of the race is in your mother's longing.

My father and mother desired a child and they begot me.
And I wanted a mother and a father and I begot night and the sea.

Some of our children are our justifications and some are but our regrets.

When night comes and you too are dark, lie down and be dark with a will.

And when morning comes and you are still dark stand up and say to the day with a will, "I am still dark."

It is stupid to play a role with the night and the day.

They would both laugh at you.

The mountain veiled in mist is not a hill; an oak tree in the rain is not a weeping willow.

Behold here is a paradox; the deep and high are nearer to one another than the mid-level to either.

When I stood a clear mirror before you, you gazed into me and saw your image.

Then you said, "I love you."

But in truth you loved yourself in me.

When you enjoy loving your neighbor it ceases to be a virtue.

Love which is not always springing is always dying.

You cannot have youth and the knowledge of it at the same time;
For youth is too busy living to know, and knowledge is too busy seeking itself to live.

You may sit at your window watching the passersby. And watching you may see a nun walking toward your right hand, and a prostitute toward your left hand.

And you may say in your innocence, "How noble is the one and how ignoble is the other."

But should you close your eyes and listen awhile you would hear a voice whispering in the ether, "One seeks me in prayer, and the other in pain. And in the spirit of each there is a bower for my spirit."

Once every hundred years Jesus of Nazareth meets Jesus of the Christian in a garden among the hills of Lebanon. And they talk long; and each time Jesus of Nazareth goes away saying to Jesus of the Christian, "My friend, I fear we shall never, never agree."

May God feed the over-abundant!

A great man has two hearts; one bleeds and the other forbears.

Should one tell a lie which does not hurt you nor anyone else, why not say in your heart that the house of his facts is too small for his fancies, and he had to leave it for larger space?

Behind every closed door is a mystery sealed with seven seals.

Waiting is the hoofs of time.

What if trouble should be a new window in the Eastern wall of your house?

You may forget the one with whom you have laughed, but never the one with whom you have wept.

There must be something strangely sacred in salt. It is in our tears and in the sea.

Our God in His gracious thirst will drink us all, the dewdrop and the tear.

You are but a fragment of your giant self, a mouth that seeks bread, and a blind hand that holds the cup for a thirsty mouth.

If you would rise but a cubit above race and country and self you would indeed become godlike.

If I were you I would not find fault with the sea at low tide.
It is a good ship and our Captain is able; it is only your stomach that is in disorder.

Should you sit upon a cloud you would not see the boundary line between one country and another, nor the boundary stone between a farm and a farm.
It is a pity you cannot sit upon a cloud.

Seven centuries ago seven white doves rose from a deep valley flying to the snow-white summit of the mountain. One of the seven men who watched the flight said, "I see a black spot on the wing of the seventh dove."

Today the people in that valley tell of seven black doves who flew to the summit of the snowy mountain.

In the autumn I gathered all my sorrows and buried them in my garden.

And when April returned and spring came to wed the earth, there grew in my garden beautiful flowers unlike all other flowers.

And my neighbors came to behold them, and they all said to me, "When autumn comes again, at seeding time, will you not give us of the seeds of these flowers that we may have them in our gardens?"

It is indeed misery if I stretch an empty hand to men and receive nothing; but it is hopelessness if I stretch a full hand and find none to receive.

I long for eternity because there I shall meet my unwritten poems and my unpainted pictures.

Art is a step from nature toward the Infinite.

A work of art is a mist carved into an image.

Even the hands that make crowns of thorns are better than idle hands.

Our most sacred tears never seek our eyes.

Every man is the descendant of every king and every slave that ever lived.

If the great-grandfather of Jesus had known what was hidden within him, would he not have stood in awe of himself?

Was the love of Judas' mother of her son less than the love of Mary for Jesus?

There are three miracles of our Brother Jesus not yet recorded in the Book: the first that He was a man like you and me, the second that He had a sense of humour, and the third that He knew He was a conqueror though conquered.

Crucified One, you are crucified upon my heart; and the nails that pierce your hands pierce the walls of my heart.

And tomorrow when a stranger passes by this Golgotha he will not know that two bled here.

He will deem it the blood of one man.

You may have heard of the Blessed Mountain.

It is the highest mountain in our world.

Should you reach the summit you would have only one desire, and that to descend and be with those who dwell in the deepest valley.

That is why it is called the Blessed Mountain.

Every thought I have imprisoned in expression I must free by my deeds.

THE BROKEN WINGS

Foreword

I was eighteen years of age when love opened my eyes with its magic rays and touched my spirit for the first time with its fiery fingers, and Selma Karamy was the first woman who awakened my spirit with her beauty and led me into the garden of high affection, where days pass like dreams and nights like weddings.

Selma Karamy was the one who taught me to worship beauty by the example of her own beauty and revealed to me the secret of love by her affection; se was the one who first sang to me the poetry of real life.

Every young man remembers his first love and tries to recapture that strange hour, the memory of which changes his deepest feeling and makes him so happy in spite of all the bitterness of its mystery.

In every young man's life there is a "Selma" who appears to him suddenly while in the spring of life and transforms his solitude into happy moments and fills the silence of his nights with music.

I was deeply engrossed in thought and contemplation and seeking to understand the meaning of nature and the revelation of books and scriptures when I heard LOVE whispered into my ears through Selma's lips. My life was a coma, empty like that of Adam's in Paradise, when I saw Selma standing before me like a column of light. She was the Eve of my heart who filled it with secrets and wonders and made me understand the meaning of life.

The first Eve led Adam out of Paradise by her own will, while Selma made me enter willingly into the paradise of pure love and virtue by her sweetness and love; but what happened to the first man also happened to me, and the fiery word which chased Adam out of Paradise was like the one which frightened me by its glittering edge and forced me away from paradise of my love without having disobeyed any order or tasted the fruit of the forbidden tree.

Today, after many years have passed, I have nothing left out of that beautiful dream except painful memories flapping like invisible wings around me, filling the depths of my heart with sorrow, and bringing tears to my eyes; and my beloved, beautiful Selma, is dead and nothing is left to commemorate her except my broken heart and tomb surrounded by cypress trees. That tomb and this heart are all that is left to bear witness of Selma.

The silence that guards the tomb does not reveal God's secret in the obscurity of the coffin, and the rustling of the branches whose roots suck the body's elements do not tell the mysteries of the grave, by the agonized sighs of my heart announce to the living the drama which love, beauty, and death have performed.

Oh, friends of my youth who are scattered in the city of Beirut, when you pass by the cemetery near the pine forest, enter it silently and walk slowly so the tramping of your feet will not disturb the slumber of the dead, and stop humbly by Selma's tomb and greet the earth that encloses her corpse and mention my name with deep sigh and say to yourself, "here, all the hopes of Gibran, who is living as prisoner of love beyond the seas, were buried. On this spot he lost his happiness, drained his tears, and forgot his smile."

By that tomb grows Gibran's sorrow together with the cypress trees, and above the tomb his spirit flickers every night commemorating Selma, joining the branches of the trees in sorrowful wailing, mourning and lamenting the going of Selma, who, yesterday was a beautiful tune on the lips of life and today is a silent secret in the bosom of the earth.

Oh, comrades of my youth! I appeal to you in the names of those virgins whom your hearts have loved, to lay a wreath of flowers on the forsaken tomb of my beloved, for the flowers you lay on Selma's tomb are like falling drops of dew for the eyes of dawn on the leaves of withering rose.

Silent Sorrow

My neighbours, you remember the dawn of youth with pleasure and regret its passing; but I remember it like a prisoner who recalls the bars and shackles of his jail. You speak of those years between infancy and youth as a golden era free from confinement and cares, but I call those years an era of silent sorrow which dropped as a seed into my heart and grew with it and could find no outlet to the world of Knowledge and wisdom until love came and opened the heart's doors and lighted its corners. Love provided me with a tongue and tears. You people remember the gardens and orchids and the meeting places and street corners that witnessed your games and heard your innocent whispering; and I remember, too, the beautiful spot in North Lebanon. Every time I close my eyes I see those valleys full of magic and dignity and those mountains covered with glory and greatness trying to reach the sky. Every time I shut my ears to the clamour of the city I hear the murmur of the rivulets and the rustling of the branches. All those beauties which I speak of now and which I long to see, as a child longs for his mother's breast, wounded my spirit, imprisoned in the darkness of youth, as a falcon suffers in its cage when it sees a flock of birds flying freely in the spacious sky. Those valleys and hills fired my imagination, but bitter thoughts wove round my heart a net of hopelessness.

Every time I went to the fields I returned disappointed, without understanding the cause of my disappointment. Every time I looked at the grey sky I felt my heart contract. Every time I heard the singing of the birds and babbling of the spring I suffered without understanding the reason for my suffering. It is said that unsophistication makes a man empty and that emptiness makes him carefree. It may be true among those who were born dead and who exist like frozen corpses; but the sensitive boy who feels much and knows little is the most unfortunate creature under the sun, because he is torn by two forces. the first force elevates him and shows him the beauty of existence through a cloud of dreams; the second ties him down to the earth and fills his eyes with dust and overpowers him with fears and darkness.

Solitude has soft, silky hands, but with strong fingers it grasps the heart and makes it ache with sorrow. Solitude is the ally of sorrow as well as a companion of spiritual exaltation.

The boy's soul undergoing the buffeting of sorrow is like a white lily just unfolding. It trembles before the breeze and opens its heart to day break and folds its leaves back when the shadow of night comes. If that boy does not have diversion or friends or companions in his games his life will be like a narrow prison in which he sees nothing but spider webs and hears nothing but the crawling of insects.

That sorrow which obsessed me during my youth was not caused by lack of amusement, because I could have had it; neither from lack of friends, because I could have found them. That sorrow was caused by an inward ailment which made me love solitude. It killed in me the inclination for games and amusement. It removed from my shoulders the wings of youth and made me like a pong of water between mountains which reflects in its calm surface the shadows of ghosts and the colours of clouds and trees, but cannot find an outlet by which to pass singing to the sea.

Thus was my life before I attained the age of eighteen. That year is like a mountain peak in my life, for it awakened knowledge in me and made me understand the vicissitudes of mankind. In that year I was reborn and unless a person is born again his life will remain like a blank sheet in the book of existence. In that year, I saw the angels of heaven looking at me through the eyes of a beautiful woman. I also saw the devils of hell raging in the heart of an evil man. He who does not see the angels and devils in the beauty and malice of life will be far removed from knowledge, and his spirit will be empty of affection.

The Hand of Destiny

In the spring of the that wonderful year, I was in Beirut. The gardens were full of Nisan flowers and the earth was carpeted with green grass, and like a secret of earth revealed to Heaven. The orange trees and apple trees, looking like houris or brides sent by nature to inspire poets and excite the imagination, were wearing white garments of perfumed blossoms.

Spring is beautiful everywhere, but it is most beautiful in Lebanon. It is a spirit that roams round the earth but hovers over Lebanon, conversing with kings and prophets, singing with the rives the songs of Solomon, and repeating with the Holy Cedars of Lebanon the memory of ancient glory. Beirut, free from the mud of winter and the dust of summer, is like a bride in the spring, or like a mermaid sitting by the side of a brook drying her smooth skin in the rays of the sun.

One day, in the month of Nisan, I went to visit a friend whose home was at some distance from the glamorous city. As we were conversing, a dignified man of about sixty-five entered the house. As I rose to greet him, my friend introduced him to me as Farris Effandi Karamy and then gave him my name with flattering words. The old man looked at me a moment, touching his forehead with the ends of his fingers as if he were trying to regain his memory. Then he smilingly approached me saying, " You are the son of a very dear friend of mine, and I am happy to see that friend in your person."

Much affected by his words, I was attracted to him like a bird whose instinct leads him to his nest before the coming of the tempest. As we sat down, he told us about his friendship with my father, recalling the time which they spent together. An old man likes to return in memory to the days of his youth like a stranger who longs to go back to his own country. He delights to tell stories of the past like a poet who takes pleasure in reciting his best poem. He lives spiritually in the past because the present passes swiftly, and the future seems to him an approach to the oblivion of the grave. An hour full of old memories passed like the shadows of the trees over the grass. When Farris Effandi started to leave, he put his left hand on my shoulder and shook my right hand, saying, " I have not seen your father for twenty years. I hope you will l take his place in frequent visits to my house." I promised gratefully to do my duty toward a dear friend of my father.

Then the old man left the house, I asked my friend to tell me more about him. He said, "I do not know any other man in Beirut whose wealth has made him kind and whose kindness has made him wealthy. He is one of the few who come to this world and leave it without harming any one, but people of that kind are usually miserable and oppressed because they are not clever enough to save themselves from the crookedness of others. Farris Effandi has one daughter whose character is similar to his and whose beauty and gracefulness are beyond description, and she will also be miserable because her father's wealth is placing her already at the edge of a horrible precipice."

As he uttered these words, I noticed that his face clouded. Then he continued, "Farris Effandi is a good old man with a noble heart, but he lacks will power. People lead him like a blind man. His daughter obeys him in spite of her pride and intelligence, and this is the secret which lurks in the life of father and daughter. This secret was discovered by an evil man who is a bishop and whose wickedness hides in the shadow of his Gospel. He makes the people believe that he is kind and noble. He is the head of religion in this land of the religions. The people obey and worship him. he leads them like a flock of lambs to the slaughter house. This bishop has a nephew who is full of hatefulness and corruption. The day will come sooner or later when he will place his nephew on his right and Farris Effandi's daughter on this left, and, holding with his evil hand the wreath of matrimony over their heads, will tie a pure virgin to a filthy degenerate, placing the heart of the day in the bosom of the night.

That is all I can tell you about Farris Effandi and his daughter, so do not ask me any more questions."

Saying this, he turned his head toward the window as if he were trying to solve the problems of human existence by concentrating on the beauty of the universe.

As I left the house I told my friend that I was going to visit Farris Effandi in a few days for the purpose of fulfilling my promise and for the sake of the friendship which had joined him and my father. He stared at me for a moment, and I noticed a change in his expression as if my few simple words had revealed to him a new idea. Then he looked straight through my eyes in a strange manner, a look of love, mercy, and fear — the look of a prophet who foresees what no one else can divine. Then his lips trembled a little, but he said nothing when I started towards the door. That strange look followed me, the meaning of which I could not understand until I grew up in the world of experience, where hearts understand each other intuitively and where spirits are mature with knowledge.

Entrance to the Shrine

In a few days, loneliness overcame me; and I tired of the grim faces of books; I hired a carriage and started for the house of Farris Effandi. As I reached the pine woods where people went for picnics, the driver took a private way, shaded with willow trees on each side. Passing through , we could see the beauty of the green grass, the grapevines, and the many coloured flowers of Nisan just blossoming.

In a few minutes the carriage stopped before a solitary house in the midst of a beautiful garden. The scent of roses, gardenia, and jasmine filled the air. As I dismounted and entered the spacious garden, I saw Farris Effandi coming to meet me. He ushered me into his house with a hearty welcome and sat by me, like a happy father when he sees his son, showering me with questions on my life, future and education. I answered him, my voice full of ambition and zeal; for I heard ringing in my ears the hymn of glory, and I was sailing the calm sea of hopeful dreams. Just then a beautiful young woman, dressed in a gorgeous white silk gown, appeared from behind the velvet curtains of the door and walked toward me. Farris Effandi and I rose from our seats.

This is my daughter Selma," said the old man. Then he introduced me to her, saying, "Fate has brought back to me a dear old friend of mine in the person of his son." Selma stared at me a moment as if doubting that a visitor could have entered their house. Her hand, when I touched it, was like a white lily, and a strange pang pierced my heart.

We all sat silent as if Selma had brought into the room with her heavenly spirit worthy of mute respect. As she felt the silence she smiled at me and said," Many a times my father has repeated to me the stories of his youth and of the old days he and your father spent together. If your father spoke to you in the same way, then this meeting is not the first one between us."

The old man was delighted to hear his daughter talking in such a manner and said, "Selma is very sentimental. She sees everything through the eyes of the spirit." Then he resumed his conversation with care and tact as if he had found in me a magic which took him on the wings of memory to the days of the past.

As I considered him, dreaming of my own later years, he looked upon me, as a lofty old tree that has withstood storms and sunshine throws its shadow upon a small sapling which shakes before the breeze of dawn.

But Selma was silent. Occasionally, she looked first at me and then at her father as if reading the first and last chapters of life's drama. The day passed faster in that garden, and I could see through the window the ghostly yellow kiss of sunset on the mountains of Lebanon. Farris Effandi continued to recount his experiences and I listened entranced and responded with such enthusiasm that his sorrow was changed to happiness.

Selma sat by the window, looking on with sorrowful eyes and not speaking, although beauty has its own heavenly language, loftier than he voices of tongues and lips. It is a timeless language, common to all humanity, a calm lake that attracts the singing rivulets to its depth and makes them silent.

Only our spirits can understand beauty, or live and grow with it. It puzzles our minds; we are unable to describe it in words; it is a sensation that our eyes cannot see, derived from both the one who observes and the one who is looked upon. Real beauty is a ray which emanates from the holy of holies of the spirit, and illuminates the body, as life comes from the depths of the earth and gives colour and scent to a flower.

Real beauty lies in the spiritual accord that is called love which can exist between a man and a woman.

Did my spirit and Selma's reach out to each other that day when we met, and did that yearning make me see her as the most beautiful woman under the sun? Or was I intoxicated with the wine of youth which made me fancy that which never existed.?

Did my youth blind my natural eyes and make me imagine the brightness of her eyes, the sweetness of her mouth, and the grace of her figure? Or was it that her brightness, sweetness, and grace opened my eyes and showed me the happiness and sorrow of love?

It is hard to answer these questions, but I say truly that in that hour I felt an emotion that I had never felt before, a new affection resting calmly in my heart, like the spirit hovering over the waters at the creation of the world, and from that affection was born my happiness and my sorrow. Thus ended the hour of my first meeting with Selma, and thus the will of Heaven freed me from the bondage of youth and solitude and let me walk in the procession of love.

Love is the only freedom in the world because it so elevates the spirit that the laws of humanity and the phenomena of nature do not alter its course.

As I rose from my seat to depart, Farris Effandi came close to me and said soberly, "Now my son, since you know your way to this house, you should come often and feel that you are coming to your father's house. Consider me as a father and Selma as a sister." Saying this, he turned to Selma as if to ask confirmation of his statement. She nodded her head positively and then looked at me as one who has found an old acquaintance.

Those words uttered by Farris Effandi Karamy placed me side by side with his daughter at the altar of love. Those words were a heavenly song which started with exaltation and ended with sorrow; they raised our spirits to the realm of light and searing flame; they were the cup from which we drank happiness and bitterness.

I left the house. The old man accompanied me to the edge of the garden, while my heart throbbed like the trembling lips of a thirsty man.

The White Torch

The month of Nisan had nearly passed. I continued to visit the home of Farris Effendi and to meet Selma in that beautiful garden, gazing upon her beauty, marvelling at her intelligence, and hearing the stillness of sorrow. I felt an invisible hand drawing me to her.

Every visit gave me a new meaning to her beauty and a new insight into her sweet spirit, Until she became a book whose pages I could understand and whose praises I could sing, but which I could never finish reading. A woman whom Providence has provided with beauty of spirit and body is a truth, at the same time both open and secret, which we can understand only by love, and touch only by virtue; and when we attempt to describe such a woman she disappears like vapour.

Selma Karamy had bodily and spiritual beauty, but how can I describe her to one who never knew her? Can a dead man remember the singing of a nightingale and the fragrance of a rose and the sigh of a brook? Can a prisoner who is heavily loaded with shackles follow the breeze of the dawn? Is not silence more painful than death? Does pride prevent me from describing Selma in plain words since I cannot draw her truthfully with luminous colours? A hungry man in a desert will not refuse to eat dry bread if Heaven does not shower him with manna and quails.

In her white silk dress, Selma was slender as a ray of moonlight coming through the window. She walked gracefully and rhythmically. Her voice was low and sweet; words fell from her lips like drops of dew falling from the petals of flowers when they are disturbed by the wind.

But Selma's face! No words can describe its expression, reflecting first great internal suffering, then heavenly exaltation.

The beauty of Selma's face was not classic; it was like a dream of revelation which cannot be measured or bound or copied by the brush of a painter or the chisel of a sculptor. Selma's beauty was not in her golden hair, but in the virtue of purity which surrounded it; not in her large eyes, but in the light which emanated from them; not in her red lips, but in the sweetness of her words; not in her ivory neck, but in its slight bow to the front. Nor was it in her perfect figure, but in the nobility of her spirit, burning like a white torch between earth and sky. her beauty was like a gift of poetry. But poets care unhappy people, for, no matter how high their spirits reach, they will still be enclosed in an envelope of tears.

Selma was deeply thoughtful rather than talkative, and her silence was a kind of music that carried one to a world of dreams and made him listen to the throbbing of his heart, and see the ghosts of his thoughts and feelings standing before him, looking him in the eyes.

She wore a cloak of deep sorrow through her life, which increased her strange beauty and dignity, as a tree in blossom is more lovely when seen through the mist of dawn.

Sorrow linked her spirit and mine, as if each saw in the other's face what the heart was feeling and heard the echo of a hidden voice. God had made two bodies in one, and separation could be nothing but agony.

The sorrowful spirit finds rest when united with a similar one. They join affectionately, as a stranger is cheered when he sees another stranger in a strange land. Hearts that are united through the medium of sorrow will not be separated by the glory of happiness. Love that is cleansed by tears will remain externally pure and beautiful.

The Tempest

One day Farris Effandi invited me to dinner at his home. I accepted, my spirit hungry for the divine bread which Heaven placed in the hands of Selma, the spiritual bread which makes our hearts hungrier the more we eat of it. It was this bread which Kais, the Arabian poet, Dante, and Sappho tasted and which set their hearts afar; the bread which the Goddess prepares with the sweetness of kisses and the bitterness of tears.

As I reached the home of Farris Effandi, I saw Selma sitting on a bench in the garden resting her head against a tree and looking like a bride in her white silk dress, or like a sentinel guarding that place.

Silently and reverently I approached and sat by her. I could not talk; so I resorted to silence, the only language of the heart, but I felt that Selma was listening to my wordless call and watching the ghost of my soul in my eyes.

In a few minutes the old man came out and greeted me as usual. When he stretched his hand toward me, I felt as if he were blessing the secrets that united me and his daughter. Then he said, "Dinner is ready, my children; let us eat. "We rose and followed him, and Selma's eyes brightened; for a new sentiment had been added to her love by her father's calling us his children.

We sat at the table enjoying the food and sipping the old wine, but our souls were living in a world far away. We were dreaming of the future and its hardships.

Three persons were separated in thoughts, but united in love; three innocent people with much feeling but little knowledge; a drama was being performed by an old man who loved his daughter and cared for her happiness, a young woman of twenty looking into the future with anxiety, and a young man, dreaming and worrying, who had tasted neither the wine of life nor its vinegar, and trying to reach the height of love and knowledge but unable to life himself up. We three sitting in twilight were eating and drinking in that solitary home, guarded by Heaven's eyes, but at the bottoms of our glasses were hidden bitterness and anguish.

As we finished eating, one of the maids announced the presence of a man at the door who wished to see Farris Effandi. "Who is he?" asked the old man. "The Bishop's messenger," said the maid. There was a moment of silence during which Farris Effandi stared at his daughter like a prophet who gazes at Heaven to divine its secret. Then he said to the maid, "Let the man in."

As the maid left, a man, dressed in oriental uniform and with big moustache curled at the ends, entered and greeted the old man, saying "His Grace, the Bishop, has sent me for you with his private carriage; he wishes to discuss important business with you." The old man's face clouded and his smile disappeared. After a moment of deep thought he came close to me and said in a friendly voice, "I hope to find you here when I come back, for Selma will enjoy your company in this solitary place."

Saying this, he turned to Selma and, smiling, asked if she agreed. She nodded her head, but her cheeks became red, and with a voice sweeter than the music of the lyre she said, "I will do my best, Father, to make our guest happy."

Selma watched the carriage that had taken her father and the Bishop's messenger until it disappeared. Then she came and sat opposite me on a divan covered with green silk. She looked like a lily bent to the carpet of green grass by the breeze of dawn. It was the will of Heaven that I should be with Selma alone, at night, in her beautiful home surrounded by trees, where silence, love, beauty and virtue dwelt together.

We were both silent, each waiting for the other to speak, but speech is not the only means of understanding between two souls. It is not the syllables that come from the lips and tongues that bring hearts together.

There is something greater and purer than what the mouth utters. Silence illuminates our souls, whispers to our hearts, and brings them together. Silence separates us from ourselves, makes us sail the firmament of spirit, and brings us closer to Heaven; it makes us feel that bodies are no more than prisons and that this world is only a place of exile.

Selma looked at me and her eyes revealed the secret of her heart. Then she quietly said, "Let us go to the garden and sit under the trees and watch the moon come up behind the mountains." Obediently I rose from my seat, but I hesitated.

Don't you think we had better stay here until the moon has risen and illuminates the garden?" And I continued, "The darkness hides the trees and flowers. We can see nothing."

Then she said, "If darkness hides the trees and flowers from our eyes, it will not hide love from our hearts."

Uttering these words in a strange tone, she turned her eyes and looked through the window. I remained silent, pondering her words, weighing the true meaning of each syllable. Then she looked at me as if she regretted what she had said and tried to take away those words from my ears by the magic of her eyes. But those eyes, instead of making me forget what she had said, repeated through the depths of my heart more clearly and effectively the sweet words which had already become graven in my memory for eternity.

Every beauty and greatness in this world is created by a single thought or emotion inside a man. Every thing we see today, made by past generation, was, before its appearance, a thought in the mind of a man or an impulse in the heart of a woman. The revolutions that shed so much blood and turned men's minds toward liberty were the idea of one man who lived in the midst of thousands of men. The devastating wars which destroyed empires were a thought that existed in the mind of an individual. The supreme teachings that changed the course of humanity were the ideas of a man whose genius separated him from his environment. A single thought build the Pyramids, founded the glory of Islam, and caused the burning of the library at Alexandria.

One thought will come to you at night which will elevate you to glory or lead you to asylum. One look from a woman's eye makes you the happiest man in the world. One word from a man's lips will make you rich or poor.

That word which Selma uttered that night arrested me between my past and future, as a boat which is anchored in the midst of the ocean. That word awakened me from the slumber of youth and solitude and set me on the stage where life and death play their parts.

The scent of flowers mingled with the breeze as we came into the garden and sat silently on a bench near a jasmine tree, listening to the breathing of sleeping nature, while in the blue sky the eyes of heaven witnessed our drama.

The moon came out from behind Mount Sunnin and shone over the coast, hills, and mountains; and we could see the villages fringing the valley like apparitions which have suddenly been conjured from nothing. We could see the beauty of Lebanon under the silver rays of the moon.

Poets of the West think of Lebanon as a legendary place, forgotten since the passing of David and Solomon and the Prophets, as the Garden of Eden became lost after the fall of Adam and Eve. To those Western poets, the word "Lebanon" is a poetical expression associated with a mountain whose sides are drenched with the incense of the Holy Cedars. It reminds them of the temples of copper and marble standing stern and impregnable and of a herd of deer feeding in the valleys. That night I saw Lebanon dream-like with the eyes of a poet.

Thus, the appearance of things changes according to the emotions, and thus we see magic and beauty in them, while the magic and beauty are really in ourselves.

As the rays of the moon shone on the face, neck, and arms of Selma, she looked like a statue of ivory sculptured by the fingers of some worshiper of Ishtar, goddess of beauty and love. As she looked at me, she said, "Why are you silent? Why do you not tell me something about your past?" As I gazed at her, my muteness vanished, and I opened my lips and said, "Did you not hear what I said when we came to this orchard? The spirit that hears the whispering of flowers and the singing of silence can also hear the shrieking of my soul and the clamour of my heart."

She covered her face with her hands and said in a trembling voice, "Yes, I heard you — I heard a voice coming from the bosom of night and a clamour raging in the heart of the day."

Forgetting my past, my very existence — everything but Selma — I answered her, saying, "And I heard you, too, Selma. I heard exhilarating music pulsing in the air and causing the whole universe to tremble."

Upon hearing these words, she closed her eyes and her lips I saw a smile of pleasure mingled with sadness. She whispered softly, "Now I know that there is something higher than heaven and deeper than the ocean and stranger than life and death and time. I know now what I did not know before."

At that moment Selma became dearer than a friend and closer than a sister and more beloved than a sweetheart. She became a supreme thought, a beautiful, an overpowering emotion living in my spirit.

It is wrong to think that love comes from long companionship and persevering courtship. Love is the offspring of spiritual affinity and unless that affinity is created in a moment, it will not be created in years or even generations.

Then Selma raised her head and gazed at the horizon where Mount Sunnin meets the sky, and said, "Yesterday you were like a brother to me, with whom I lived and by whom I sat calmly under my father's care. Now, I feel the presence of something stranger and sweeter than brotherly affection, an unfamiliar commingling of love and fear that fills my heart with sorrow and happiness."

I responded, "This emotion which we fear and which shakes us when it passes through our hearts is the law of nature that guides the moon around the earth and the sun around the God."

She put her hand on my head and wove her fingers through my hair. Her face brightened and tears came out of her eyes like drops of dew on the leaves of a lily, and she said, "Who would believe our story — who would believe that in this hour we have surmounted the obstacles of doubt? Who would believe that the month of Nisan which brought us together for the first time, is the month that halted us in the Holy of Holies of life?"

Her hand was still on my head as she spoke, and I would not have preferred a royal crown or a wreath of glory to that beautiful smooth hand whose fingers were twined in my hair.

Then I answered her: "People will not believe our story because they do not know what love is the only flower that grows and blossoms without the aid of seasons, but was it Nisan that brought us together for the first time, and is it this hour that has arrested us in the Holy of Holies of life? Is it not the hand of God that brought our souls close together before birth and made us prisoners of each other for all the days and nights? Man's life does not commence in the womb and never ends in the grave; and this firmament, full of moonlight and stars, is not deserted by loving souls and intuitive spirits."

As she drew her hand away from my head, I felt a kind of electrical vibration at the roots of my hair mingled with the night breeze. Like a devoted worshiper who receives his blessing by kissing the altar in a shrine, I took Selma's hand, placed my burning lips on it, and gave it a long kiss, the memory of which melts my heart and awakens by its sweetness all the virtue of my spirit.

An hour passed, every minute of which was a year of love. The silence of the night, moonlight, flowers, and trees made us forget all reality except love, when suddenly we heard the galloping of horses and rattling of carriage wheels. Awakened from our pleasant swoon and plunged from the world of dreams into the world of perplexity and misery, we found that the old man had returned from his mission. We rose and walked through the orchard to meet him.

Then the carriage reached the entrance of the garden, Farris Effandi dismounted and slowly walked towards us, bending forward slightly as if he were carrying a heavy load. He approached Selma and placed both of his hands on her shoulders and stared at her. Tears coursed down his wrinkled cheeks and his lips trembled with sorrowful smile. In a choking voice, he said, "My beloved Selma, very soon you will be taken away from the arms of your father to the arms of another man. Very soon fate will carry you from this lonely home to the world's spacious court, and this garden will miss the pressure of your footsteps, and your father will become a stranger to you. All is done; may God bless you."

Hearing these words, Selma's face clouded and her eyes froze as if she felt a premonition of death. Then she screamed, like a bird shot down, suffering, and trembling, and in a choked voice said, "What do you say? What do you mean? Where are you sending me?"

Then she looked at him searchingly, trying to discover his secret. In a moment she said, "I understand. I understand everything. The Bishop has demanded me from you and has prepared a cage for this bird with broken wings. Is this your will, Father?"

His answer was a deep sigh. Tenderly he led Selma into the house while I remained standing in the garden, waves of perplexity beating upon me like a tempest upon autumn leaves. Then I followed them into the living room, and to avoid embarrassment, shook the old man's hand, looked at Selma, my beautiful star, and left the house.

As I reached the end of the garden I heard the old man calling me and turned to meet him. Apologetically he took my hand and said, "Forgive me, my son. I have ruined your evening with the shedding of tears, but please come to see me when my house is deserted and I am lonely and desperate. Youth, my dear son, does not combine with senility, as morning does not have meet the night; but you will come to me and call to my memory the youthful days which I spent with your father, and you will tell me the news of life which does not count me as among its sons any longer. Will you not visit me when Selma leaves and I am left here in loneliness?"

While he said these sorrowful words and I silently shook his hand, I felt the warm tears falling from his eyes upon my hand. Trembling with sorrow and filial affection. I felt as if my heart were choked with grief. When I raised my head and he saw the tears in my eyes, he bent toward me and touched my forehead with his lips. "Good-bye, son, Good-bye."

In old man's tear is more potent than that of a young man because it is the residuum of life in his weakening body. A young man's tear is like a drop of dew on the leaf of a rose, while that of an old man is like a yellow leaf which falls with the wind at the approach of winter.

As I left the house of Farris Effandi Karamy, Selma's voice still rang in my ears, her beauty followed me like a wraith, and her father's tears dried slowly on my hand.

My departure was like Adam's exodus from Paradise, but the Eve of my heart was not with me to make the whole world an Eden. That night, in which I had been born again, I felt that I saw death's face for the first time.

Thus the sun enlivens and kills the fields with its heat.

The Lake of Fire

Everything that a man does secretly in the darkness of night will be clearly revealed in the daylight. Words uttered in privacy will become unexpectedly common conversation. Deed which we hide today in the corners of our lodgings will be shouted on every street tomorrow.

Thus the ghosts of darkness revealed the purpose of Bishop Bulos Galib's meeting with Farris Effandi Karamy, and his conversation was repeated all over the neighbourhood until it reached my ears.

The discussion that took place between Bishop Bulos Galib and Farris Effandi that night was not over the problems of the poor or the widows and orphans. The main purpose for sending after Farris Effandi and bringing him in the Bishops' private carriage was the betrothal of Selma to the Bishop's nephew, Mansour Bey Galib.

Selma was the only child of the wealthy Farris Effandi, and the Bishop's choice fell on Selma, not on account of her beauty and noble spirit, but on account of her father's money which would guarantee Mansour Bey a good and prosperous fortune and make him an important man.

The heads of religion in the East are not satisfied with their own munificence, but they must strive to make all members of their families superiors and oppressors. The glory of a prince goes to his eldest son by inheritance, but the exaltation of a religious head is contagious among his brothers and nephews. Thus the Christian bishop and the Moslem imam and the Brahman priest become like sea reptiles who clutch their prey with many tentacles and suck their blood with numerous mouths.

Then the Bishop demanded Selma's hand for his nephew, the only answer that he received from her father was a deep silence and falling tears, for he hated to lose his only child. Any man's soul trembles when he is separated from his only daughter whom he has reared to young womanhood.

The sorrow of parents at the marriage of a daughter is equal to their happiness at the marriage of a son, because a son brings to the family a new member, while a daughter, upon her marriage, is lost to them.

Farris Effandi perforce granted the Bishop's request, obeying his will unwillingly, because Farris Effandi knew the Bishop's nephew very well, knew that he was dangerous, full of hate, wickedness, and corruption.

In Lebanon, no Christian could oppose his bishop and remain in good standing. No man could disobey his religious head and keep his reputation. The eye could not resist a spear without being pierced, and the hand could not grasp a sword without being cut off.

Suppose that Farris Effandi had resisted the Bishop and refused his wish; then Selma's reputation would have been ruined and her name would have been blemished by the dirt of lips and tongues. In the opinion of the fox, high bunches of grapes that can't be reached are sour.

Thus destiny seized Selma and led her like a humiliated slave in the procession of miserable oriental woman, and thus fell that noble spirit into the trap after having flown freely on the white wings of love in a sky full of moonlight scented with the odour of flowers.

In some countries, the parent's wealth is a source of misery for the children. The wide strong box which the father and mother together have used for the safety of their wealth becomes a narrow, dark prison for the souls of their heirs. The Almighty Dinar which the people worship becomes a demon which punished the spirit and deadens the heart. Selma Karamy was one of those who were the victims of their parents' wealth and bridegrooms' cupidity. Had it not been for her father's wealth, Selma would still be living happily.

A week had passed. The love of Selma was my sole entertainer, singing songs of happiness for me at night and waking me at dawn to reveal the meaning of life and the secrets of nature. It is a heavenly love that is free from jealousy, rich and never harmful to the spirit. It is deep affinity that bathes the soul in contentment; a deep hunger for affection which, when satisfied, fills the soul with bounty; a tenderness that creates hope without agitating the soul, changing earth to paradise and life to a sweet and a beautiful dream. In the morning, when I walked in the fields, I saw the token of Eternity in the awakening of nature, and when I sat by the seashore I heard the waves singing the song of Eternity. And when I walked in the streets I saw the beauty of life and the splendour of humanity in the appearance of passers-by and movements of workers.

Those days passed like ghosts and disappeared like clouds, and soon nothing was left for me but sorrowful memories. The eye with which I used to look at the beauty of spring and the awakening of nature, could see nothing but the fury of the tempest and the misery of winter. The ears with which I formerly heard with delight the song of the waves, could hear only the howling of the wind and the wrath of the sea against the precipice. The soul which had observed happily the tireless vigour of mankind and the glory of the universe, was tortured by the knowledge of disappointment and failure. Nothing was more beautiful than those days of love, and nothing was more bitter than those horrible nights of sorrow.

When I could no longer resist the impulse, I went, on the weekend, once more to Selma's home — the shrine which Beauty had erected and which Love had blessed, in which the spirit could worship and the heart kneel humbly and pray. When I entered the garden I felt a power pulling me away from this world and placing me in a sphere supernaturally free from struggle and hardship. Like a mystic who receives a revelation of Heaven, I saw myself amid the trees and flowers, and as I approached the entrance of the house I beheld Selma sitting on the bench in the shadow of a jasmine tree where we both had sat the week before, on that night which Providence had chosen for the beginning of my happiness and sorrow.

She neither moved nor spoke as I approached her. She seemed to have known intuitively that I was coming, and when I sat by her she gazed at me for a moment and sighed deeply, then turned her head and looked at the sky. And, after a moment full of magic silence, she turned back toward me and tremblingly took my hand and said in a faint voice, "Look at me, my friend; study my face and I read in it that which you want to know and which I can not recite. Look at me, my beloved... look at me, my brother."

I gazed at her intently and saw that those eyes, which a few days ago were smiling like lips and moving like the wings of a nightingales, were already sunken and glazed with sorrow and pain. Her face, that had resembled the unfolding, sun kissed leaves of a lily, had faded and become colourless. Her sweet lips were like two withering roses that autumn has left on their stems.

Her neck, that had been a column of ivory, was bent forward as if it no longer could support the burden of grief in her head.

All these changes I saw in Selma's face, but to me they were like a passing cloud that covered the face of the moon and makes it more beautiful. A look which reveals inward stress adds more beauty to the face, no matter how much tragedy and pain it bespeaks; but the face which, in silence, does not announce hidden mysteries is not beautiful, regardless of the symmetry of its features. The cup does not entice our lips unless the wine's colour is seen through the transparent crystal.

Selma, on that evening, was like a cup full of heavenly wine concocted of the bitterness and sweetness of life. Unaware, she symbolized the oriental woman who never leaves her parents' home until she puts upon her neck the heavy yoke of her husband, who never leaves her loving mother's arms until she must live as a slave, enduring the harshness of her husband's mother.

I continued to look at Selma and listen to her depressed spirit and suffer with her until I felt that time has ceased and the universe had faded from existence. I could see only her two large eyes staring fixedly at me and could feel only her cold, trembling hand holding mine.

I woke from my swoon hearing Selma saying quietly, "Come by beloved, let us discuss the horrible future before it comes, My father has just left the house to see the man who is going to be my companion until death. My father, whom God chose for the purpose of my existence, will meet the man whom the world has selected to be my master for the rest of my life. In the heart of this city, the old man who accompanied me during my youth will meet the young man who will be my companion for the coming years. Tonight the two families will set the marriage date. What a strange and impressive hour! Last week at this time, under this jasmine tree, Love embraced my soul for the first time, okay. While Destiny was writing the first word of my life's story at the Bishop's mansion. Now, while my father and my suitor are planning the day of marriage, I see your spirit quivering around me as a thirsty bird flickers above a spring of water guarded by a hungry serpent. Oh, how great this night is! And how deep is its mystery!"

Learning these words, I felt that dark ghost of complete despondency was seizing our love to choke it in its infancy, and I answered her, "That bird will remain flickering over that spring until thirst destroys him or falls into the grasp of a serpent and becomes its prey."

She responded, "No, my beloved, this nightingale should remain alive and sing until dark comes, until spring passes, until the end of the world, and keep on singing eternally. His voice should not be silenced, because he brings life to my heart, his wings should not be broken, because their motion removes the cloud from my heart.

When I whispered, "Selma, my beloved, thirst will exhaust him, and fear will kill him."

She replied immediately with trembling lips, "The thirst of soul is sweeter than the wine of material things, and the fear of spirit is dearer than the security of the body. But listen, my beloved, listen carefully, I am standing today at the door of a new life which I know nothing about. I am like a blind man who feels his way so that he will not fall. My father's wealth has placed me in the slave market, and this man has bought me. I neither know nor love him, but I shall learn to love him, and I shall obey him, serve him, and make him happy. I shall give him all that a weak woman can give a strong man.

But you, my beloved, are still in the prime of life. You can walk freely upon life's spacious path, carpeted with flowers. You are free to traverse the world, making of your heart a torch to light your way. You can think, talk, and act freely; you can write your name on the face of life because you are a man; you can live as a master because your father's wealth will not place you in the slave market to be bought and sold; you can marry the woman of your choice and, before she lives in your home, you can let her reside in your heart and can exchange confidences without hindrances."

Silence prevailed for a moment, and Selma continued, "But, is it now that Life will tear us apart so that you may attain the glory of a man and I the duty of a woman? Is it for this that the valley swallows the song of the nightingale in its depths, and the wind scatters the petals of the rose, and the feet tread upon the wind cup? Were all those nights we spent in the moonlight by the jasmine tree, where our souls united, in vain? Did we fly swiftly toward the stars until our wings tired, and are we descending now into the abyss? Or was Love asleep when he came to us, and did he, when he woke, become angry and decide to punish us? Or did our spirits turn the nights' breeze into a wind that tore us to pieces and blew us like dust to the depth of the valley? We disobeyed no commandment, nor did we taste of forbidden fruit, so what is making us leave this paradise? We never conspired or practised mutiny, then why are we descending to hell? No, no, the moments which united us are greater than centuries, and the light that illuminated our spirits is stronger than the dark; and if the tempest separates us on this rough ocean, the waves will unite us on the calm shore; and if this life kills us, death will unite us. A woman's heart will change with time or season; even if it dies eternally, it will never perish. A woman's heart is like a field turned into a battleground; after the trees are uprooted and the grass is burned and the rocks are reddened with blood and the earth is planted with bones and skulls, it is calm and silent as if nothing has happened; for the spring and autumn come at their intervals and resume their work.

And now, my beloved, what shall we do? How shall we part and when shall we meet? Shall we consider love a strange visitor who came in the evening and left us in the morning? Or shall we suppose this affection a dream that came in our sleep and departed when we awoke?

Shall we consider this week an hour of intoxication to be replaced by soberness? Raise your head and let me look at you, my beloved; open your lips and let me hear your voice. Speak to me! Will you remember me after this tempest has sunk the ship of our love? Will you hear the whispering of my wings in the silence of the night? Will you hear my spirit fluttering over you? Will you listen to my sighs? Will you see my shadow approach with the shadows of dusk and disappear with the flush of dawn? Tell me, my beloved, what will you be after having been magic ray to my eyes, sweet song to my ears, and wings to my soul? What will you be?"

Learning these words, my heart melted, and I answered her, "I will be as you want me to be, my beloved."

Then she said, " I want you to love me as a poet loves his sorrowful thoughts. I want you to remember me as a traveller remembers a calm pool in which his image was reflected as he drank its water. I want you to remember me as a mother remember her child that died before it saw the light, and I want you to remember me as a merciful king remembers a prisoner who died before his pardon reached him. I want you to be my companion, and I want you to visit my father and console him in his solitude because I shall be leaving him soon and shall be a stranger to him.

I answered her, saying, " I will do all you have said and will make my soul an envelope for your soul, and my heart a residence for your beauty and my breast a grave for your sorrows. I shall love you , Selma, as the prairies love the spring, and I shall live in you in the life of a flower under the sun's rays. I shall sing your name as the valley sings the echo of the bells of the village churches; I shall listen to the language of your soul as the shore listens to the story of the waves. I shall remember you as a stranger remembers his beloved country, and as a hungry man remembers a banquet, and as a dethroned king remembers the days of his glory, and as a prisoner remembers the hours of ease and freedom. I shall remember you as a sower remembers the bundles of wheat on his threshing flour, and as a shepherd remembers the green prairies the sweet brooks."

Selma listened to my words with palpitating heart, and said "Tomorrow the truth will become ghostly and the awakening will be like a dream. Will a lover be satisfied embracing a ghost, or will a thirsty man quench his thirst from the spring or a dream?"

I answered her, "Tomorrow, destiny will put you in the midst of a peaceful family, but it will send me into the world of struggle and warfare. You will be in the home of a person whom chance has made most fortunate through your beauty and virtue, while I shall be living a life of suffering and fear. You will enter the gate of life, while I shall enter the gate of death. You will be received hospitably, while I shall exist in solitude, but I shall erect a statue of love and worship it in the valley of death. Love will be my sole comforter, and I shall drink love like wine and wear it like garment. At dawn, Love will wake me from slumber and take me to the distant field, and at noon will lead me to the shadows of trees, where I will find shelter with the birds from the heat of the sun. In the evening, it will cause me to pause before sunset to hear nature's farewell song to the light of day and will show me ghostly clouds sailing in the sky. At night, Love will embrace me, and I shall sleep, dreaming of the heavenly world where the spirits of lovers and poets abide. In the Spring I shall walk side by side with love among violets and jasmines and drink the remaining drops of winter in the lily cups. In Summer we shall make the bundles of hay our pillows and the grass our bed, and the blue sky will cover us as we gaze at the stars and the moon.

In Autumn, Love and I will go to the vineyard and sit by the wine press and watch the grapevines being denuded of their golden ornaments, and the migrating flocks of birds will wing over us. In Winter, we shall sit by the fireside reciting stories of long ago and chronicles of far countries. During my youth, Love will be my teacher; in middle age, my help; and in old age, my delight. Love, my beloved Selma, will stay with me to the end of my life, and after death the hand of God will unite us again."

All these words came from the depths of my heart like flames of fire which leap raging from the hearth and then disappear in the ashes. Selma was weeping as if her eyes were lips answering me with tears.

Those whom love has not given wings cannot fly the cloud of appearances to see the magic world in which Selma's spirit and mine existed together in that sorrowfully happy hour. Those whom Love has not chosen as followers do not hear when Love calls. This story is not for them. Even if they should comprehend these pages, they would not be able to grasp the shadowy meanings which are not clothed in words and do not reside on paper, but what human being is he who has never sipped the wine from the cup of love, and what spirit is it that has never stood reverently before that lighted altar in the temple whose pavement is the hearts of men and women and whose ceiling is the secret canopy of dreams? What flower is that on whose leaves the dawn has never poured a drop of dew; what streamlet is that which lost its course without going to the sea?

Selma raised her face toward the sky and gazed at the heavenly stars which studded the firmament. She stretched out her hands; her eyes widened, and her lips trembled. On her pale face, I could see the signs of sorrow, oppression, hopelessness, and pain. Then she cried, " Oh, Lord, what has a woman done that hath offended Thee? What sin has she committed to deserve such a punishment? For what crime has she been awarded everlasting castigation? Oh, Lord, Thou art strong, and I am weak. Why hast Thou made me suffer pain? Thou art great and almighty, while I am nothing but a tiny creature crawling before Thy throne. Why hast Thou crushed me with Thy foot? Thou art a raging tempest, and I am like dust; why, my Lord, hast Thou flung me upon the cold earth? Thou art powerful, and I am helpless; why art Thou fighting me? Thou art considerate, and I am prudent; why art Thou destroying me? Thou hast created woman with love, and why, with love, dost Thou ruin her? With Thy right hand dost Thou lift her, and with Thy left hand dost Thou strike her into the abyss, and she knows not why. In her mouth Thou blowest the breath of Life, and in her heart Thou sowest the seeds of death. Thou dost show her the path of happiness, but Thou leadest her in the road of misery; in her mouth Thou dost place a song of happiness, but then Thou dost close her lips with sorrow and dost fetter her tongue with agony. With Thy mysterious fingers dost Thou dress her wounds, and with Thine hands Thou drawest the dread of pain round her pleasures. In her bed Thou hidest pleasure and peace, but beside it Thou dost erect obstacles and fear. Thou dost excite her affection through Thy will, and from her affection does shame emanate. By Thy will Thou showest her the beauty of creation, but her love for beauty becomes a terrible famine. Thou dost make her drink life in the cup of death, and death in the cup of life. Thou purifiest her with tears, and in tears her life streams away. Oh, Lord, Thou hast opened my eyes with love, and with love Thou hast blinded me. Thou hast kissed me with Thy lips and struck me with Thy strong hand. Thou has planted in my heart a white rose, but around the rose a barrier of thorns. Thou hast tied my present with the spirit of a young man whom I love, but my life with the body of an unknown man. So help me, my Lord, to be strong in this deadly struggle and assist me to be truthful and virtuous until death. Thy will be done. Oh , Lord God."

Silence continued. Selma looked down, pale and frail; her arms dropped, and her head bowed and it seemed to me as if a tempest had broken a branch from a tree and cast it down to dry and perish.

I took her cold hand and kissed it, but when I attempted to console her it was I who needed consolation more than she did. I kept silent, thinking of our plight and listening to my heartbeats. Neither of us said more.

Extreme torture is mute, and so we sat silent, petrified, like columns of marble buried under the sand of an earthquake. Neither wished to listen to the other because our heart-threads had become weak and even breathing would have broken them.

It was midnight, and we could see the crescent moon rising from behind Mount Sunnin, and it looked in the midst of the stars, like the face of a corpse, in a coffin surrounded by the dim lights of candles. And Lebanon looked like an old man whose back was bent with age and whose eyes were a haven for insomnia, watching the dark and waiting for dawn, like asking sitting on the ashes of his throne in the debris of his palace.

The mountains, trees, and rivers change their appearance with the vicissitudes of times and seasons, as a man changes with his experiences and emotions. The lofty poplar that resembles a bride in the daytime, will look like a column of smoke in the evening; the huge rock that stands impregnable at noon, will appear to be a miserable pauper at night, with earth for his bed and the sky for his cover; and the rivulet that we see glittering in the morning and hear singing the hymn of Eternity, will, in the evening, turn to a stream of tears wailing like a mother bereft of her child, and Lebanon, that had looked dignified a week before, when the moon was full and our spirits were happy, looked sorrowful and lonesome that night.

We stood up and bade each other farewell, but love and despair stood between us like two ghosts, one stretching his wings with his fingers over our throats, one weeping and the other laughing hideously.

As I took Selma's hand and put it to my lips, she came close to me and placed a kiss on my forehead, then dropped on the wooden bench. She shut her eyes and whispered softly, "Oh, Lord God, have mercy on me and mend my broken wings!"

As I left Selma in the garden, I felt as if my senses were covered with a thick veil, like a lake whose surface is concealed by fog.

The beauty of trees, the moonlight, the deep silence, everything about me looked ugly and horrible. The true light that had showed me the beauty and wonder of the universe was converted to a great flame of fire that seared my heart; and the Eternal music I used to hear became a clamour, more frightening than the roar of a lion.

I reached my room, and like a wounded bird shot down by a hunter, I fell on my bed, repeating the words of Selma: "Oh, Lord God, have mercy on me and mend my broken wings!"

Before the Throne of Death

Marriage in these days is a mockery whose management is in the hands of young men and parents. In most countries the young men win while the parents lose. The woman is looked upon as a commodity, purchased and delivered from one house to another. In time her beauty fades and she becomes like an old piece of furniture left in a dark corner.

Modern civilization has made woman a little wiser, but it has increased her suffering because of man's covetousness. The woman of yesterday was a happy wife, but the woman of today is a miserable mistress. In the past she walked blindly in the light, but now she walks open-eyed in the dark. She was beautiful in her ignorance, virtuous in her simplicity, and strong in her weakness. Today she has become ugly in her ingenuity, superficial and heartless in her knowledge. Will the day ever come when beauty and knowledge, ingenuity and virtue, and weakness of body and strength of spirit will be united in a woman?

I am one of those who believe that spiritual progress is a rule of human life, but the approach to perfection is slow and painful. If a woman elevates herself in one respect and is retarded in another, it is because the rough trail that leads to the mountain peak is not free of ambushes of thieves and lairs of wolves.

This strange generation exists between sleeping and waking. It holds in its hands the soil of the past and the seeds of the future. However, we find in every city a woman who symbolizes the future.

In the city of Beirut, Selma Karamy was the symbol of the future Oriental woman, but, like many who lie ahead of their time, she became the victim of the present; and like a flower snatched from its stem and carried away by the current of a river, she walked in the miserable procession of the defeated.

Mansour Bey Galib and Selma were married, and lived together in a beautiful house at Ras Beyrouth, where all the wealthy dignitaries resided. Farris Effandi Karamy was left in his solitary home in the midst of his garden and orchards like a lonely shepherd amid his flock.

The days and merry nights of the wedding passed, but the honeymoon left memories of times of bitter sorrow, as wars leave skulls and dead bones on the battlefield. The dignity of an Oriental wedding inspires the hearts of young men and women, but its termination may drop them like millstones to the bottom of the sea. Their exhilaration is like footprints on sand which remain only till they are washed away by the waves.

Spring departed, and so did summer and autumn, but my love for Selma increased day by day until it became a kind of mute worship, the feeling that an orphan has toward the soul of his mother in Heaven. My yearning was converted to blind sorrow that could see nothing but itself, and the passion that drew tears from my eyes was replaced by perplexity that sucked the blood from my heart, and my sighs of affection became a constant prayer for the happiness of Selma and her husband and peace for her father.

My hopes and prayers were in vain, because Selma's misery was an internal malady that nothing but death could cure.

Mansour Bey was a man to whom all the luxuries of life came easily; but, in spite of that, he was dissatisfied and rapacious. After marrying Selma, he neglected her father in his loneliness and prayed for his death so that he could inherit what was left of the old man's wealth.

Mansour Bey's character was similar to his uncle's; the only difference between the two was that the Bishop got everything he wanted secretly, under the protection of his ecclesiastical robe and the golden cross which he wore on his chest, while his nephew did everything publicly. The Bishop went to church in the morning and spent the rest of the day pilfering from the widows, orphans, and simple minded people. But Mansour Bey spent his days in pursuit of sexual satisfaction. On Sunday, Bishop Bulos Galib preached his Gospel; but during weekdays he never practiced what he preached, occupying himself with political intrigues of the locality. And, by means of his uncle's prestige and influence, Mansour Bey made it his business to secure political plums for those who could offer a sufficient bribe.

Bishop Bulos was a thief who hid himself under the cover of night, while his nephew, Mansour Bey, was a swindler who walked proudly in daylight. However, the people of Oriental nations place trust in such as they— wolves and butchers who ruin their country through covetousness and crush their neighbours with an iron hand.

Why do I occupy these pages with words about the betrayers of poor nations instead of reserving all the space for the story of a miserable woman with a broken heart? Why do I shed tears for oppressed peoples rather than keep all my tears for the memory of a weak woman whose life was snatched by the teeth of death?

But my dear readers, don't' you think that such a woman is like a nation that is oppressed by priests and rulers? Don't you believe that thwarted love which leads a woman to the grave is like the despair which pervades the people of the earth? A woman is to a nation as light is to a lamp. Will not the light be dim if the oil in the lamp is low?

Autumn passed, and the wind blew the yellow leaves form the trees, making way for winter, which came howling and crying. I was still in the City of Beirut without a companion save my dreams, which would lift my spirit to the sky and then bury it deep in the bosom of the earth.

The sorrowful spirit finds relaxation in solitude. It abhors people, as a wounded deer deserts the herd and lives in a cave until it is healed or dead.

One day I heard Farris Effandi was ill. I left my solitary abode and walked to his home, taking a new route, a lonely path between olive trees, avoiding the main road with its rattling carriage wheels.

Arriving at the old man's house, I entered and found Farris Effandi lying on his bed, weak and pale. His eyes were sunken and looked like two deep, dark valleys haunted by the ghosts of pain. The smile which had always enlivened his face was choked with pain and agony; and the bones of his gentle hands looked like naked branches trembling before the tempest. As I approached him and inquired as to his health, he turned his pale face toward me, and on his trembling lips appeared a smile, and he said in a weak voice, "Go — go, my son, to the other room and comfort Selma and bring her to sit by the side of my bed."

I entered the adjacent room and found Selma lying on a divan, covering her head with her arms and burying her face in a pillow so that her father would not hear her weeping. Approaching slowly, I pronounced her name in a voice that seemed more like sighing than whispering. She moved fearfully, as if she had been interrupted in a terrible dream, and sat up, looking at me with glazed eyes, doubting whether I was a ghost or a living being. After a deep silence which took us back on the wings of memory to that hour when we were intoxicated with wine of love, Selma wiped away her tears and said, "See how time has changed us! See how time has changed the course of our lives and left us in these ruins. In this place spring united us in a bond of love, and in this place has brought us together before the throne of death. How beautiful was spring, and how terrible is this winter!"

Speaking thus, she covered her face again with her hands as if she were shielding her eyes from the spectre of the past standing before her. I put my hand on her head and said, "Come, Selma, come and let us be as strong towers before the tempest. Let us stand like brave soldiers before the enemy and face his weapons. If we are killed, we shall die as martyrs; and if we win, we shall live as heroes. Braving obstacles and hardships is nobler than retreat to tranquillity. The butterfly that hovers around the lamp until it dies is more admirable than the mole that lives in a dark tunnel. Come, Selma, let us walk this rough path firmly, with our eyes toward the sun so that we may not see the skulls and serpents among the rocks and thorns. if fear should stop us in middle of the road, we would hear only ridicule from the voices of the night, but if we reach the mountain peak bravely we shall join the heavenly spirits in songs of triumph and joy. Cheer up, Selma, wipe away your tears and remove the sorrow from your face. Rise, and let us sit by the bed of your father, because his life depends on your life, and your smile is his only cure."

Kindly and affectionately she looked at me and said, "Are you asking me to have patience, while you are in need of it yourself? Will a hungry man give his bread to another hungry man? Or will sick man give medicine to another which he himself needs badly?"

She rose, her head bent slightly forward and we walked to the old man's room and sat by the side of his bed. Selma forced a smile and pretended to be patient, and her father tried to make her believe that he was feeling better and getting stronger; but both father and daughter were aware of each other's sorrow and heard the unvoiced sighs. They were like two equal forces, wearing each other away silently. The father's heart was melting because of his daughter's plight. They were two pure souls, one departing and the other agonized with grief, embracing in love and death; and I was between the two with my own troubled heart. We were three people, gathered and crushed by the hands of destiny; an old man like a dwelling ruined by flood, a young woman whose symbol was a lily beheaded by the sharp edge of a sickle, and a young man who was a weak sapling, bent by a snowfall; and all of us were toys in the hands of fate.

Farris Effandi moved slowly and stretched his weak hand toward Selma, and in a loving and tender voice said, "Hold my hand, my beloved." Selma held his hand; then he said, "I have lived long enough, and I have enjoyed the fruits of life's seasons. I have experienced all its phases with equanimity. I lost your mother when you were three years of age, and she left you as a precious treasure in my lap. I watched you grow, and your face reproduced your mother's features as stars reflected in a calm pool of water. Your character, intelligence, and beauty are your mother's, even your manner of speaking and gestures. You have been my only consolation in this life because you were the image of your mother in every deed and word. Now, I grow old, and my only resting place is between the soft wings of death. Be comforted, my beloved daughter, because I have lived long enough to see you as a woman. Be happy because I shall live in you after my death. My departure today would be no different from my going tomorrow or the day after, for our days are perishing like the leaves of autumn. The hour of my days are perishing like the leaves of autumn. The hour of my death approaches rapidly, and my soul is desirous of being united with your mother's."

As he uttered these words sweetly and lovingly, his face was radiant. Then he put his hand under his pillow and pulled out a small picture in a gold frame. With his eyes on the little photograph, he said, "Come, Selma, come and see your mother in this picture."

Selma wiped away her tears, and after gazing long at the picture, she kissed it repeatedly and cried, "Oh, my beloved mother! Oh, mother!" Then she placed her trembling lips on the picture as if she wished to pour her soul into that image.

The most beautiful word on the lips of mankind is the word "Mother," and the most beautiful call is the call of "My mother." it is a word full of hope and love, a sweet and kind word coming from the depths of the heart. The mother is every thing — she is our consolation in sorrow, our hope in misery, and our strength in weakness. She is the source of love, mercy, sympathy, and forgiveness. He who loses his mother loses a pure soul who blesses and guards him constantly.

Every thing in nature bespeaks the mother. The sun is the mother of earth and gives it its nourishment of hear; it never leaves the universe at night until it has put the earth to sleep to the song of the sea and the hymn of birds and brooks. And this earth is the mother of trees and flowers. It produces them, nurses them, and weans them. The trees and flowers become kind mothers of their great fruits and seeds. And the mother, the prototype of all existence, is the eternal spirit, full of beauty and love.

Selma Karamy never knew her mother because she had died when Selma was an infant, but Selma wept when she saw the picture and cried, "Oh, mother!" The word mother is hidden in our hearts, and it comes upon our lips in hours of sorrow and happiness as the perfume comes from the heart of the rose and mingles with clear and cloudy air.

Selma stared at her mother's picture, kissing it repeatedly, until she collapsed by her father's bed.

The old man placed both hands on her head and said, "I have shown you, my dear child, a picture of your mother on paper. Now listen to me and I shall let you hear her words."

She lifted her head like a little bird in the nest that hears its mother's wing, and looked at him attentively.

Farris Effandi opened his mouth and said, 'Your mother was nursing you when she lost her father; she cried and wept at his going, but she was wise and patient. She sat by me in this room as soon as the funeral was over and held my hand and said, 'Farris, my father is dead now and you are my only consolation in this world. The heart's affections are divided like the branches of the cedar tree; if the tree loses one strong branch, it will suffer but it does not die. It will pour all its vitality into the next branch so that it will grow and fill the empty place.' This is what your mother told me when her father died, and you should say the same thing when death takes my body to its resting place and my soul to God's care.'

Selma answered him with falling tears and broken heart, "When Mother lost her father, you took his place; but who is going to take yours when you are gone? She was left in the care of a loving and truthful husband; she found consolation in her little daughter, and who will be my consolation when you pass away? You have been my father and mother and the companion of my youth."

Saying these words, she turned and looked at me, and, holding the side of my garment, said, "This is the only friend I shall have after you are gone, but how can he console me when he is suffering also? How can a broken heart find consolation in a disappointed soul? A sorrowful woman cannot be comforted by her neighbour's sorrow, nor can a bird fly with broken wings. He is the friend of my soul, but I have already placed a heavy burden of sorrow upon him and dimmed his eyes with my tears till he can see nothing but darkness. he is a brother whom I dearly love, but he is like all brothers who share my sorrow and help me shed tears which increase my bitterness and burn my heart."

Selma's words stabbed my heart, and I felt that I could bear no more. The old man listened to her with depressed spirit. The old man listened to her with depressed spirit, trembling like the light of a lamp before the wind. Then he stretched out his hand and said, "Let me go peacefully, my child. I have broken the bars of this cage; let me fly and do not stop me, for your mother is calling me. The sky is clear and the sea is calm and the boat is ready to sail; do not delay its voyage. Let my body rest with those who are resting; let my dream end and my soul awaken with the dawn; let your soul embrace mine and give me the kiss of hope; let no drops of sorrow or bitterness fall upon my body lest the flowers and grass refuse their nourishment. Do not shed tears of misery upon my hand, for they may grow thorns upon my grave. Do not draw lines of agony upon my forehead, for the wind may pass and read them and refuse to carry the dust of my bones to the green prairies... I love you, my child, while I lived, and I shall love you when I am dead, and my soul shall always watch over you and protect you."

When Farris Effandi looked at me with his eyes half closed and said, "My son, be a real brother to Selma as your father was to me. Be her help and friend in need, and do not let her mourn, because mourning for the dead is a mistake. Repeat to her pleasant tales and sing for her the songs of life so that she may forget her sorrows. Remember me to your father; ask him to tell you the stories of your youth and tell him that I loved him in the person of his son in the last hour of my life."

Silence prevailed, and I could see the pallor of death on the old man's face. Then he rolled his eyes and looked at us and whispered, "Don't call the physician, for he might extend my sentence in this prison by his medicine. The days of slavery are gone, and my soul seeks the freedom of the skies. And do not call the priest to my bedside, because his incantations would not save me if I were a sinner, nor would it rush me to Heaven if I were innocent. The will of humanity cannot change the will of God, as an astrologer cannot change the course of the stars. But after my death let the doctors and priest do what they please, for my ship will continue sailing until it reaches its destination."

At midnight Farris Effandi opened his tired eyes for the last time and focused them on Selma, who was kneeling by his bedside. He tried to speak, but could not, for death had already choked his voice; but he finally managed to say, "The night has passed... Oh, Selma...Oh...Oh, Selma..." Then he bent his head, his face turned white, and I could see a smile on his lips as he breathed his last.

Selma felt her father's hand. It was cold. Then she raised her head and looked at his face. It was covered with the veil of death. Selma was so choked that she could not shed tears, nor sigh, nor even move. For a moment she stared at him with fixed eyes like those of a statue; then she bent down until her forehead touched the floor, and said, "Oh, Lord, have mercy and mend our broken wings."

Farris Effandi Karamy died; his soul was embraced by Eternity, and his body was returned to the earth. Mansour Bey Galib got possession of his wealth, and Selma became a prisoner of life—a life of grief and misery.

I was lost in sorrow and reverie. Days and nights preyed upon me as the eagle ravages its victim. Many a time I tried to forget my misfortune by occupying myself with books and scriptures of past generation, but it was like extinguishing fire with oil, for I could see nothing in the procession of the past but tragedy and could hear nothing but weeping and wailing. The

Book of Job was more fascinating to me than the Psalms and I preferred the Elegies of Jeremiah to the Song of Solomon. Hamlet was closer to my heart than all other dramas of western writers. Thus despair weakens our sight and closes our ears. We can see nothing but spectres of doom and can hear only the beating of our agitated hearts.

Between Christ and Ishtar

In the midst of the gardens and hills which connect the city of Beirut with Lebanon there is a small temple, very ancient, dug out of white rock , surrounded by olive, almond, and willow trees. Although this temple is a half mile from the main highway, at the time of my story very few people interested in relics and ancient ruins had visited it. It was one of many interesting places hidden and forgotten in Lebanon. Due to its seclusion, it had become a haven for worshippers and a shrine for lonely lovers.

As one enters this temple he sees on the wall at the east side an old Phoenician picture, carved in the rock depicting Ishtar, goddess of love and beauty, sitting on her throne, surrounded by seven nude virgins standing in different posses. The first one carries a torch; the second, a guitar; the third, a censer; the fourth a jug of wine; the fifth, a branch of roses; the sixth, a wreath of laurel; the seventh, a bow and arrow; and all of them look at Ishtar reverently.

In the second wall there is another picture, more modern than the first one, symbolizing Christ nailed to the cross, and at His side stand His sorrowful mother and Mary Magdalene and two other women weeping. This Byzantine picture shows that it was carved in the fifteenth or sixteenth century.*

In the west side wall there are two round transits through which the sun's rays enter the temple and strike the pictures and make them look as if they were painted with gold water colour. In the middle of the temple there is a square marble with old paintings on its sides, some of which can hardly be seen under the petrified lumps of blood which show that the ancient people offered sacrifices on this rock and poured perfume, wine, and oil upon it.

There is nothing else in that little temple except deep silence, revealing to the living the secrets of the goddess and speaking wordlessly of past generations and the evolution of religions. Such a sight carries the poet to a world far away from the one in which he dwells and convinces the philosopher that men were born religious; they felt a need for that which they could not see and drew symbols, the meaning of which divulged their hidden secrets and their desires in life and death.

In that unknown temple, I met Selma once every month and spent the hours with her, looking at those strange pictures, thinking of the crucified Christ and pondering upon the young Phoenician men and women who lived, loved and worshipped beauty in the person of Ishtar by burning incense before her statue and pouring perfume on her shrine, people for whom nothing is left to speak except the name, repeated by the march of time before the face of Eternity.

It is hard to write down in words the memories of those hours when I met Selma — those heavenly hours, filled with pain, happiness, sorrow, hope, and misery.

We met secretly in the old temple, remembering the old days, discussing our present, fearing our future, and gradually bringing out the hidden secrets in the depths of our hearts and complaining to each other of our misery and suffering, trying to console ourselves with imaginary hopes and sorrowful dreams. Every now and then we would become calm and wipe our tears and start smiling, forgetting everything except Love; we embraced each other until our hearts melted; then Selma would print a pure kiss on my forehead and fill my heart with ecstasy; I would return the kiss as she bent her ivory neck while her cheeks became gently red like the first ray of dawn on the forehead of hills. We silently looked at the distant horizon where the clouds were coloured with the orange ray of sunset.

Our conversation was not limited to love; every now and then we drifted on to current topics and exchanged ideas. During the course of conversation Selma spoke of woman's place in society, the imprint that the past generation had left on her character, the relationship between husband and wife, and the spiritual diseases and corruption which threatened married life. I remember her saying: "The poets and writers are trying to understand the reality of woman, but up to this day they have not understood the hidden secrets of her heart, because they look upon her from behind the sexual veil and see nothing but externals; they look upon her through the magnifying glass of hatefulness and find nothing except weakness and submission.

In another occasion she said, pointing to the carved pictures on the walls of the temple, "In the heart of this rock there are two symbols depicting the essence of a woman's desires and revealing the hidden secrets of her soul, moving between love and sorrow — between affection and sacrifice, between Ishtar sitting on the throne and Mary standing by the cross. The man buys glory and reputation, but the woman pays the price."

No one knew about our secret meetings except God and the flock of birds which flew over the temple. Selma used to come in her carriage to a place named Pasha park and from there she walked to the temple, where she found me anxiously waiting for her.

We feared not the observer's eyes, neither did our consciences bother us; the spirit which is purified by fire and washed by tears is higher than what the people call shame and disgrace; it is free from the laws of slavery and old customs against the affections of the human heart. That spirit can proudly stand unashamed before the throne of God.

Human society has yielded for seventy centuries to corrupted laws until it cannot understand the meaning of the superior and eternal laws. A man's eyes have become accustomed to the dim light of candles and cannot see the sunlight. Spiritual disease is inherited from one generation to another until it has become a part of people, who look upon it, not as a disease, but as a natural gift, showered by God upon Adam. If those people found someone free from the germs of this disease, they would think of him with shame and disgrace.

Those who think evil of Selma Karamy because she left her husband's home and met me in the temple are the diseased and weak-minded kind who look upon the healthy and sound as rebels. They are like insects crawling in the dark for fear of being stepped upon by the passer-by.

The oppressed prisoners, who can break away from his jail and does not do so, is a coward. Selma, an innocent and oppressed prisoner, was unable to free herself from slavery. Was she to blame because she looked through the jail window upon the green fields and spacious sky? Will the people count her as being untruthful to her husband because she came from his home to sit by me between Christ and Ishtar? Let the people say what they please; Selma had passed the marshes which submerge other spirits and had landed in a world that could not be reached by the howling of wolves and rattling of snakes. People may say what they want about me, for the spirit who has seen the spectre of death cannot be scared by the faces of thieves; the soldier who has seen the swords glittering over his head and streams of blood under his feet does not care about rocks thrown at him by the children on the streets.

The Sacrifice

One day in the late part of June, as the people left the city for the mountain to avoid the heat of summer, I went as usual to the temple to meet Selma, carrying with me a little book of Andalusian poems. As I reached the temple I sat there waiting for Selma, glancing at intervals at the pages of my book, reciting those verses which filled my heart with ecstasy and brought to my soul the memory of the kings, poets, and knights who bade farewell to Granada, and left, with tears in their eyes and sorrow in their hearts, their palaces, institutions and hopes behind. In an hour I saw Selma walking in the midst of the gardens and I approaching the temple, leaning on her parasol as if she were carrying all the worries of the world upon her shoulders. As she entered the temple and sat by me, I noticed some sort of change in her eyes and I was anxious to inquire about it.

Selma felt what was going on in my mind, and she put her hand on my head and said, "Come close to me, come my beloved, come and let me quench my thirst, for the hour of separation has come."

I asked her, "Did your husband find out about our meeting her?" She responded, "My husband does not care about me, neither does he know how I spend my time, for he is busy with those poor girls whom poverty has driven into the houses of ill fame; those girls who sell their bodies for bread, kneaded with blood and tears."

I inquired, "What prevents you from coming to this temple and sitting by me reverently before God? Is your soul requesting our separation.?"

She answered with tears in her eyes, "No, my beloved, my spirit did not ask for separation, for you are a part of me. My eyes never get tired of looking at you, for you are their light; but if destiny ruled that I should walk the rough path of life loaded with shackles, would I be satisfied if your fate should be like mine?" Then she added, "I cannot say everything, because the tongue is mute with pain and cannot talk; the lips are sealed with misery and cannot move; all I can say to you is that I am afraid you may fall in the same trap I fell in."

When I asked, "What do you mean, Selma, and of whom are you afraid?" She covered her face with her hands and said, "The Bishop has already found out that once a month I have been leaving the grave which he buried me in."

I inquired, "Did the Bishop find out about our meetings here?" She answered, "If he did, you would not see me here sitting by you, but he is getting suspicious and he informed all his servants and guards to watch me closely. I am feeling that the house I live in and the path I walk on are all eyes watching me, and fingers pointing at me, and ears listening to the whisper of my thoughts."

She was silent for a while, and then she added, with tears pouring down her cheeks, "I am not afraid of the Bishop, for wetness does not scare the drowned, but I am afraid you might fall into the trap and become his prey; you are still young and free as the sunlight. I am not frightened of fate which has shot all its arrows in my breast, but I am afraid the serpent might bite your feet and detain you from climbing the mountain peak where the future awaits you with its pleasure and glory."

I said, "He who has not been bitten by the serpents of light and snapped at by the wolves of darkness will always be deceived by the days and nights. But listen, Selma, listen carefully; is separation the only means of avoiding people's evils and meanness? Has the path of love and freedom been closed and is nothing left except submission to the will of the slaves of death?"

She responded, "Nothing is left save separation and bidding each other farewell."

With rebellious spirit I took her hand and said excitedly, "We have yielded to the people's will for a long time; since the time we met until this hour we have been led by the blind and have worshipped with them before their idols. Since the time I met you we have been in the hands of the Bishop like two balls which he has thrown around as he pleased. Are we going to submit to his will until death takes us away? Did God give us the breath of life to place it under death's feet? Did He give us liberty to make it a shadow of slavery? He who extinguishes his spirit's fire with his own hands is an infidel in the eyes of Heaven, for Heaven set the fire that burns in our spirits. He who does not rebel against oppression is doing himself injustice. I love you, Selma, and you love me, too; and Love is a precious treasure, it is God's gift to sensitive and great spirits. Shall we throw this treasure away and let the pigs scatter it and trample on it? This world is full of wonder and beauty. Why are we living in this narrow tunnel which the Bishop and his assistants have dug out for us? Life is full of happiness and freedom; why don't we take this heavy yoke off our shoulders and break the chains tied to our feet, and walk freely toward peace? Get up and let us leave this small temple for God's great temple. Let us leave this country and all its slavery and ignorance for another country far away and unreached by the hands of the thieves. Let us go to the coast under the cover of night and catch a boat that will take us across the oceans, where we can find a new life full of happiness and understanding. Do not hesitate, Selma for these minutes are more precious to us than the crowns of kings and more sublime than the thrones of angels. Let us follow the column of light that leads us from this arid desert into the green fields where flowers and aromatic plants grow."

She shook her head and gazed at something invisible on the ceiling of the temple; a sorrowful smile appeared on her lips; then she said, "No, no my beloved. Heaven placed in my hand a cup, full of vinegar and gall; I forced myself to drink it in order to know the full bitterness at the bottom until nothing was left save a few drops, which I shall drink patiently. I am not worthy of a new life of love and peace; I am not strong enough for life's pleasure and sweetness, because a bird with broken wings cannot fly in the spacious sky. The eyes that are accustomed to the dim light of a candle are not strong enough to stare at the sun. Do not talk to me of happiness; its memory makes me suffer. Mention not peace to me; its shadow frightens me; but look at me and I will show you the holy torch which Heaven has lighted in the ashes of my heart — you know that I love you as a mother loves her only child, and Love only taught me to protect you even from myself. It is Love, purified with fire, that stops me from following you to the farthest land. Love kills my desires so that you may live freely and virtuously. Limited love asks for possession of the beloved, but the unlimited asks only for itself. Love that comes between the naiveté and awakening of youth satisfies itself with possessing, and grows with embraces. But Love which is born in the firmament's lap and has descended with the night's secrets is not contended with anything but Eternity and immortality; it does not stand reverently before anything except deity.

When I knew that the Bishop wanted to stop me from leaving his nephew's house and to take my only pleasure away from me, I stood before the window of my room and looked toward the sea, thinking of the vast countries beyond it and the real freedom and personal independence which can be found there. I felt that I was living close to you, surrounded by the shadow of your spirit, submerged in the ocean of your affection. But all these thoughts which illuminate a woman's heart and make her rebel against old customs and live in the shadow of freedom and justice, made me believe that I am weak and that our love is limited and feeble, unable to stand before the sun's face. I cried like a king whose kingdom and treasure have been usurped, but immediately I saw your face through my tears and your eyes gazing at me and I remembered what you said to me once (Come, Selma, come and let us be strong towers before the tempest. Let us stand like brave soldiers before the enemy and face his weapons. If we are killed, we shall die as martyrs; and if we win, we shall live as heroes. Braving obstacles and hardships is nobler than retreat to tranquillity.) These words, my beloved, you uttered when the wings of death were hovering around my father's bed; I remembered them yesterday when the wings of despair were hovering above my head. I strengthened myself and felt, while in the darkness of my prison, some sort of precious freedom easing our difficulties and diminishing our sorrows. I found out that our love was as deep as the ocean and as high as the stars and as spacious as the sky. I came here to see you, and in my weak spirit there is a new strength, and this strength is the ability to sacrifice a great thing in order to obtain a greater one; it is the sacrifice of my happiness so that you may remain virtuous and honourable in the eyes of the people and be far away from their treachery and persecution.

In the past, when I came to this place I felt as if heavy chains were pulling down on me, but today I came here with a new determination that laughs at the shackles and shortens the way. I used to come to this temple like a scared phantom, but today I came like a brave woman who feels the urgency of sacrifice and knows the value of suffering, a woman who likes to protect the one she loves from the ignorant people and from her hungry spirit. I used to sit by you like a trembling shadow, but today I came here to show you my true self before Ishtar and Christ.

I am a tree, grown in the shade, and today I stretched my branches to tremble for a while in the daylight. I came here to tell you good-bye, my beloved, and it is my hope that our farewell will be great and awful like our love. Let our farewell be like fire that bends the gold and makes it more resplendent."

Selma did not allow me to speak or protest, but she looked at me, her eyes glittering, her face retaining its dignity, seeming like an angel worthy of silence and respect. Then she flung herself upon me, something which she had never done before, and put her smooth arms around me and printed a long, deep, fiery kiss on my lips.

As the sun went down, withdrawing its rays from those gardens and orchards, Selma moved to the middle of the temple and gazed along at its walls and corners as if she wanted to pour the light of her eyes on its pictures and symbols. Then she walked forward and reverently knelt before the picture of Christ and kissed His feet, and she whispered, "Oh, Christ, I have chosen Thy Cross and deserted Ishtar's world of pleasure and happiness; I have worn the wreath of thorns and discarded the wreath of laurel and washed myself with blood and tears instead of perfume and scent; I have drunk vinegar and gall from a cup which was meant for wine and nectar; accept me, my Lord, among Thy followers and lead me toward Galilee with those who have chosen Thee, contended with their sufferings and delighted with their sorrows."

When she rose and looked at me and said, "Now I shall return happily to my dark cave, where horrible ghosts reside, Do not sympathize with me, my beloved, and do not feel sorry for me, because the soul that sees the shadow of God once will never be frightened, thereafter, of the ghosts of devils. And the eye that looks on heaven once will not be closed by the pains of the world."

Uttering these words, Selma left the place of worship; and I remained there lost in a deep sea of thoughts, absorbed in the world of revelation where God sits on the throne and the angels write down the acts of human beings, and the souls recite the tragedy of life, and the brides of Heaven sing the hymns of love, sorrow and immortality.

Night had already come when I awakened from my swoon and found myself bewildered in the midst of the gardens, repeating the echo of every word uttered by Selma and remembering her silence, ,her actions, her movements, her expression and the touch of her hands, until I realized the meaning of farewell and the pain of lonesomeness. I was depressed and heart-broken. It was my first discovery of the fact that men, even if they are born free, will remain slaves of strict laws enacted by their forefathers; and that the firmament, which we imagine as unchanging, is the yielding of today to the will of tomorrow and submission of yesterday to the will of today — Many a time, since the night, I have thought of the spiritual law which made Selma prefer death to life, and many a time I have made a comparison between nobility of sacrifice and happiness of rebellion to find out which one is nobler and more beautiful; but until now I have distilled only one truth out of the whole matter, and this truth is sincerity, which makes all our deeds beautiful and honourable. And this sincerity was in Selma Karamy.

The Rescuer

Five years of Selma's marriage passed without bringing children to strengthen the ties of spiritual relation between her and her husband and bind their repugnant souls together.

A barren woman is looked upon with disdain everywhere because of most men's desire to perpetuate themselves through posterity.

The substantial man considers his childless wife as an enemy; he detests her and deserts her and wishes her death. Mansour Bey Galib was that kind of man; materially, he was like earth, and hard like steel and greedy like a grave. His desire of having a child to carry on his name and reputation made him hate Selma in spite of her beauty and sweetness.

A tree grown in a cave does not bear fruit; and Selma, who lived in the shade of life, did not bear children.....

The nightingale does not make his nest in a cage lest slavery be the lot of its chicks.... Selma was a prisoner of misery and it was Heaven's will that she would not have another prisoner to share her life. The flowers of the field are the children of sun's affection and nature's love; and the children of men are the flowers of love and compassion.....

The spirit of love and compassion never dominated Selma's beautiful home at Ras Beyrouth; nevertheless, she knelt down on her knees every night before Heaven and asked God for a child in whom she would find comfort and consolation... She prayed successively until Heaven answered her prayers....

The tree of the cave blossomed to bear fruit at last. The nightingale in the cage commenced making its nest with the feathers of its wings.

Selma stretched her chained arms toward Heaven to receive God's precious gift and nothing in the world could have made her happier than becoming a potential mother.

She waited anxiously, counting the days and looking forward to the time when Heaven's sweetest melody, the voice of her child, should ring in her ears....

She commenced to see the dawn of a brighter future through her tears.

It was the month of Nisan when Selma was stretched on the bed of pain and labour, where life and death were wrestling. The doctor and the midwife were ready to deliver to the world a new guest. Late at night Selma started her successive cry... a cry of life's partition from life... a cry of continuance in the firmament of nothingness.. a cry of a weak force before the stillness of great forces... the cry of poor Selma who was lying down in despair under the feet of life and death.

At dawn Selma gave birth to a baby boy. When she opened her eyes she saw smiling faces all over the room, then she looked again and saw life and death still wrestling by her bed. She closed her eyes and cried, saying for the first time, "Oh, my son." The midwife wrapped the infant with silk swaddles and placed him by his mother, but the doctor kept looking at Selma and sorrowfully shaking his head.

The voices of joy woke the neighbours, who rushed into the house to felicitate the father upon the birth of his heir, but the doctor still gazed at Selma and her infant and shook his head....

The servants hurried to spread the good news to Mansour Bey, but the doctor stared at Selma and her child with a disappointed look on his face.

As the sun came out, Selma took the infant to her breast; he opened his eyes for the first time and looked at his mother; then he quivered and close them for the last time. The doctor took the child from Selma's arms and on his cheeks fell tears; then he whispered to himself, "He is a departing guest."

The child passed away while the neighbours were celebrating with the father in the big hall at the house and drinking to the health of their heir; and Selma looked at the doctor, and pleaded, "Give me my child and let me embrace him."

Though the child was dead, the sounds of the drinking cups increased in the hall.....

He was born at dawn and died at sunrise...

He was born like a thought and died like a sigh and disappeared like a shadow.

He did not live to console and comfort his mother.

His life began at the end of the night and ended at the beginning of the day, like a drop of few poured by the eyes of the dark and dried by the touch of the light.

A pearl brought by the tide to the coast and returned by the ebb into the depth of the sea....

A lily that has just blossomed from the bud of life and is mashed under the feet of death.

A dear guest whose appearance illuminated Selma's heart and whose departure killed her soul.

This is the life of men, the life of nations, the life of suns, moons and stars.

And Selma focused her eyes upon the doctor and cried, "Give me my child and let me embrace him; give me my child and let me nurse him."

Then the doctor bent his head. His voice choked and he said, "Your child is dead, Madame, be patient.

Upon hearing her doctor's announcement, Selma uttered a terrible cry. Then she was quiet for a moment and smiled happily. Her face brightened as if she had discovered something, and quietly she said, "Give me my child; bring him close to me and let me see him dead."

The doctor carried the dead child to Selma and placed him between her arms. She embraced him, then turned her face toward the wall and addressed the dead infant saying, "You have come to take me away my child; you have come to show me the way that leads to the coast. Here I am my child; lead me and let us leave this dark cave.

And in a minute the sun's ray penetrated the window curtains and fell upon two calm bodies lying on a bed, guarded by the profound dignity of silence and shaded by the wings of death. The doctor left the room with tears in his eyes, and as he reached the big hall the celebrations was converted into a funeral, but Mansour Bey Galib never uttered a word or shed a tear. He remained standing motionless like a statue, holding a drinking cup with his right hand.

* * *

The second day Selma was shrouded with her white wedding dress and laid in a coffin; the child's shroud was his swaddle; his coffin was his mother's arms; his grave was her calm breast. Two corpses were carried in one coffin, and I walked reverently with the crowd accompanying Selma and her infant to their resting place.

Arriving at the cemetery, Bishop Galib commenced chanting while the other priests prayed, and on their gloomy faces appeared a veil of ignorance and emptiness.

As the coffin went down, one of the bystanders whispered, "This is the first time in my life I have seen two corpses in one coffin." Another one said, "It seems as if the child had come to rescue his mother from her pitiless husband."

A third one said, "Look at Mansour Bey: he is gazing at the sky as if his eyes were made of glass. He does not look like he has lost his wife and child in one day." A fourth one added, "His uncle, the Bishop, will marry him again tomorrow to a wealthier and stronger woman.

The Bishop and the priests kept on singing and chanting until the grave digger was through filing the ditch. Then, the people, individually, approached the Bishop and his nephew and offered their respects to them with sweet words of sympathy, but I stood lonely aside without a soul to console me, as if Selma and her child meant nothing to me.

The farewell-bidders left the cemetery; the grave digger stood by the new grave holding a shovel with his hand.

As I approached him, I inquired, "Do you remember where Farris Effandi Karamy was buried?"

He looked at me for a moment, then pointed at Selma's grave and said, "Right here; I placed his daughter upon him and upon his daughter's breast rests her child, and upon all I put the earth back with this shovel."

Then I said, "In this ditch you have also buried my heart."

As the grave digger disappeared behind the poplar trees, I could not resist anymore; I dropped down on Selma's grave and wept.

A TEAR AND A SMILE

The Creation

The God separated a spirit from Himself and fashioned it into Beauty. He showered upon her all the blessings of gracefulness and kindness. He gave her the cup of happiness and said, "Drink not from this cup unless you forget the past and the future, for happiness is naught but the moment." And He also gave her a cup of sorrow and said, "Drink from this cup and you will understand the meaning of the fleeting instants of the joy of life, for sorrow ever abounds."

And the God bestowed upon her a love that would desert he forever upon her first sigh of earthly satisfaction, and a sweetness that would vanish with her first awareness of flattery.

And He gave her wisdom from heaven to lead to the all-righteous path, and placed in the depth of her heart and eye that sees the unseen, and created in he an affection and goodness toward all things. He dressed her with raiment of hopes spun by the angels of heaven from the sinews of the rainbow. And He cloaked her in the shadow of confusion, which is the dawn of life and light.

Then the God took consuming fire from the furnace of anger, and searing wind from the desert of ignorance, and sharp-cutting sands from the shore of selfishness, and coarse earth from under the feet of ages, and combined them all and fashioned Man. He gave to Man a blind power that rages and drives him into a madness which extinguishes only before gratification of desire, and placed life in him which is the spectre of death.

And the god laughed and cried. He felt an overwhelming love and pity for Man, and sheltered him beneath His guidance.

Two Infants

A prince stood on the balcony of his palace addressing a great multitude summoned for the occasion and said, "Let me offer you and this whole fortunate country my congratulations upon the birth of a new prince who will carry the name of my noble family, and of whom you will be justly proud. He is the new bearer of a great and illustrious ancestry, and upon him depends the brilliant future of this realm. Sing and be merry!" The voices of the throngs, full of joy and thankfulness, flooded the sky with exhilarating song, welcoming the new tyrant who would affix the yoke of oppression to their necks by ruling the weak with bitter authority, and exploiting their bodies and killing their souls. For that destiny, the people were singing and drinking ecstatically to the heady of the new Emir.

Another child entered life and that kingdom at the same time. While the crowds were glorifying the strong and belittling themselves by singing praise to a potential despot, and while the angels of heaven were weeping over the people's weakness and servitude, a sick woman was thinking. She lived in an old, deserted hovel and, lying in her hard bed beside her newly born infant wrapped with ragged swaddles, was starving to death. She was a penurious and miserable young wife neglected by humanity; her husband had fallen into the trap of death set by the prince's oppression, leaving a solitary woman to whom God had sent, that night, a tiny companion to prevent her from working and sustaining life.

As the mass dispersed and silence was restored to the vicinity, the wretched woman placed the infant on her lap and looked into his face and wept as if she were to baptize him with tears. And with a hunger weakened voice she spoke to the child saying, "Why have you left the spiritual world and come to share with me the bitterness of earthly life? Why have you deserted the angels and the spacious firmament and come to this miserable land of humans, filled with agony, oppression, and heartlessness? I have nothing to give you except tears; will you be nourished on tears instead of milk?

I have no silk clothes to put on you; will my naked, shivering arms give you warmth? The little animals graze in the pasture and return safely to their shed; and the small birds pick the seeds and sleep placidly between the branches. But you, my beloved, have naught save a loving but destitute mother."

Then she took the infant to her withered breast and clasped her arms around him as if wanting to join the two bodies in one, as before. She lifted her burning eyes slowly toward heaven and cried, "God! Have mercy on my unfortunate countrymen!"

At that moment the clouds floated from the face of the moon, whose beams penetrated the transom of that poor home and fell upon two corpses.

The House of Fortune

My wearied heart bade me farewell and left for the House of Fortune. As he reached that holy city which the soul had blessed and worshipped, he commenced wondering, for he could not find what he had always imagined would be there. The city was empty of power, money, and authority.

And my heart spoke to the daughter of Love saying, "Oh Love, where can I find Contentment? I heard that she had come here to join you."

And the daughter of Love responded, "Contentment has already gone to preach her gospel in the city, where greed and corruption are paramount; we are not in need of her."

Fortune craves not Contentment, for it is an earthly hope, and its desires are embraced by union with objects, while Contentment is naught but heartfelt.

The eternal soul is never contented; it ever seeks exaltation. Then my heart looked upon Life of Beauty and said: "Thou art all knowledge; enlighten me as to the mystery of Woman." And he answered, "Oh human heart, woman is your own reflection, and whatever you are, she is; wherever you live, she lives; she is like religion if not interpreted by the ignorant, and like a moon, if not veiled with clouds, and like a breeze, if not poisoned with impurities."

And my heart walked toward Knowledge, the daughter of Love and Beauty, and said, "Bestow upon me wisdom, that I might share it with the people." And she responded, "Say not wisdom, but rather fortune, for real fortune comes not from outside, but begins in the Holy of Holies of life. Share of thyself with the people."

A Poet's Death Is his Life

The dark wings of night enfolded the city upon which Nature had spread a pure white garment of snow; and men deserted the streets for their houses in search of warmth, while the north wind probed in contemplation of laying waste the gardens. There in the suburb stood an old hut heavily laden with snow and on the verge of falling. In a dark recess of that hovel was a poor bed in which a dying youth was lying, staring at the dim light of his oil lamp, made to flicker by the entering winds. He a man in the spring of life who foresaw fully that the peaceful hour of freeing himself from the clutches of life was fast nearing. He was awaiting Death's visit gratefully, and upon his pale face appeared the dawn of hope; and on his lops a sorrowful smile; and in his eyes forgiveness.

He was poet perishing from hunger in the city of living rich. He was placed in the earthly world to enliven the heart of man with his beautiful and profound sayings. He as noble soul, sent by the Goddess of Understanding to soothe and make gentle the human spirit. But alas! He gladly bade the cold earth farewell without receiving a smile from its strange occupants.

He was breathing his last and had no one at his bedside save the oil lamp, his only companion, and some parchments upon which he had inscribed his heart's feeling. As he salvaged the remnants of his withering strength he lifted his hands heavenward; he moved his eyes hopelessly, as if wanting to penetrate the ceiling in order to see the stars from behind the veil clouds.

And he said, "Come, oh beautiful Death; my soul is longing for you. Come close to me and unfasten the irons life, for I am weary of dragging them. Come, oh sweet Death, and deliver me from my neighbours who looked upon me as a stranger because I interpret to them the language of the angels. Hurry, oh peaceful Death, and carry me from these multitudes who left me in the dark corner of oblivion because I do not bleed the weak as they do. Come, oh gentle Death, and enfold me under your white wings, for my fellowmen are not in want of me. Embrace me, oh Death, full of love and mercy; let your lips touch my lips which never tasted a mother's kiss, not touched a sister's cheeks, not caresses a sweetheart's fingertips. Come and take me, by beloved Death."

Then, at the bedside of the dying poet appeared an angel who possessed a supernatural and divine beauty, holding in her hand a wreath of lilies. She embraced him and closed his eyes so he could see no more, except with the eye of his spirit. She impressed a deep and long and gently withdrawn kiss that left and eternal smile of fulfilment upon his lips. Then the hovel became empty and nothing was lest save parchments and papers which the poet had strewn with bitter futility.

Hundreds of years later, when the people of the city arose from the diseases slumber of ignorance and saw the dawn of knowledge, they erected a monument in the most beautiful garden of the city and celebrated a feast every year in honour of that poet, whose writings had freed them. Oh, how cruel is man's ignorance!

The Criminal

A young man of strong body, weakened by hunger, sat on the walker's portion of the street stretching his hand toward all who passed, begging and repeating his hand toward all who passed, begging and repeating the sad song of his defeat in life, while suffering from hunger and from humiliation.

When night came, his lips and tongue were parched, while his hand was still as empty as his stomach.

He gathered himself and went out from the city, where he sat under a tree and wept bitterly. Then he lifted his puzzled eyes to heaven while hunger was eating his inside, and he said, "Oh Lord, I went to the rich man and asked for employment, but he turned me away because of my shabbiness; I knocked at the school door, but was forbidden solace because I was empty-handed; I sought any occupation that would give me bread, but all to no avail. In desperation I asked alms, but They worshippers saw me and said "He is strong and lazy, and he should not beg."

"Oh Lord, it is Thy will that my mother gave birth unto me, and now the earth offers me back to You before the Ending."

His expression then changed. He arose and his eyes now glittered in determination. He fashioned a thick and heavy stick from the branch of the tree, and pointed it toward the city, shouting, "I asked for bread with all the strength of my voice, and was refused. Not I shall obtain it by the strength of my muscles! I asked for bread in the name of mercy and love, but humanity did not heed. I shall take it now in the name of evil!"

The passing years rendered the youth a robber, killer and destroyer of souls; he crushed all who opposed him; he amassed fabulous wealth with which he won himself over to those in power. He was admired by colleagues, envied by other thieves, and feared by the multitudes.

His riches and false position prevailed upon the Emir to appoint him deputy in that city – the sad process pursued by unwise governors. Thefts were then legalized; oppression was supported by authority; crushing of the weak became commonplace; the throngs curried and praised.

Thus does the first touch of humanity's selfishness make criminals of the humble, and make killers of the sons of peace; thus does the early greed of humanity grow and strike back at humanity a thousand fold!

Song of Fortune

Man and I are sweethearts
He craves me and I long for him,
But alas!
Between us has appeared a rival who brings us misery.
She is cruel and demanding,
Possessing empty lure.
Her name is Substance.
She follows wherever we go
And watches like a sentinel,
Bringing restlessness to my lover.

I ask for my beloved in the forest,
Under the trees, by the lakes.
I cannot find him,
For Substance has spirited him to the clamorous city
And placed him on the throne
Of quaking, metal riches.

I call for him with the voice of knowledge
And the song of Wisdom.
He does not hearken,
For Substance has enticed him into the dungeon
Of selfishness, where avarice dwells.

I seek him in the field of Contentment,
But I am alone,
For my rival has imprisoned him ,
I the cave of gluttony and greed,
And locked him there
With painful chains of gold.

I call to him at dawn, when Nature smiles,
But he does not hear,
For excess has laden his drugged eyes with sick slumber.

I beguile him at eventide, when Silence rules
And the flowers sleep.
But he responds not,
For his fear over what the morrow will bring shadows his thoughts.

He yearns to love me;
He asks for me in this own acts.
But he will find me not except in God's acts.
He seeks me in the edifices of his glory
Which he has built upon the bones of others;
He whispers to me from among his heaps of gold and silver;
But he will find me only by coming to the house of Simplicity
Which God has built at the brink of the stream of affection.

He desires to kiss me before his coffers,
But his lips will never touch mine,
Except in the richness of the pure breeze.

He asks me to share with him his fabulous wealth,
But I will not forsake God's fortune;
I will not cast off my cloak of beauty.

He seeks deceit for medium;
I seek only the medium of his heart.
He bruises his heart in his narrow cell;
I would enrich his heart with all my love.

My beloved has learned how to shriek and cry for my enemy, Substance;
I would teach him how to shed tears of affection
And mercy from the eyes of his soul
For all things,
And utter sighs of contentment through those tears.

Man is my sweetheart;
I want to belong to him.

Song of the Rain

I am dotted silver threads dropped from heaven by the gods.
Nature then takes me, to adorn her fields and valleys.

I am beautiful pearls,
Plucked from the crown of Ishtar by the daughter of Dawn to embellish the gardens.

When I cry the hills laugh;
When I humble myself the flowers rejoice;
When I bow, all things are elated.

The field and the cloud are lovers
And between them I am a messenger of mercy.
I quench the thirst of one;
I cure the ailment of the other.

The voice of thunder declares my arrival;
The rainbow announces my departure.
I am like earthly life,
Which begins at the feet of the mad elements
And ends under the upraised wings of death.

I emerge from the heard of the sea
Soar with the breeze.
When I see a field in need,
I descend and embrace the flowers and the trees in a million little ways.

I touch gently at the windows with my soft fingers,
And my announcement is a welcome song all can hear
But only the sensitive can understand.

The heat in the air gives birth to me,
But in turn I kill it,
As woman overcomes man with the strength she takes from him.

I am the sigh of the sea;
The laughter of the field;
The tears of heaven.

So with love –
Sighs from the deep sea of affection;
Laughter from the colourful field of the spirit;
Tears from the endless heaven of memories.

The Poet

He is a link between this and the coming world.
He is a pure spring from which all thirsty souls may drink.

He is a tree watered by the River of Beauty,
Bearing fruit which the hungry heart craves;

He is a nightingale,
Soothing the depressed spirit with his beautiful melodies;
He is a white cloud appearing over the horizon,
Ascending and growing until it fills the face of the sky.
Then it falls on the flows in the field of Life,
Opening their petals to admit the light.

He is an angel,
Sent by the goddess to preach the Deity's gospel;
He is a brilliant lamp,
Unconquered by darkness
And inextinguishable by the wind.
It is filled with oil by Ihstar of Love,
And lighted by Apollon of Music.

He is a solitary figure,
Robed in simplicity and kindness;
He sits upon the lap of Nature to draw his inspiration,
And stays up in the silence of the night,
Awaiting the descending of the spirit.

He is a sower
Who sows the seeds of his heart in the prairies of affection,
And humanity reaps the harvest for her nourishment.

This is the poet – whom the people ignore in this life,
And who is recognized only when he bids the earthly world farewell
And returns to his arbour in heaven.

This is the poet – who asks naught of humanity but a smile.
This is the poet – whose spirit ascends and fills the firmament with beautiful sayings;
Yet the people deny themselves his radiance.

Until when shall the people remain asleep?
Until when shall they continue to glorify those who attain greatness by moments of advantage?
How long shall they ignore those who enable them to see the beauty of their spirit,
Symbol of peace and love?

Until when shall human beings honour the dead and forget the living,
Who spend their lives encircled in misery,
And who consume themselves,
Like burning candles to illuminate the way
For the ignorant and lead them into the path of light?

Poet, you are the life of this life,
And you have triumphed over the ages of despite their severity.

Poet, you will one day rule the hearts,
And therefore, your kingdom has no ending.

Poet, examine your crown of thorns;
You will find concealed in it a budding wreath of laurel.

Laughter and Tears

As the Sun withdrew his rays from the garden, and the moon threw cushioned beams upon the flowers, I sat under the trees pondering upon the phenomena of the atmosphere, looking through the branches at the strewn stars which glittered like chips of silver upon a blue carpet; and I could hear from a distance the agitated murmur of the rivulet singing its way briskly into the valley.

When the birds took shelter among the boughs, and the flowers folded their petals, and tremendous silence descended, I heard a rustle of feet though the grass. I took heed and saw a young couple approaching my arbour. The say under a tree where I could see them without being seen.

After he looked about in every direction, I heard the young man saying, "Sit by me, my beloved, and listen to my heart; smile, for your happiness is a symbol of our future; be merry, for the sparkling days rejoice with us.

"My soul is warning me of the doubt in your heart, for doubt in love is a sin. "Soon you will be the owner of this vast land, lighted by this beautiful moon; soon you will be the mistress of my palace, and all the servants and maids will obey your commands.

"Smile, my beloved, like the gold smiles from my father's coffers.

"My heart refuses to deny you its secret. Twelve months of comfort and travel await us; for a year we will spend my father's gold at the blue lakes of Switzerland, and viewing the edifices of Italy and Egypt, and resting under the Holy Cedars of Lebanon; you will meet the princesses who will envy you for your jewels and clothes.

"All these things I will do for you; will you be satisfied?"

In a little while I saw them walking and stepping on flowers as the rich step upon the hearts of the poor. As they disappeared from my sight, I commenced to make comparison between love and money, and to analyze their position in the heart.

Money! The source of insincere love; the spring of false light and fortune; the well of poisoned water; the desperation of old age!

I was still wandering in the vast desert of contemplation when a forlorn and spectre-like couple passed by me and sat on the grass; a young man and a young woman who had left their farming shacks in the nearby fields for this cool and solitary place.

After a few moments of complete silence, I heard the following words uttered with sighs from weather-bitten lips, "Shed not tears, my beloved; love that opens our eyes and enslaves our hearts can give us the blessing of patience. Be consoled in our delay our delay, for we have taken an oath and entered Love's shrine; for our love will ever grow in adversity; for it is in Love's name that we are suffering the obstacles of poverty and the sharpness of misery and the emptiness of separation. I shall attack these hardships until I triumph and place in your hands a strength that will help over all things to complete the journey of life.

"Love – which is God – will consider our sighs and tears as incense burned at His altar and He will reward us with fortitude. Good-bye, my beloved; I must leave before the heartening moon vanishes."

A pure voice, combined of the consuming flame of love, and the hopeless bitterness of longing and the resolved sweetness of patience, said, "Good-bye, my beloved."

They separated, and the elegy to their union was smothered by the wails of my crying heart.

I looked upon slumbering Nature, and with deep reflection discovered the reality of a vast and infinite thing – something no power could demand, influence acquire, nor riches purchase. Nor could it be effaced by the tears of time or deadened by sorrow; a thing which cannot be discovered by the blue lakes of Switzerland or the beautiful edifices of Italy.

It is something that gathers strength with patience, grows despite obstacles, warms in winter, flourishes in spring, casts a breeze in summer, and bears fruit in autumn – I found Love.

Vision

There in the middle of the field, by the side of a crystalline stream, I saw a bird-cage whose rods and hinges were fashioned by an expert's hands. In one corner lay a dead bird, and in another were two basins – one empty of water and the other of seeds. I stood there reverently, as if the lifeless bird and the murmur of the water were worthy of deep silence and respect – something worth of examination and meditation by the heard and conscience.

As I engrossed myself in view and thought, I found that the poor creature had died of thirst beside a stream of water, and of hunger in the midst of a rich field, cradle of life; like a rich man locked inside his iron safe, perishing from hunger amid heaps of gold.

Before my eyes I saw the cage turned suddenly into a human skeleton, and the dead bird into a man's heart which was bleeding from a deep wound that looked like the lips of a sorrowing woman. A voice came from that wound saying, "I am the human heart, prisoner of substance and victim of earthly laws.

"In God's field of Beauty, at the edge of the stream of life, I was imprisoned in the cage of laws made by man.

"In the centre of beautiful Creation I died neglected because I was kept from enjoying the freedom of God's bounty.

"Everything of beauty that awakens my love and desire is a disgrace, according to man's conceptions; everything of goodness that I crave is but naught, according to his judgment.

"I am the lost human heart, imprisoned in the foul dungeon of man's dictates, tied with chains of earthly authority, dead and forgotten by laughing humanity whose tongue is tied and whose eyes are empty of visible tears."

All these words I heard, and I saw them emerging with a stream of ever thinning blood from that wounded heart.

More was said, but my misted eyes and crying should prevented further sight or hearing.

Two Wishes

In the silence of the night Death descended from God toward the earth. He hovered above a city and pierced the dwellings with his eyes. He say the spirits floating on wings of dreams, and the people who were surrendered to the Slumber.

When the moon fell below the horizon and the city became black, Death walked silently among the houses – careful to touch nothing – until he reached a palace. He entered through the bolted gates undisturbed, and stood by the rich man's bed; and as Death touched his forehead, the sleeper's eyes opened, showing great fright.

When he saw the spectre, he summoned a voice mingled with fear and anger, and said, "God away, oh horrible dream; leave me, you dreadful ghost. Who are you? How did you enter this place? What do you want? Leave this place at once, for I am the lord of the house and will call my slaves and guards, and order them to kill you!"

Then Death spoke, softly but with smouldering thunder, "I am Death. Stand and bow!"

The man responded, "What do you want? What have you come here when I have not yet finished my affairs? What see you from strength such as mine? Go to the weak man, and take him away!

"I loathe the sight of your bloody paws and hollow face, and my eyes take sick at your horrible ribbed winds and cadaverous body."

After a moment of fearful realization he added, "No, No, oh merciful Death! Mind not talk, for even fear reveals what the heart forbids.

"Take a bushelful of my gold, or a handful of my slave's souls, but leave me. I have accounts with Life requiring settling; I have due from people much gold; my ships have not reached the harbour; my demand, but spare my life. Death, I own harems of supernatural beauty; your choice is my gift to you. Give heed, Death – I have but one child, and I love him dearly for he is my only joy in this life. I offer supreme sacrifice – take him, but spare me!"

Death murmured, "You are not rich, but pitifully poor." Then Death took the hand of that earthly slave, removed his reality, and gave to the angels the heavy task of correction.

And Death walked slowly amidst the dwellings of the poor until he reached the most miserable he could find. He entered and approached a bed upon which a youth slept fitfully. Death touched his eyes; the lad sprang up as he saw Death standing by, and, with a voice full of love and hope he said, "Here I am, my beautiful Death. Accept my soul, for you are the hope of my dreams. Be their accomplishment! Embrace me, oh beloved Death! You are merciful; do not leave me. You are God's messenger; deliver me to Him. You are the right hand of Truth and the heart of Kindness; do not neglect me.

"I have begged for you many times, but you did not come; I have sought you, but you avoided me; I called out to you, but you listened not. You hear me now – embrace my soul, beloved Death!"

Death placed his softened hand upon the trembling lips, removed all reality, and enfolded it beneath his wings for secure conduct. And returning to the sky, Death looked back and whispered his warning:

"Only those return to Eternity. Who on earth seek out Eternity."

Yesterday and Today

The gold-hoarder walked in his palace park and with him walked his troubles. And over his head hovered worries as a vulture hovers over a carcass, until he reached a beautiful lake surrounded by magnificent marble statuary.

He sat there pondering the water which poured from the mouths of the statues like thoughts flowing freely from a lover's imagination, and contemplating heavily his palace which stood upon a knoll like a birthmark upon the cheek of a maiden. His fancy revealed to him the pages of his life's drama which he read with falling tears that veiled his eyes and prevented him from viewing man's feeble additions to Nature.

He looked back with piercing regret to the images of his early life, woven into pattern by the gods, until he could no longer control his anguish. He said aloud, "Yesterday I was grazing my sheep in the green valley, enjoying my existence, sounding my flute, and holding my head high. Today I am a prisoner of greed. Gold leads into gold, then into restlessness and finally into crushing misery.

"Yesterday I was like a singing bird, soaring freely here and there in the fields. Today I am a slave to fickle wealth, society's rules, and city's customs, and purchased friends, pleasing the people by conforming to the strange and narrow laws of man. I was born to be free and enjoy the bounty of life, but I find myself like a beast of burden so heavily laden with gold that his back is breaking.

"Where are the spacious plains, the singing brooks, the pure breeze, the closeness of Nature? Where is my deity? I have lost all! Naught remains save loneliness that saddens me, gold that ridicules me, slaves who curse to my back, and a palace that I have erected as a tomb for my happiness, and in whose greatness I have lost my heart.

"Yesterday I roamed the prairies and the hills together with the Bedouin's daughter; Virtue was our companion, Love our delight, and the moon our guardian. Today I am among women with shallow beauty who sell themselves for gold and diamonds.

"Yesterday I was carefree, sharing with the shepherds all the joy of life; eating, playing, working, singing, and dancing together to the music of the heart's truth. Today I find myself among the people like a frightened lamb among the wolves. As I walk in the roads, they gaze at me with hateful eyes and point at me with scorn and jealousy, and as I steal through the park I see frowning faces all about me.

"Yesterday I was rich in happiness and today I am poor in gold.

"Yesterday I was a happy shepherd looking upon his head as a merciful king looks with pleasure upon his contented subjects. Today I am a slave standing before my wealth, my wealth which robbed me of the beauty of life I once knew.

"Forgive me, my Judge! I did not know that riches would put my life in fragments and lead me into the dungeons of harshness and stupidity. What I thought was glory is naught but an eternal inferno."

He gathered himself wearily and walked slowly toward the palace, sighing and repeating, "Is this what people call wealth? Is this the god I am serving and worshipping? Is this what I seek of the earth? Why can I not trade it for one particle of contentment? Who would sell me one beautiful thought for a ton of gold? Who would give me one moment of love for a handful of gems? Who would grant me an eye that can see others' hearts, and take all my coffers in barter?"

As he reached the palace gates he turned and looked toward the city as Jeremiah gazed toward Jerusalem. He raised his arms in woeful lament and shouted, "Oh people of the noisome city, who are living in darkness, hastening toward misery, preaching falsehood, and speaking with stupidity... until when shall you remain ignorant? Unit when shall you abide in the filth of life and continue to desert its gardens? Why wear you tattered robes of narrowness while the silk raiment of Nature's beauty is fashioned for you? The lamp of wisdom is dimming; it is time to furnish it with oil. The house of true fortune is being destroyed; it is time to rebuild it and guard it. The thieves of ignorance have stolen the treasure of your peace; it is time to retake it!"

At that moment a poor man stood before him and stretched forth his hand for alms. As he looked at the beggar, his lips parted, his eyes brightened with a softness, and his face radiated kindness. It was as if the yesterday he had lamented by the lake had come to greet him. He embraced the pauper with affection and filled his hands with gold, and with a voice sincere with the sweetness of love he said, "Come back tomorrow and bring with you your fellow sufferers. All your possessions will be restored."

He entered his palace saying, "Everything in life is good; even gold, for it teaches a lesson. Money is like a stringed instrument; he who does not know how to use it properly will hear only discordant music. Money is like love; it kills slowly and painfully the one who withholds it, and it enlivens the other who turns it upon his fellow man."

Leave Me, My Blamer

Leave me, my blamer,
For the sake of the love which unites your soul with that of your beloved one;
For the sake of that which joins spirit with mothers affection,
And ties your heart with filial love.
Go, and leave me to my own weeping heart.

Let me sail in the ocean of my dreams;
Wait until Tomorrow comes,
For tomorrow is free to do with me as he wishes.
Your laying is naught but shadow
That walks with the spirit to the tomb of abashment,
And shows heard the cold, solid earth.

I have a little heart within me
And I like to bring him out of his prison and carry him on the palm of my hand
To examine him In depth and extract his secret.
Aim not your arrows at him,
Lest he takes fright and vanish 'ere he pours the secret blood
As a sacrifice at the altar of his own faith,
Given him by Deity
When he fashioned him of love and beauty.

The sun is rising and the nightingale Is singing,
And the myrtle is breathing its fragrance into space.
I want to free myself from the quilted slumber of wrong.
Do not detain me, my blamer!

Cavil me not by mention of the lions of the forest
Or the snakes of the valley,
For me soul knows no fear of earth
And accepts no warning of evil before evil comes.

Advise me not, my blamer,
For calamities have opened my heart
And tears have cleansed my eyes,
And errors have taught me the language of the hearts.

Talk not of banishment, for conscience is my judge
And he will justify me and protect me if I am innocent,
And will deny me of life if I am a criminal.

Love's procession is moving;
Beauty is waving her banner;
Youth is sounding the trumpet of joy;
Disturb not my contrition, my blamer.
Let me walk, for the path is rich with roses and mint,
And the air is scented with cleanliness.

Relate not the tales of wealth and greatness,
For my soul is rich with bounty and great with God's glory.

Speak not of peoples and laws and kingdoms,
For the whole earth is my birthplace
And all humans are my brothers.

Go from me, for you are taking away life –
Giving repentance and bringing needless words.

The Beauty of Death

Part One – The Calling

Let me sleep, for my soul is intoxicated with love and
Let me rest, for my spirit has had its bounty of days and nights;
Light the candles and burn the incense around my bed, and
Scatter leaves of jasmine and roses over my body;
Embalm my hair with frankincense and sprinkle my feet with perfume,
And read what the hand of Death has written on my forehead.

Let me rest in the arms of Slumber, for my open eyes are tired;
Let the silver-stringed lyre quiver and soothe my spirit;
Weave from the harp and lute a veil around my withering heart.

Sing of the past as you behold the dawn of hope in my eyes, for
It's magic meaning is a soft bed upon which my heart rests.

Dry your tears, my friends, and raise your heads as the flowers
Raise their crowns to greet the dawn.
Look at the bride of Death standing like a column of light
Between my bed and the infinite;
Hold your breath and listen with me to the beckoning rustle of her
white wings.

Come close and bid me farewell;
Touch my eyes with smiling lips.
Let the children grasp my hands with soft and rosy fingers;
Let the ages place their veined hands upon my head and bless me;
Let the virgins come close and see the shadow of God in my eyes,
And hear the echo of His will racing with my breath.

Part Two – The Ascending

I have passed a mountain peak
And my soul is soaring in the firmament of complete and unbound freedom;
I am far, far away, my companions,
And the clouds are hiding the hills from my eyes.
The valleys are becoming flooded with an ocean of silence,
And the hands of oblivion are engulfing the roads and the houses;
The prairies and fields are disappearing behind a white spectre
That looks like the spring cloud, yellow as the candlelight
And red as the twilight.

The songs of the waves and the hymns of the streams are scattered,
And the voices of the throngs reduced to silence;
And I can hear naught but the music of Eternity
In exact harmony with the spirit's desires.
I am cloaked in full whiteness;
I am in comfort; I am in peace.

Part Three – The Remains

Unwrap me from this white linen shroud
And clothe me with leaves of jasmine and lilies;
Take my body from the ivory casket and let it rest
Upon pillows of orange blossoms.
Lament me not, but sing songs of youth and joy;
Shed not tears upon me, but sing of harvest and the winepress;
Utter no sigh of agony,
But draw upon my face with your finger the symbol of Love and Joy.
Disturb not the air's tranquillity with chanting and requiems,
But let your hearts sing with me the song of Eternal Life;
Mourn me not with apparel of black,
But dress in colour and rejoice with me;
Talk not of my departure with sighs in your hearts;
Close your eyes and you will see me with you forevermore.

Place me upon clusters of leaves
And carry my upon your friendly shoulders
And walk slowly to the deserted forest.
Take me not to the crowded burying ground
Lest my slumber be disrupted by the rattling of bones and skulls.
Carry me to the cypress woods
And dig my grave where violets and poppies grow not in the other's shadow;
Let my grave be deep
So that the flood will not carry my bones to the open valley;
Let my grace be wide,
So that the twilight shadows will come and sit by me.

Take from me all earthly raiment
And place me deep in my Mother Earth;
And place me with care upon my mother's breast.
Cover me with soft earth,
And let each handful be mixed with seeds of jasmine, lilies and myrtle;
And when they grow above me,
And thrive on my body's element they will breathe the fragrance of my heart into space;
And reveal even to the sun the secret of my peace;
And sail with the breeze and comfort the wayfarer.

Leave me then, friends – leave me and depart on mute feet,
As the silence walks in the deserted valley;
Leave me to God and disperse yourselves slowly,
As the almond and apple blossoms disperse under the vibration of Nisan's breeze.
Go back to the joy of your dwellings
And you will find there that which Death cannot remove from you and me.
Leave with place, for what you see here is far away in meaning
From the earthly world. Leave me.

A Poet's Voice

Part One

The power of charity sows deep in my heart, and I reap and gather the wheat in bundles and give them to the hungry.

My soul gives life to the grapevine and I press its bunches and give the juice to the thirsty.

Heaven fills my lamp with oil and I place it at my window to direct the stranger through the dark.

I do all these things because I live in them; and if destiny should tie my hands and prevent me from so doing, then death would be my only desire. For I am a poet, and if I cannot give, I shall refuse to receive.

Humanity rages like a tempest, but I sigh in silence for I know the storm must pass away while a sigh goes to God.

Human kinds cling to earthly things, but I seek ever to embrace the torch of love so it will purify me by its fire and sear inhumanity from my heart.

Substantial things deaden a man without suffering; love awakens him with enlivening pains.

Humans are divided into different clans and tribes, and belong to countries and towns. But I find myself a stranger to all communities and belong to no settlement. The universe is my country and the human family is my tribe.

Men are weak, and it is sad that they divide amongst themselves. The world is narrow and it is unwise to cleave it into kingdoms, empires, and provinces.

Human kinds unite themselves one to destroy the temples of the soul, and they join hands to build edifices for earthly bodies. I stand alone listening to the voice of hope in my deep self saying, "As love enlivens a man's heart with pain, so ignorance teaches him the way of knowledge." Pain and ignorance lead to great joy and knowledge because the Supreme Being has created nothing vain under the sun.

Part Two

I have a yearning for my beautiful country, and I love its people because of their misery. But if my people rose, stimulated by plunder and motivated by what they call "patriotic spirit" to murder, and invaded my neighbour's country, then upon the committing of any human atrocity I would hate my people and my country.

I sing the praise of my birthplace and long to see the home of my children; but if the people in that home refused to shelter and feed the needy wayfarer, I would convert my praise into anger and my longing to forgetfulness. My inner voice would say, "The house that does not comfort the need is worthy of naught by destruction."

I love my native village with some of my love for my country; and I love my country with part of my love for the earth, all of which is my country; and I love the earth will all of myself because it is the haven of humanity, the manifest spirit of God.

Humanity is the spirit of the Supreme Being on earth, and that humanity is standing amidst ruins, hiding its nakedness behind tattered rags, shedding tears upon hollow cheeks, and calling for its children with pitiful voice. But the children are busy singing their clan's anthem; they are busy sharpening the swords and cannot hear the cry of their mothers.

Humanity appeals to its people but they listen not. Were one to listen, and console a mother by wiping her tears, other would say, "He is weak, affected by sentiment."

Humanity is the spirit of the Supreme Being on earth, and that Supreme Being preaches love and good-will. But the people ridicule such teachings. The Nazarene Jesus listened, and crucifixion was his lot; Socrates heard the voice and followed it, and he too fell victim in body. The followers of The Nazarene and Socrates are the followers of Deity, and since people will not kill them, they deride them, saying, "Ridicule is more bitter than killing."

Jerusalem could not kill The Nazarene, nor Athens Socrates; they are living yet and shall live eternally. Ridicule cannot triumph over the followers of Deity. They live and grow forever.

Part Three

Thou art my brother because you are a human, and we both are sons of one Holy Spirit; we are equal and made of the same earth.

You are here as my companion along the path of life, and my aid in understanding the meaning of hidden Truth. You are a human, and, that fact sufficing, I love you as a brother. You may speak of me as you choose, for Tomorrow shall take you away and will use your talk as evidence for his judgment, and you shall receive justice.

You may deprive me of whatever I possess, for my greed instigated the amassing of wealth and you are entitled to my lot if it will satisfy you.

You may do unto me whatever you wish, but you shall not be able to touch my Truth.

You may shed my blood and burn my body, but you cannot kill or hurt my spirit.

You may tie my hands with chains and my feet with shackles, and put me in the dark prison, but who shall not enslave my thinking, for it is free, like the breeze in the spacious sky.

You are my brother and I love you. I love you worshipping in your church, kneeling in your temple, and praying in your mosque. You and I and all are children of one religion, for the varied paths of religion are but the fingers of the loving hand of the Supreme Being, extended to all, offering completeness of spirit to all, anxious to receive all.

I love you for your Truth, derived from your knowledge; that Truth which I cannot see because of my ignorance. But I respect it as a divine thing, for it is the deed of the spirit. Your Truth shall meet my Truth in the coming world and blend together like the fragrance of flowers and becoming one whole and eternal Truth, perpetuating and living in the eternity of Love and Beauty.

I love you because you are weak before the strong oppressor, and poor before the greedy rich. For these reasons I shed tears and comfort you; and from behind my tears I see you embraced in the arms of Justice, smiling and forgiving your persecutors. You are my brother and I love you.

Part Four

You are my brother, but why are you quarrelling with me? Why do you invade my country and try to subjugate me for the sake of pleasing those who are seeking glory and authority?

Why do you leave your wife and children and follow Death to the distant land for the sake of those who buy glory with your blood, and high honour with your mother's tears?

Is it an honour for a man to kill his brother man? If you deem it an honour, let it be an act of worship, and erect a temple to Cain who slew his brother Abel.

Is self-preservation the first law of Nature? Why, then, does Greed urge you to self-sacrifice in order only to achieve his aim in hurting your brothers? Beware, my brother, of the leader who says, "Love of existence obliges us to deprive the people of their rights!" I say unto you but this: protecting others' rights is the noblest and most beautiful human act; if my existence requires that I kill others, then death is more honourable to me, and if I cannot find someone to kill me for the protection of my honour, I will not hesitate to take my life by my own hands for the sake of Eternity before Eternity comes.

Selfishness, my brother, is the cause of blind superiority, and superiority creates clanship, and clanship creates authority which leads to discord and subjugation.

The soul believes in the power of knowledge and justice over dark ignorance; it denies the authority that supplies the swords to defend and strengthen ignorance and oppression – that authority which destroyed Babylon and shook the foundation of Jerusalem and left Rome in ruins. It is that which made people call criminals great mean; made writers respect their names; made historians relate the stories of their inhumanity in manner of praise.

The only authority I obey is the knowledge of guarding and acquiescing in the Natural Law of Justice.

What justice does authority display when it kills the killer? When it imprisons the robber? When it descends on a neighbourhood country and slays its people? What does justice think of the authority under which a killer punishes the one who kills, and a thief sentences the one who steals?

You are my brother, and I love you; and Love is justice with its full intensity and dignity. If justice did not support my love for you, regardless of your tribe and community, I would be a deceiver concealing the ugliness of selfishness behind the outer garment of pure love.

Conclusion

My soul is my friend who consoles me in misery and distress of life. He who does not befriend his soul is an enemy of humanity, and he who does not find human guidance within himself will perish desperately. Life emerges from within, and derives not from environs.

I came to say a word and I shall say it now. But if death prevents its uttering, it will be said by Tomorrow, for Tomorrow never leaves a secret in the book of Eternity.

I came to live in the glory of Love and the light of Beauty, which are the reflections of God. I am here living, and the people are unable to exile me from the domain of life for they know I will live in death. If they pluck my eyes I will hearken to the murmurs of Love and the songs of Beauty.

If they close my ears I will enjoy the touch of the breeze mixed with the incense of Love and the fragrance of Beauty.

If they place me in a vacuum, I will live together with my soul, the child of Love and Beauty.

I came here to be for all and with all, and what I do today in my solitude will be echoed by Tomorrow to the people.

What I say now with one heart will be said tomorrow by many hearts.

The Life of Love

Spring

Come, my beloved; let us walk amidst the knolls,
For the snow is water,
And life is alive from its slumber and is roaming the hills and valleys.
Let us follow the footprints of Spring into the distant fields,
And mount the hilltops to draw inspiration high above the cool green plains.

Dawn of Spring has unfolded her winter-kept garment
And placed it on the peach and citrus trees;
And they appear as brides in the ceremonial custom of the Night of Kedre.

The sprigs of grapevine embrace each other like sweethearts,
And the brooks burst out in dance between the rocks,
Repeating the song of joy;
And the flowers bud suddenly from the heart of nature,
Like foam from the rich heart of the sea.

Come, my beloved; let us drink the last of Winter's tears from the cupped lilies,
And soothe our spirits with the shower of notes from the birds,
And wander in exhilaration through the intoxicating breeze.

Let us sit by that rock, where violets hide;
Let us pursue their exchange of the sweetness of kisses.

Summer

Let us go into the fields, my beloved,
For the time of harvest approaches,
And the sun's eyes are ripening the grain.
Let us tend the fruit of the earth,
As the spirit nourishes the grains of joy from the seeds of Love, sowed deep in our hearts.
Let us fill our bins with the products of nature,
As life fills so abundantly the domain of our hearts with her endless bounty.
Let us make the flowers our bed,
And the sky our blanket,
And rest our heads together upon pillows of soft hay.
Let us relax after the day's toil, and listen to the provoking murmur of the brook.

Autumn

Let us go and gather grapes in the vineyard for the winepress,
And keep the wine in old vases,
As the spirit keeps Knowledge of the ages in eternal vessels.

Let us return to our dwelling,
For the wind has caused the yellow leaves to fall
And shroud the withering flowers that whisper elegy to Summer.
Come home, my eternal sweetheart,
For the birds have made pilgrimage to warmth
And lest the chilled prairies suffering pangs of solitude.
The jasmine and myrtle have no more tears.

Let us retreat, for the tired brook has ceased its song;
And the bubblesome springs are drained of their copious weeping;
And their cautious old hills have stored away their colourful garments.

Come, my beloved; Nature is justly weary
And is bidding her enthusiasm farewell
With quiet and contented melody.

Winter

Come close to me, oh companion of my full life;
Come close to me and let not Winter's touch enter between us.
Sit by me before the hearth,
For fire is the only fruit of Winter.

Speak to me of the glory of your heart,
For that is greater than the shrieking elements beyond our door.
Bind the door and seal the transoms,
For the angry countenance of the heaven depresses my spirit,
And the face of our snow-laden fields makes my soul cry.

Feed the lamp with oil and let it not dim,
And place it by you,
So I can read with tears what your life with me has written upon your face.

Bring Autumn's wine.
Let us drink and sing the song of remembrance to Spring's carefree sowing,
And Summer's watchful tending,
And Autumn's reward in harvest.

Come close to me, oh beloved of my soul;
The fire is cooling and fleeing under the ashes.
Embrace me, for I fear loneliness;
The lamp is dim, and the wine which we pressed is closing our eyes.
Let us look upon each other before they are shut.
Find me with your arms and embrace me;
Let slumber then embrace our souls as one.
Kiss me, my beloved, for Winter has stolen all but our moving lips.

You are close by me, my Forever.
How deep and wide will be the ocean of Slumber,
And how recent was the dawn!

Song of the Wave

The strong shore is my beloved
And I am his sweetheart.
We are at last united by love,
And then the moon draws me from him.
I go to him in haste and depart
Reluctantly, with many little farewells.

I steal swiftly from behind the blue horizon,
To cast the silver of my foam upon the gold of his sand,
And we blend in melted brilliance.

I quench his thirst and submerge his heart;
He softens my voice and subdues my temper.
At dawn I recite the rules of love upon his ears,
And he embraces me longingly.

At eventide I sing to him the song of hope,
And then print smooth kisses upon his face;
I am swift and fearful, but he is quiet, patient, and thoughtful.
His broad bosom soothes my restlessness.

As the tide comes we caress each other,
When it withdraws, I drop to his feet in prayer.

Many times have I danced around mermaids
As they rose from the depths
And rested upon my crest to watch the stars;
Many times have I heard lovers complain of their smallness,
And I helped them to sigh.

Many times have I teased the great rocks
And fondled them with a smile,
But never have I received laughter from them;
Many times have I lifted drowning souls
And carried them tenderly to my beloved shore.
He gives them strength as he takes mine.

Many times have I stolen gems from the depths
And presented them to my beloved shore.
He takes them in silence,
But still I give for he welcomes me ever.

In the heaviness of night,
When all creatures seek the ghost of slumber,
I sit up, singing at one time and sighing at another.
I am awake always.

Alas! Sleeplessness has weakened me!
But I am a lover, and the truth of love is strong.
I may be weary, but I shall never die.

Peace

The tempest calmed after bending the branches of the trees and leaning heavily upon the grain in the field. The stars appeared as broken remnants of lightning, but now silence prevailed over all, as if Nature's war had never been fought.

At that hour a young woman entered her chamber and knelt by her bed sobbing bitterly. Her heart flamed with agony but she could finally open her lips and say, "Oh Lord, bring him home safely to me. I have exhausted my tears and can offer no more, oh Lord, full of love and mercy. My patience is drained and calamity is seeking possession of my heart. Save him, oh Lord, from the iron paws of War; deliver him from such unmerciful Death, for he is weak, governed by the strong. Oh Lord, save my beloved, who is Thine own son, from the foe, who is Thy foe. Keep him from the forced pathway to Death's door; let him see me, or come and take me to him." Uietly a young man entered. His head was wrapped in bandage soaked with escaping life.

He approached he with a greeting of tears and laughter, then took her hand and placed against it his flaming lips. And with a voice with bespoke past sorrow, and joy of union, and uncertainty of her reaction, he said, "Fear me not, for I am the object of your plea. Be glad, for Peace has carried me back safely to you, and humanity has restored what greed essayed to take from us. Be not sad, but smile, my beloved. Do not express bewilderment, for Love has power that dispels Death; charm that conquers the enemy. I am your one. Think me not a spectre emerging from the House of Death to visit your Home of Beauty.

"Do not be frightened, for I am now Truth, spared from swords and fire to reveal to the people the triumph of Love over War. I am Word uttering introduction to the play of happiness and peace."

Then the young man became speechless and his tears spoke the language of the heart; and the angels of Joy hovered about that dwelling, and the two hearts restored the singleness which had been taken from them.

At dawn the two stood in the middle of the field contemplating the beauty of Nature injured by the tempest. After a deep and comforting silence, the soldier said to his sweetheart, "Look at the Darkness, giving birth to the Sun."

The Playground of Life

One hour devoted to the pursuit of beauty and love is worth a full century of glory given by the frightened weak to the strong.

From that hour comes man's Truth; and during that century truth sleeps between the restless arms of disturbing dreams.

In that hour the soul sees for herself the natural law, and for that century she imprisons herself behind the law of man; and she is shackled with irons of oppression.

That hour was the inspiration of the Songs Of Solomon, and that century was the blind power which destroyed the temple of Baalbek.

That hour was the birth of the Sermon on the Mount, and that century wrecked the castles of Palmyra and the Tower of Babylon.

That hour was the Hegira of Mohammed and that century forgot Allah, Golgotha, and Sinai.

One hour devoted to mourning and lamenting the stolen equality of the weak is nobler than a century filled with greed and usurpation.

It is at that hour when the heart is purified by flaming sorrow and illuminated by the torch of love.

And in that century, desires for truth are buried in the bosom of the earth.

That hour is the root which must flourish.

That hour of meditation, the hour of prayer, and the hour of a new era of good.

And that century is a life of Nero spent on self-investment taken solely from earthly substance.

This is life.

Portrayed on the stage for ages; recorded earthly for centuries; lived in strangeness for years; sung as a hymn for days; exalted but for an hour, but the hour is treasured by eternity as a jewel

The City of the Dead

Yesterday I drew myself from the noisome throngs and proceeded into the field until I reached a knoll upon which Nature had spread her comely garments. Now I could breathe.

I looked back, and the city appeared with its magnificent mosques and stately residences veiled by the smoke of the shops.

I commenced analyzing man's mission, but could conclude only that most of his life was identified with struggle and hardship. Then I tried not to ponder over what the sons of Adam had done, and centred my eyes on the field which is the throne of God's glory. In one secluded corner of the field I observed a burying ground surrounded by poplar trees.

There, between the city of the dead and the city of the living, I meditated. I thought of the eternal silence in the first and the endless sorrow in the second.

In the city of the living I found hope and despair; love and hatred, joy and sorrow, wealth and poverty, faith and infidelity.

In the city of the dead there is buried earth in earth that Nature converts, in the night's silence, into vegetation, and then into animal, and then into man. As my mind wandered in this fashion, I saw a procession moving slowly and reverently, accompanied by pieces of music that filled the sky with sad melody. It was an elaborate funeral. The dead was followed by the living who wept and lamented his going. As the cortege reached the place of interment the priests commenced praying and burning incense, and musicians blowing and plucking their instruments, mourning the departed. Then the leaders came forward one after the other and recited their eulogies with fine choice of words.

At last the multitude departed, leaving the dead resting in a most spacious and beautiful vault, expertly designed in stone and iron, and surrounded by the most expensively-entwined wreaths of flowers.

The farewell-bidders returned to the city and I remained, watching them from a distance and speaking softly to myself while the sun was descending to the horizon and Nature was making her many preparations for slumber.

Then I saw two men labouring under the weight of a wooden casket, and behind them a shabby-appearing woman carrying an infant on her arms. Following last was a dog who, with heartbreaking eyes, stared first at the woman and then at the casket.

It was a poor funeral. This guest of Death left to cold society a miserable wife and an infant to share her sorrows and a faithful dog whose heart knew of his companion's departure.

As they reached the burial place they deposited the casket into a ditch away from the tended shrubs and marble stones, and retreated after a few simple words to God. The dog made one last turn to look at his friend's grave as the small group disappeared behind the trees.

I looked at the city of the living and said to myself, "That place belongs to the few." Then I looked upon the trim city of the dead and said, "That place, too, belongs to the few. Oh Lord, where is the haven of all the people?"

As I said this, I looked toward the clouds, mingled with the sun's longest and most beautiful golden rays. And I heard a voice within me saying, "Over there!"

The Widow and her Son

Night fell over North Lebanon and snow was covering the villages surrounded by the Kadeesha Valley, giving the fields and prairies the appearance of a great sheet of parchment upon which the furious Nature was recording her many deeds. Men came home from the streets while silence engulfed the night.

In a lone house near those villages lived a woman who sat by her fireside spinning wool, and at her side was her only child, staring now at the fire and then at his mother.

A terrible roar of thunder shook the house and the little boy shook with fright. He threw his arms about his mother, seeking protection from Nature in her affection. She took him to her bosom and kissed him; then she say him on her lap and said, "Do not fear, my son, for Nature is but comparing her great power to man's weakness. There is a Supreme Being beyond the falling snow and the heavy clouds and the blowing wind, and He knows the needs of the earth, for He made it; and He looks upon the weak with merciful eyes.

"Be brave, my boy. Nature smiles in Spring and laughs in Summer and yawns in Autumn, but now she is weeping; and with her tears she waters life, hidden under the earth.

"Sleep, my dear child; your father is viewing us from Eternity. The snow and thunder bring us closer to him at this time.

"Sleep, my beloved, for this white blanket which makes us cold, keeps the seeds warm, and these war-like things will produce beautiful flowers when Nisan comes.

"Thus, my child, man cannot reap love until after sad and revealing separation, and bitter patience, and desperate hardship. Sleep, my little boy; sweet dreams will find your soul who is unafraid of the terrible darkness of night and the biting frost."

The little boy looked upon his mother with sleep-laden eyes and said, "Mother, my eyes are heavy, but I cannot go to bed without saying my prayer."

The woman looked at his angelic face, her vision blurred by misted eyes, and said, "Repeat with me, my boy – 'God, have mercy on the poor and protect them from the winter; warm their thin-clad bodies with Thy merciful hands; look upon the orphans who are sleeping in wretched houses, suffering from hunger and cold. Hear, oh Lord, the call of widows who are helpless and shivering with fear for their young. Open, oh Lord, the hearts of all humans, that they may see the misery of the weak. Have mercy upon the sufferers who knock on doors, and lead the wayfarers into warm places. Watch, oh Lord, over the little birds and protect the trees and fields from the anger of the storm; for Thou art merciful and full of love.'"

As Slumber captured the boy's spirit, his mother placed him in the bed and kissed his eyes with quivering lips. Then she went back and sat by the hearth, spinning the wool to make him raiment.

Song of the Soul

In the depth of my soul there is a wordless song
A song that lives in the seed of my heart.
It refuses to melt with ink on parchment;
It engulfs my affection in a transparent cloak
And flows but not upon my lips.

How can I sigh it?
I fear it may mingle with earthly ether;
To whom shall I sing it?
It dwells in the house of my soul,
In fear of harsh ears.

When I look into my inner eyes I see the shadow of its shadow;
When I touch my fingertips I feel its vibrations.

The deeds of my hands heed its presence as a lake must reflect the glittering stars;
My tears reveal it, as bright drops of dew reveal the secret of a withering rose.

It is a song composed by contemplation,
And published by silence,
And shunned by clamour,
And folded by truth,
And repeated by dreams,
And understood by love,
And hidden by awakening,
And sung by the soul.

It is the song of love;
What Cain or Esau could sing it?

It is more fragrant than jasmine;
What voice could enslave it?

It is heartbound, as a virgin's secret;
What string could quiver it?

Who dares unite the roar of the sea
And the singing of the nightingale?
Who dares compare the shrieking tempest
To the sigh of an infant?
Who dares speak aloud the words
Intended for the heart to speak?
What human dares sing in voice
The song of God?

Song of the Flower

I am a kind word uttered and repeated by the voice of nature;
I am a star fallen from the blue tent upon the green carpet.
I am the daughter of the elements with whom winter conceived;
To whom Spring gave birth;
I was reared in the lap of Summer and I slept in the bed of Autumn.

At dawn I unite with the breeze to announce the coming of light;
At eventide I join the birds in bidding the light farewell.

The plains are decorated with my beautiful colours,
And the air is scented with my fragrance.

As I embrace slumber the eyes of night watch over me,
And as I awaken I stare at the sun,
Which is the only eye of the day.

I drink dew for wine, and harken to the voices of the birds,
And dance to the rhythmic swaying of the grass.

I am the lover's gift; I am the wedding wreath;
I am the memory of a moment of happiness;
I am the last gift of the living to the dead;
I am a part of joy and a part of sorrow.

But I look up high to see only the light,
And never look down to see my shadow.
This is wisdom which man must learn.

Song of Love

I am the lover's eyes, and the spirit's wine, and the heart's nourishment.
I am a rose.
My heart opens at dawn and the virgin kisses me and places me upon her breast.

I am the house of true fortune, and the origin of pleasure, and the beginning of peace and tranquillity.
I am the gentle smile upon his lips of beauty.
When youth overtakes me he forgets his toil,
And his whole life becomes reality of sweet dreams.

I am the poet's elation,
And the artist's revelation,
And the musician's inspiration.

I am a sacred shrine in the heart of a child, adored by a merciful mother.

I appear to a heart's cry; I shun a demand;
My fullness pursues the heart's desire;
It shuns the empty claim of the voice.

I appeared to Adam through Eve
And exile was his lot;
Yet I revealed myself to Solomon, and he drew wisdom from my presence.

I smiled at Helena and she destroyed Tarwada;
Yet I crowned Cleopatra and peace dominated the Valley of the Nile.

I am like the ages – building today and destroying tomorrow;
I am like a god, who creates and ruins;
I am sweeter than a violet's sigh;
I am more violent than a raging tempest.

Gifts alone do not entice me;
Parting does not discourage me;
Poverty does not chase me;
Jealousy does not prove my awareness;
Madness does not evidence my presence.

Oh seekers, I am Truth, beseeching Truth;
And your Truth in seeking and receiving
And protecting me shall determine my behaviour.

Song of Man

I was here from the moment of the beginning, and here I am still.
And I shall remain here until the end of the world,
For there is no ending to my grief-stricken being.

I roamed the infinite sky, and soared in the ideal world, and floated through the firmament.
But here I am, prisoner of measurement.

I heard the teachings of Confucius;
I listened to Brahma's wisdom;
I sat by Buddha under the Tree of Knowledge.
Yet here I am, existing with ignorance and heresy.

I was on Sinai when Jehovah approached Moses;
I saw the Nazarene's miracles at the Jordan;
I was in Medina when Mohammed visited.
Yet I here I am, prisoner of bewilderment.

Then I witnessed the might of Babylon;
I learned of the glory of Egypt;
I viewed the warring greatness of Rome.
Yet my earlier teachings showed the weakness and sorrow of those achievements.

I conversed with the magicians of Ain Dour;
I debated with the priests of Assyria;
I gleaned depth from the prophets of Palestine.
Yet, I am still seeking truth.

I gathered wisdom from quiet India;
I probed the antiquity of Arabia;
I heard all that can be heard.
Yet, my heart is deaf and blind.

I suffered at the hands of despotic rulers;
I suffered slavery under insane invaders;
I suffered hunger imposed by tyranny;
Yet, I still possess some inner power with which I struggle to greet each day.

My mind is filled, but my heart is empty;
My body is old, but my heart is an infant.
Perhaps in youth my heart will grow,
But I pray to grow old and reach the moment of my return to God.
Only then will my heart fill!

I was here from the moment of the beginning, and here I am still.
And I shall remain here until the end ff world,
For there is no ending to my grief-stricken being.

Before the Throne of Beauty

One heavy day I ran away from the grim face of society and the dizzying clamour of the city and directed my weary step to the spacious alley. I pursued the beckoning course of the rivulet and the musical sounds of the birds until I reached a lonely spot where the flowing branches of the trees prevented the sun from the touching the earth.

I stood there, and it was entertaining to my soul – my thirsty soul who had seen naught but the mirage of life instead of its sweetness.

I was engrossed deeply in thought and my spirits were sailing the firmament when a hour, wearing a sprig of grapevine that covered part of her naked body, and a wreath of poppies about her golden hair, suddenly appeared to me. As she realized my astonishment, she greeted me saying, "Fear me not; I am the Nymph of the Jungle."

"How can beauty like yours be committed to live in this place? Please tell me who your are, and whence you come?" I asked. She sat gracefully on the green grass and responded, "I am the symbol of nature! I am the ever virgin your forefathers worshipped, and to my honour they erected shrines and temples at Baalbek and Jbeil." And I dared say, "But those temples and shrines were laid waste and the bones of my adoring ancestors became a part of the earth; nothing was left to commemorate their goddess save a pitiful few and the forgotten pages in the book of history."

She replied, "Some goddesses live in the lives of their worshippers and die in their deaths, while some live an eternal and infinite life. My life is sustained by the world of beauty which you will see where ever you rest your eyes, and this beauty is nature itself; it is the beginning of the shepherds joy among the hills, and a villagers happiness in the fields, and the pleasure of the awe filled tribes between the mountains and the plains. This Beauty promotes the wise into the throne the truth."

Then I said, "Beauty is a terrible power!" And she retorted, "Human beings fear all things, even yourselves. You fear heaven, the source of spiritual peace; you fear nature, the haven of rest and tranquillity; you fear the God of goodness and accuse him of anger, while he is full of love and mercy."

After a deep silence, mingled with sweet dreams, I asked, "Speak to me of that beauty which the people interpret and define, each one according to his own conception; I have seen her honoured and worshipped in different ways and manners."

She answered, "Beauty is that which attracts your soul, and that which loves to give and not to receive. When you meet Beauty, you feel that the hands deep within your inner self are stretched forth to bring her into the domain of your heart. It is the magnificence combined of sorrow and joy; it is the Unseen which you see, and the Vague which you understand, and the Mute which you hear – it is the Holy of Holies that begins in yourself and ends vastly beyond your earthly imagination."

Then the Nymph of the Jungle approached me and laid her scented hands upon my eyes. And as she withdrew, I found me alone in the valley. When I returned to the city, whose turbulence no longer vexed me, I repeated her words:

"Beauty is that which attracts your soul, and that which loves to give and not to receive."

A Lover's Call

Where are you, my beloved? Are you in that little paradise, watering the flowers who look upon you as infants look upon the breast of their mothers?

Or are you in your chamber where the shrine of virtue has been placed in your honour, and upon which you offer my heart and soul as sacrifice?

Or amongst the books, seeking human knowledge, while you are replete with heavenly wisdom?

Oh companion of my soul, where are you? Are you praying in the temple? Or calling Nature in the field, haven of your dreams?

Are you in the huts of the poor, consoling the broken-hearted with the sweetness of your soul, and filling their hands with your bounty?

You are God's spirit everywhere; you are stronger than the ages.

Do you have memory of the day we met, when the halo of your spirit surrounded us, and the Angels of Love floated about, singing the praise of the soul's deed?

Do you recollect our sitting in the shade of the branches, sheltering ourselves from humanity, as the ribs protect the divine secret of the heart from injury?

Remember you the trails and forest we walked, with hands joined, and our heads leaning against each other, as if we were hiding ourselves within ourselves?

Recall you the hour I bade you farewell, and the maritime kiss you placed on my lips? That kiss taught me that joining of lips in love reveals heavenly secrets which the tongue cannot utter!

That kiss was introduction to a great sigh, like the Almighty's breath that turned earth into man.

That sigh led my way into the spiritual world announcing the glory of my soul; and there it shall perpetuate until again we meet.

I remember when you kissed me and kissed me, with tears coursing your cheeks, and you said, "earthly bodies must often separate for earthly purpose, and must live apart impelled by worldly intent.

"But the spirit remains joined safely in the hands of love, until death arrives and takes joined souls to God.

"Go, my beloved; love has chosen you her delegate; over her, for she is beauty who offers to her follower the cup of the sweetness of life. as for my own empty arms, your love shall remain my comforting groom; you memory, my eternal wedding."

Where are you now, my other self? Are you awake in the silence of the night? Let the clean breeze convey to you my heart's every beat and affection.

Are you fondling my face in your memory? That image is no longer my own, for sorrow has dropped his shadow on my happy countenance of the past.

Sobs have withered my eyes which reflected your beauty and dried my lips which you sweetened with kisses.

Where are you, my beloved? Do you hear my weeping from beyond the ocean? Do you understand my need? Do you know the greatness of my patience?

Is there any spirit in the air capable of conveying to you the breath of this dying youth? Is there any secret communication between angels that will carry to you my complaint?

Where are you, my beautiful star? The obscurity of life has cast me upon its bosom; sorrow has conquered me.

Sail your smile into the air; it will reach and enliven me! breathe your fragrance into the air; it will sustain me!

Where are you, my beloved?

Oh, how great is Love!

And how little am I!

The Palace and the Hut

Part One

As night fell and the light glittered in the great house, the servants stood at the massive door awaiting the coming of the guests; and upon their velvet garments shown golden buttons.

The magnificent carriages drew into the palace park and the nobles entered, dressed in gorgeous raiment and decorated with jewels. The instruments filled the air with pleasant melodies while the dignitaries danced to the soothing music.

At midnight the finest and most palatable foods were served on a beautiful table embellished with all kinds of the rarest flowers. The feasters dined and drank abundantly, until the sequence of the wine began to play its part. At dawn the throng dispersed boisterously, after spending a long night of intoxication and gluttony which hurried their worn bodies into their deep beds with unnatural sleep.

Part Two

At eventide, a man attired in the dress of heavy work stood before the door of his small house and knocked at the door. As it opened, he entered and greeted the occupants in a cheerful manner, and then sat between his children who were playing at the fireplace. In a short time, his wife had the meal prepared and they sat at a wooden table consuming their food. After eating they gathered around the oil lamp and talked of the day's events. When the early night had lapsed, all stood silently and surrendered themselves to the King of Slumber with a song of praise and a prayer of gratitude on their lips.

TWENTY DRAWINGS

Towards the Infinite

On the Art of Kahlil Gibran

"The lives of former generations are a lesson to posterity." This quotation from the volume which is currently accepted as the masterpiece of ancient Arabic literature, The Thousand and One Nights, serves in a slightly paraphrased form as a fitting introduction to the work of the most authoritative artist and poet of modern Arabia—Kahlil Gibran.

In the near East there are over a hundred million whose native language is Arabic and the poetry of Gibran has become so incorporated with the national traditions of these people that one is not quoting lightly in saying that "the works of the present generation are a lesson to posterity." But Gibran the poet, who has been known to the Arabian world of letters as poet, critic and historian for twenty-four years, has already been introduced to the English reading public by his book "The Madman," a collection of poems and parables, some translated by him for his own works in Arabic and others written directly in English with an admirable fluency and command of the Western tongue.

It is Gibran the painter whose drawings are now being brought to the attention of his American audience and the following interpretation of his art will perhaps serve as a clue to the ever entrancing mystery of the harmonies and dissonances which exist between the East and the West.

Kahlil Gibran was born in Mt. Lebanon and although he has deliberately chosen to identify himself with the new world and its surging problems, his affiliations with Syria form such a vital part of his life that in this instance it seems as if the links between the old world and the new were admirably forged and adequately tempered. Despite the fact that he feels himself to be essentially a Syrian and that he is acclaimed as the authoritative spokesman for the Arabic people in the allied arts, Gibran belongs to the world outside of nationalistic interests and his art is a product of a deep sympathy with the problems which constitute the moving current of life in all nations and throughout all ages. His poetry is a blend of ancient imagery coupled with the poignant irony of modern introspection, and his painting is also a product of the abundant phantasies of the Orient set forth with as scrupulous a perfection of technique as the West has ever produced.

It is this blend of the poet and the painter which makes his work stand apart from the modern poetry of the East which we have come to know in the work of Tagore for instance, and which separates his painting from the traditional conception of Oriental art. For Gibran, in spite of his filial allegiance to Syria, is a citizen of the land of Cosmopolis—that ever moving realm, somewhat like the fabled island of Atlantis, which belongs to all times and to no particular place; so that Gibran, besides being the most widely read poet of modern Arabia, is also closely affiliated with Paris. There he worked with Rodin and he exhibited at the Salon a series of portraits, which included Debussy, Rostand, Sarah Bernhardt, and Rodin himself, who said: "I know of no one else in whom drawing and poetry are so linked together as to make him a new Blake."

His sensitive appreciation of the interrelation of the arts enables him to be the spokesman for the genius of the Arabic people to whom the Western world owes a debt which it is only beginning now to appreciate, and no poet of former generations has done more to bring about a closer understanding between the East and the West than Kahlil Gibran.

Tagore, for instance, belongs exclusively to India. Whether we read him or not—whether we incorporate his work with that of other modern schools, nevertheless this does not affect the value of Tagore to India. For he has not lived in the land of Cosmopolis nor does he lend his interests to the new era in western literature. But Gibran has chosen to co-operate with Western arts and letters and his faith in the development of our "static culture" is indeed a lesson to posterity.

He has surrendered his position as a leader in the world of the near East in order to bring the traditions and genius of the Arabic people to the attention of the Western world. And although commentators have long since acknowledged our debt in literature to the Arabs, who introduced rhyme into Europe over a thousand years ago, and historians have admitted the impetus which was given to the sciences by Arabic philosophers, yet it remains the task of a modern to introduce us in painting to the vast poetical conceptions which constitute a part of the heritage of the Arabian race mind.

Kahlil Gibran is one of the artists who are engaged in the struggle between the old and the new, or as in other times, the conflict was termed, the oscillation between the classic and the romantic tendencies in art. As a poet, he is a Romanticist, moving abreast the times and incorporating the keenly analytic spirit of our age into the ancient parable or the simple form of rhythmic prose. But in painting he is a Classicist and his work owes more to the findings of da Vinci than it does to any of our modern insurgents. Thus Gibran is also caught in the struggle which is the besetting problem of the world today, the reconstruction of an era which will adjust the imperishable legacy of the old world, the classic traditions, with the ever evolving, fluctuating tendencies in art which constitute the essence of true Romanticism.

For the cataclysm which has overwhelmed our world and is causing us to reconstruct our geographical boundaries and political tenets, also demands us to reconstruct our moral valuations and our standards in the life of the soul, of which art is one of the most profound manifestations. And as we think back upon the destruction which has separated the world with which we were familiar from the world in which we move today, we become more and more aware of the cataclysm which has so completely shattered our philosophies, dogmas and artistic beliefs.

A sombre burden has descended upon the shoulders of the coming generation, whose task it is to create a world as yet in embryo—and, if our arts are not to go down before such inspirations as the camouflage, and if science is not to be prostituted to such creations as the tank,—if a nobler expression of energy is yet to redeem man from the pit into which his destructive power has plunged him, then in the period of reconstruction he must insensibly turn to new and more vital forms of self-expression. Religion in the traditional meaning can no longer lift him out of the rut of his suffering and only in another form of expression which will portray the realities of the soul devoutly, either in terms of art, science or social creeds, will he be able to effect a transition between the death agony of the old world and the travail of the new.

But even in this dark traverse through which we are passing in an effort to win a newer life as our own, we are aware of certain germinating influences which already foreshadow the art of the future, so that the productions of an artist can never be evaluated in terms of self-expression alone but must be measured by their relation to the organic processes of which they are an integral part.

To the interpretive mind, for instance, the destruction of Carthage cannot be judged as a pyrotechnical display of military prowess, for that which is significant was the impetus of change which that act gave to civilization. With the importation of the cult of Cybele, the great Mother, Rome was placed in direct communication with the East and a contact between the modern and the ancient world was firmly established. Eventually, the religion and the art of the East not only acquired a foothold, but became an integral part of later Roman culture, so that Rome was conquered by that which centuries before it had set out to subdue. The Romans set out to conquer a rival and brought back the religion and thereby much of their rival's system of power. In this way a process which on the surface was nationalistic became fundamentally a part of the organic evolution of civilization, which redirected the cultural processes of a nation and eventually of what was, then, the modern world.

Thus the term modern loses its coin value when we see how lightly it can be shifted from era to era, denoting certain types of ideas rather than periods of time. For the life of the inner world is without boundaries other than personal limitations, without national or particularistic interests other than those we voluntarily adopt. We shift our emotional contents upon a word like "Spartacide" and it becomes a modern equivalent; it is at once cut adrift from its original connotation and it becomes vitally related to our own interests and feelings. In short the word, the symbol flashes the past to life and passes on to meaning into the present in order to stimulate the mind to seek out new intellectual pastures.

For the soul is occupied with but a few problems and these are singularly few. Life in its elemental functioning is but a transformation of the processes of Birth, Love and Death. The hunger of the appetites and the hunger of possession; the desire for adventure and the fear of the unknown; to love and to be loved; out of these essential simplicities, man has erected the vast complexities of life and to these essential simplicities the artist must return who seeks a new means of expression amidst the clutter of religions, arts and moralities.

Those who have witnessed the disintegration of a world can no longer find satisfaction in objective painting. What has the art of Messonier to say to a man who has lived in a trench? What has the art of Watteau to offer to men who have experienced shrapnel or the submarine? We know that Veronese worked amidst the voluptuous realities which he depicted; we know that Watteau phantasied the shepherd and shepherdess exquisitely, but to us this type of painting is merely interesting because of its historic value. Intrinsically, it has no message to offer us.

It is at this point in art that symbolism reveals itself as the interrelating principle between the life of the soul and objective life; that is to say that just as the symbol of the word is the interchanging coin between ancient and modern concepts, so in art, the symbolic meaning is the interchanging medium between the modern and the antique. Yet before we apply the word "symbolic" to an artist we must first come to a clear conception of its value, for it is a word which one approaches with hesitancy as its meaning has become so clouded by misusage that our mind flashes instantly to that group who were thus classified and then to the satirical lyric of the man "walking down Piccadilly with a lily in his mediaeval hand."

We can get no clearer picture of symbolism in Art than by recalling that period and school which gave every appearance of it and yet never possessed its essence. The pre-Raphaelites for instance, attempted to recreate in their mode and manner, that which was for ever past just as certain modernists attempt a crude simplicity which was only characteristic of primitive humanity. The true symbolist is concerned with the life of the inner world. To his eyes the changing cultures of man are merely transformations upon which he focusses his attention. Whereas, to the ideationist—the objective artist—each epoch, each strata in the history of man is a separate and distinct reality and he occupies himself depicting the surfaces and planes of the outer expression of life. He is in constant relation to the present; he has no personal affiliation with the vast spiritual life of the past and possesses no embryonic conception of the future.

But to the true symbolist life is a perpetual recreation and he moves in a world freed from traditions and confines. He need not attempt to escape from the limitations of the present by seeking the mannerisms of an enigmatical past. He is in direct contact with that past and hence the future is an ever fluid and ever luminous atmosphere; he is at one with fundamentals.

If we examine the work of the early Primitives we see at once how deeply imbued they were with the essence of symbolism. In fact, they cared so deeply for the spirit of the idea that the manner of its presentation caused them little concern. They covered the walls of Assisi because they wished to tell the story of Jesus that others might know and profit by it.

To them, Jesus was a reality, not a story about which to make a painting, and consequently it was a matter of indifference to Ghirlandaio whether the women attending the Virgin wore the dresses of his own age or those of antiquity. They *were* the women attending the Virgin and that which has given the Santa Maria Novella its lustre, is the power of a feeling, visioned, experienced, grasped—and then put forth again.

However, in the minds of the pre-Raphaelites, the vision was most assiduously cultivated. Their very pre-occupation proves them to have been objective artists diverted from their proper functioning. They did not seek the vision of England, which would have been their true expression, the sentimental Victorian England of their day, but they turned their eyes towards the Italy of the past and became blinded by the dust of the centuries which lay upon it. The result was narrative art, a beautiful and ingenious affectation of the source of inspiration, but the symbols of love and sorrow, of joy and pain became involved in confused mysticism. For the pre-Raphaelites sought not their own spirit but that of another, not the meaning within but that lying as far away as possible—in fact the more remote it was, the more they sought it. They reproduced instead of creating, and they have given us beautiful stories, beautiful pictures, beautiful ideas—everything except that which can never be reproduced, and that is the spirit of their own age.

In the separation of the symbolist from the ideationist, the art of the East is most concisely divided from the art of the West. To the East the lotus is a flower, but also a symbol of divinity; to the West it is a flower developing into the acanthus design and completing the circle, it becomes a decoration, and so again only a flower. Again the earth, the sun, the sea, that which is above, and that which lies beneath, are to the Western mind, materials of study to be touched, represented, understood and grasped. But to the East, it suffices that these things are and will be eternally, and that behind these realities which we visualize and know, lie other and again other forces and experiences, other suns, other seas, melting mysteriously into one another as the leaves of the lotus.

It is at this dividing line of East and West, of the symbolist and the ideationist, that the work of Kahlil Gibran presents itself as an arresting type in our conception of painting. He has accepted both the traditions of form and the inner meaning of the idea, and he exhibits both a new type of work and another method of approach to fundamental truths.

The qualities of the East and the West are blended in him with a singular felicity of expression, so that while he is the symbolist in the true sense of the word, he is not affixed to traditional expression, as he would be if he were creating in the manner of the East, and though he narrates a story as definitely as any pre-Raphaelite, it is without any fan-fare of historical circumstances or any of the accompaniment of symbolic accessories. In his art there is no conflict whether the idea shall prevail over the emotion, or whether emotion shall sway the thought, because both are so equally established that we are not conscious of one or the other as dominant. They co-exist in harmony and the result is an expression of sheer beauty in which thought and feeling are equally blended. In this fusion of two opposing tendencies the art of Gibran transcends the conflicts of schools and is beyond the fixed conceptions of the classic or romantic traditions.

An illuminating beauty informs his work; to him the idea becomes beautiful if it is true; the emotion becomes truth if it is real. He possesses a singular power of dividing what is essential from what is extraneous in the presentation of beauty and truth. And he keeps to a simplicity of manner in the portrayal of an idea which is closely akin to the spirit of the Primitives, albeit the art of the centuries has gone into the moulding of his powers; but in his statements he is simple, almost instinctively simple. In fact, he may be described as an intuitive artist—as that type of artist whose feeling is like the divining rod which leads down to shafts of golden values and who does not obfuscate his mind with intellectual conceptions of what or how he should create. And having followed his instinctive flair for truth, he now applies his conscious powers to perfect his finding and to create his embryonic expressions into paintings of beauty and value.

He needs only a small sheet of paper to give us the meaning of the "Erdgeist"; we see a body of a woman who rises out of the vast form of the All-Mother, carrying in her arms man and woman. Only the head of the unfolding mother with its mysterious smile is drawn in what we are accustomed to think of as drawing. There is the story, interpret it as you will; Erda—Amida—Ceres—Mary—the choice is a matter of time and temperament. The meaning is the same and Gibran is dealing with fundamentals.

But in the portrayal of the idea he is scrupulously faithful to the perfection of his technique. Thus beauty is the final arbiter upon the destiny of his production. He creates with intuitive feeling then shapes his work into unity with the power of thought, but both these impulses are guided and guarded by a profound love and appreciation of the beautiful which enables him to portray that which he has to say as simply and as sincerely as it is possible for him to do so. It is this quality of instinctive simplicity which makes his painting so clearly akin to the art of the sculpture, for the sculptor, unless in relief, cannot deal with anything other than the essential idea and the beauty of form. In sculpture there are no accessories of background, no gradations of colour values to attract the eye and deflect the mind from thought. Very few painters have been able to express the essentials of life in painting. Da Vinci attempted it but he was lured away from the quest by his love of subtleties, and pupils like Luini or Sodoma expressed the subtleties but failed to grasp the inner meaning which held Da Vinci to his perpetual quest.

The art of Gibran is symbolic in the deepest meaning of the word because its roots spring from those basic truths which are fundamental for all ages and all experiences. He senses the meaning of the earth and her productions; of man, the final and the consummate flower, and throughout his work he expresses the interrelating unity of man with nature. He shows us Man evolving out of the beast in a struggle with another centaur; he portrays the recumbent Mother crouched against a centaur who holds the child in his arms—the child who is already one step beyond, a conception closely parallel to that of Nietzsche. In yet another picture he shows us Man driving or being driven by a horse, divinely frenzied.

His centaurs and horses have a charm beyond their natures so that they are never wholly animal in character. They have a grace which is reminiscent of the Chinese statuettes of horses, with their square nostrils and delicate hoofs, hoofs that paw the air rather than the ground and stamp upon the mind the finest qualities of a horse, its fleetness, swiftness and strength. So that in regarding these centaurs we sense the beast that is yet man and again that man which is and must be animal; we become conscious of that evolution upwards which is in itself a miracle, although there is a barrier which will for ever prevent man from clutching the stars.

The picture of the flying figure suggests the sweeping onrush of the winged victory, man's supreme aspiration; it is symbol of the divine force which impels man for ever onward to higher levels of evolution. The study of the human body in flight has been a source of inspiration to almost every artist; in the Palazzo Ducale at Venice for instance, Tintoretto has introduced a multitude of flying figures into his great ceiling painting of "Venice as the Queen of the Adriatic." But in all these studies there are certain distortions of the human body. These forms are either too aspirant or too convulsive so that one is unpleasantly reminded of the muscular sensations of cramped arms and benumbed legs.

In the Sistine Chapel however, the great patriarchal paintings of the Jehovah creating the world, dividing the waters of the earth or sweeping through space to touch the finger of the recumbent Adam, are all so balanced and so benignly reposeful that they convey not only a sense of flight through space but the impression of the very weight of space which is able to sustain these moving bodies.

Gibran's studies of movement are akin to those of Michelangelo because he has arrived at a unity of thought and representation. Not only is he the master of the symbolic idea which he expresses but he has attained the technical grasp upon his material. Hence we are not disconcerted by false conceptions of the human body or erroneous perspectives.

His paintings are mostly wash drawings and only here and there does his pencil co-operate with his brush to suggest and complete the theme. The level of his painting is very delicate—plane suggesting another plane in the most subtle gradation so that at first there seems to be but little colour and then comes a swift realization that it is all colour—only imperceptibly diffused. In one or two of the studies like the sombre picture of the man with the cap, more vivid reds and blues are introduced and a certain greenish blue, wholly of the East, reappears constantly in his studies of definite types. But in his more profound interpretative work, the gradation of colour is delicate in the extreme. He uses colour to reveal his form unlike many painters who lose their sense of form in the pursuit of colour; that is another reason why his paintings are so suggestive of the art of the sculptor.

This impression is conveyed most powerfully in the study of a woman's head, the frontispiece to this volume, a painting which is the most complete exposition of the art of Gibran. The head is thrown back and seems to rest upon a white background that is yet not exactly white; it is the colour of the sea at an infinite distance when colour is no longer colour but merely light. The head, lying upon this luminous ground is so delicately delineated that the throat veins almost quiver and the pale lips are about to move. And as we look upon the fine profile, the sensitive, highly arched nose and the tender, compassionate mouth, it seems as if this woman's head had arisen out of those deeper waters which we call the sea of memory, as if indeed

"Our souls have sight of that immortal sea from whence we came."

There is little drawing as we are accustomed to think of drawing, but the painting is modelled in colour and is akin to the interpretation of a sculptor who usually seeks the greater freedom which larger material begets. That something flowing which alone makes the earth other than a piece of stone is revealed in almost all his work. It is the very soul of sculpture and he is but expressing it in kindred form.

Gibran is an interpreter of "the heavens above and the earth below." He recalls like a fleeting memory, the meaning of the great clouds which swept like a flock of storm gulls before the bewildered eyes of primitive man, but he has likewise sounded the pit of agony into which the soul descends during the crucifixion of its development. For Gibran is not alone interested in the story of man, he is interested in the history of life; he is not concerned merely with its portrayal, he shares its struggle. He is impelled by that force which lies beyond all things animate and inanimate—that force which produces, destroys and recreates with the same intensity, the same purpose and always to his eyes, with the same succession of beauty.

Therein lies the reason why his work is of today with its unrest and grouping in spite of its intuitive simplicity in the use of symbolic material of the past. It is of today because we are seeking to infuse a new meaning into life whereby we can accept the bitter in order to gain the sweet; we are endeavouring to come to terms with the ancient symbols and although the concepts which Gibran portrays are as old as Cronos, they are also as modern as the interpretative spirit of our age. His art arises out of the past but its appeal is to the thinking minds of today and it foreshadows a trend in the creative work of the future.

The tryptich of the crucifixion in this series of drawings shows at once how the symbol of the Christ between the two thieves can be used either to express the complete religious and mythological conception, as it would have been used by the Primitives in some large fresco, and how the same idea can be conveyed on a small sheet of paper by one who understands the inner meaning and is able to put it forth as a representation of the conflict of every self-conscious being. In this drawing a man rests upon the shoulders of two companions. There are no religious accessories either of halo or stigmata with which to associate or localize the conception and yet the story of the crucifixion is completely portrayed.

It is in this absolute simplicity of idea and intuitive revelation coupled with an instinctive grasp of the beauty of form, that Gibran attains the consummation of his powers and commands a respect meritorious of the classic. For amidst the deluge which has overwhelmed our world of art, when Cubists collide with Vorticists and both are submerged by the onrushing of the Orphicists—when school and type arise and as swiftly decline in the quest of the new and the age is seeking a picture of its soul in barbaric imitation of genuine barbarism, it is of inestimable value to come upon an artist who is fulfilling himself in his work apart from any claptrap of modern devices. Gibran has not gone to strange lands to study the new but he has walked the silent path of the meditative creator and he has brought out of his own depths these eternal verities of the history of man's inner life. He has recreated the symbolic incarnation of the All-Mother—he has divined the flying wish of humanity and he has laid bare and retold the story of the Passion.

In the poetic revelation of these psychologic conceptions of humanity he exhibits a world of consummate beauty to the younger artists of America whose life he has chosen to share. He is expressing the vast, the infinite forms of the ever fluid past and is showing us how these imperishable memories can stimulate the art of the future.

Only in the acceptance of this infinitely varied racial history as a living part of the present, will America prepare herself for the eventual renaissance of the arts and as a forerunner of this renaissance, Gibran will occupy a similar position to that of Giotto and Ghirlandaio in relation to the Italian Golden Age. The painters of the Renaissance showed the world that the human being could be portrayed as if he were divine. But to those who preceded the Renaissance the "as if" did not exist. To them—as to Gibran, human life is divine. The body reflects and represents the spirit, and art arises out of the interplay between the inner and the outer world.

It is a fact that in painting as well as in poetry, we are standing today on the tiptoes of expectation, awaiting the fusion of a closer union between the old world and the new. We are no longer bounded by New England conceptions of the poetical on the one side and by the various quasi-tragic representations of the Last of the Mohicans as a basic expression of American art on the other. In the anticipation of the eventual renaissance of the world, we in America can lend ourselves to study those who are its precursors.

For Gibran belongs to that group of artists whose message always heralds a period of transition and whose voice challenges the present to a recapitulation of its standards.

There is a tradition so old that its origin is lost in the mists of antiquity where it is acclaimed as the symbol of our common ancestor Adam. Its sign signifies "Dum voluit spiritus Mundi." Out of the illimitable past—illuminating the East, touching in turn Greece, Italy, Flanders, Germany, France and Spain,—so passed the great creative spirit in the world of art; what if this same illuminative spirit should be in turn approaching our shores, provided that we are receptive enough to understand and to assimilate its fundamental message.

Note

The illustrations have been moved so that they do not break up paragraphs.

The Greater Self

The Blind

The Mountain

Flight

Centaur and Child

Uplifted

The Rock

The Waterfall

The Burden

The Great Longing

Veiled Face

Crucified

Compassion

The Triangle

The Struggle

The Great Aloneness

Woman with Garment

Mother and Child

The Innermost

THE FORERUNNER

His Parables and Poems

Introduction

You are your own forerunner, and the towers you have built are but the foundation of your giant-self. And that self too shall be a foundation.

And I too am my own forerunner, for the long shadow stretching before me at sunrise shall gather under my feet at the noon hour. Yet another sunrise shall lay another shadow before me, and that also shall be gathered at another noon.

Always have we been our own forerunners, and always shall we be. And all that we have gathered and shall gather shall be but seeds for fields yet unploughed. We are the fields and the ploughmen, the gatherers and the gathered.

When you were a wandering desire in the mist, I too was there, a wandering desire. Then we sought one another, and out of our eagerness dreams were born. And dreams were time limitless, and dreams were space without measure.

And when you were a silent word upon Life's quivering lips, I too was there, another silent word. Then Life uttered us and we came down the years throbbing with memories of yesterday and with longing for tomorrow, for yesterday was death conquered and tomorrow was birth pursued.

And now we are in God's hands. You are a sun in His right hand and I an earth in His left hand. Yet you are not more, shining, than I, shone upon.

And we, sun and earth, are but the beginning of a greater sun and a greater earth. And always shall we be the beginning.

* * *

You are your own forerunner, you the stranger passing by the gate of my garden.

And I too am my own forerunner, though I sit in the shadows of my trees and seem motionless.

God's Fool

Once there came from the desert to the great city of Sharia a man who was a dreamer, and he had naught but his garment and a staff.

And as he walked through the streets he gazed with awe and wonder at the temples and towers and palaces, for the city of Sharia was of surpassing beauty. And he spoke often to the passersby, questioning them about their city—but they understood not his language, nor he their language.

At the noon hour he stopped before a vast inn. It was built of yellow marble, and people were going in and coming out unhindered.

"This must be a shrine," he said to himself, and he too went in. But what was his surprise to find himself in a hall of great splendour and a large company of men and women seated about many tables. They were eating and drinking and listening to the musicians.

"Nay," said the dreamer. "This is no worshipping. It must be a feast given by the prince to the people, in celebration of a great event."

At that moment a man, whom he took to be the slave of the prince, approached him, and bade him be seated. And he was served with meat and wine and most excellent sweets.

When he was satisfied, the dreamer rose to depart. At the door he was stopped by a large man magnificently arrayed.

"Surely this is the prince himself," said the dreamer in his heart, and he bowed to him and thanked him.

Then the large man said in the language of the city:

"Sir, you have not paid for your dinner." And the dreamer did not understand, and again thanked him heartily. Then the large man bethought him, and he looked more closely upon the dreamer. And he saw that he was a stranger, clad in but a poor garment, and that indeed he had not wherewith to pay for his meal. Then the large man clapped his hands and called—and there came four watchmen of the city. And they listened to the large man. Then they took the dreamer between them, and they were two on each side of him. And the dreamer noted the ceremoniousness of their dress and of their manner and he looked upon them with delight.

"These," said he, "are men of distinction."

And they walked all together until they came to the House of Judgment and they entered.

The dreamer saw before him, seated upon a throne, a venerable man with flowing beard, robed majestically. And he thought he was the king. And he rejoiced to be brought before him.

Now the watchmen related to the judge, who was the venerable man, the charge against the dreamer; and the judge appointed two advocates, one to present the charge and the other to defend the stranger. And the advocates rose, the one after the other, and delivered each his argument. And the dreamer thought himself to be listening to addresses of welcome, and his heart filled with gratitude to the king and the prince for all that was done for him.

Then sentence was passed upon the dreamer, that upon a tablet hung about his neck his crime should be written, and that he should ride through the city on a naked horse, with a trumpeter and a drummer before him. And the sentence was carried out forthwith.

Now as the dreamer rode through the city upon the naked horse, with the trumpeter and the drummer before him, the inhabitants of the city came running forth at the sound of the noise, and when they saw him they laughed one and all, and the children ran after him in companies from street to street. And the dreamer's heart was filled with ecstasy, and his eyes shone upon them. For to him the tablet was a sign of the king's blessing and the procession was in his honour.

Now as he rode, he saw among the crowd a man who was from the desert like himself and his heart swelled with joy, and he cried out to him with a shout:

"Friend! Friend! Where are we? What city of the heart's desire is this? What race of lavish hosts?—who feast the chance guest in their palaces, whose princes companion him, whose king hangs a token upon his breast and opens to him the hospitality of a city descended from heaven."

And he who was also of the desert replied not. He only smiled and slightly shook his head. And the procession passed on.

And the dreamer's face was uplifted and his eyes were overflowing with light.

Love

They say the jackal and the mole
Drink from the self-same stream
Where the lion comes to drink.

And they say the eagle and the vulture
Dig their beaks into the same carcass,
And are at peace, one with the other,
In the presence of the dead thing.

O love, whose lordly hand
Has bridled my desires,
And raised my hunger and my thirst
To dignity and pride,
Let not the strong in me and the constant
Eat the bread or drink the wine
That tempt my weaker self.

Let me rather starve,
And let my heart parch with thirst,
And let me die and perish,
Ere I stretch my hand
To a cup you did not fill,
Or a bowl you did not bless.

The King-Hermit

They told me that in a forest among the mountains lives a young man in solitude who once was a king of a vast country beyond the Two Rivers. And they also said that he, of his own will, had left his throne and the land of his glory and come to dwell in the wilderness.

And I said, "I would seek that man, and learn the secret of his heart; for he who renounces a kingdom must needs be greater than a kingdom."

On that very day I went to the forest where he dwells. And I found him sitting under a white cypress, and in his hand a reed as if it were a sceptre. And I greeted him even as I would greet a king.

And he turned to me and said gently, "What would you in this forest of serenity? Seek you a lost self in the green shadows, or is it a home-coming in your twilight?"

And I answered, "I sought but you—for I fain would know that which made you leave a kingdom for a forest."

And he said, "Brief is my story, for sudden was the bursting of the bubble. It happened thus: One day as I sat at a window in my palace, my chamberlain and an envoy from a foreign land were walking in my garden. And as they approached my window, the lord chamberlain was speaking of himself and saying, 'I am like the king; I have a thirst for strong wine and a hunger for all games of chance. And like my lord the king I have storms of temper.' And the lord chamberlain and the envoy disappeared among the trees. But in a few minutes they returned, and this time the lord chamberlain was speaking of me, and he was saying, 'My lord the king is like myself—a good marksman; and like me he loves music and bathes thrice a day.'"

After a moment he added, "On the eve of that day I left my palace with but my garment, for I would no longer be ruler over those who assume my vices and attribute to me their virtues."

And I said, "This is indeed a wonder, and passing strange."

And he said, "Nay, my friend, you knocked at the gate of my silences and received but a trifle. For who would not leave a kingdom for a forest where the seasons sing and dance ceaselessly? Many are those who have given their kingdom for less than solitude and the sweet fellowship of aloneness. Countless are the eagles who descend from the upper air to live with moles that they may know the secrets of the earth. There are those who renounce the kingdom of dreams that they may not seem distant from the dreamless. And those who renounce the kingdom of nakedness and cover their souls that others may not be ashamed in beholding truth uncovered and beauty unveiled. And greater yet than all of these is he who renounces the kingdom of sorrow that he may not seem proud and vainglorious."

Then rising he leaned upon his reed and said, "Go now to the great city and sit at its gate and watch all those who enter into it and those who go out. And see that you find him who, though born a king, is without kingdom; and him who though ruled in flesh rules in spirit—though neither he nor his subjects know this; and him also who but seems to rule yet is in truth slave of his own slaves."

After he had said these things he smiled on me, and there were a thousand dawns upon his lips. Then he turned and walked away into the heart of the forest.

And I returned to the city, and I sat at its gate to watch the passersby even as he had told me. And from that day to this numberless are the kings whose shadows have passed over me and few are the subjects over whom my shadow has passed.

The Lion's Daughter

Four slaves stood fanning an old queen who was asleep upon her throne. And she was snoring. And upon the queen's lap a cat lay purring and gazing lazily at the slaves.

The first slave spoke, and said, "How ugly this old woman is in her sleep. See her mouth droop; and she breathes as if the devil were choking her."

Then the cat said, purring, *"Not half so ugly in her sleep as you in your waking slavery."*

And the second slave said, "You would think sleep would smooth her wrinkles instead of deepening them. She must be dreaming of something evil."

And the cat purred, "Would that you might sleep also and dream of your freedom."

And the third slave said, "Perhaps she is seeing the procession of all those that she has slain."

And the cat purred, "Aye, she sees the procession of your forefathers and your descendants."

And the fourth slave said, "It is all very well to talk about her, but it does not make me less weary of standing and fanning."

And the cat purred, "You shall be fanning to all eternity; for as it is on earth so it is in heaven."

At this moment the old queen nodded in her sleep, and her crown fell to the floor.

And one of the slaves said, "That is a bad omen."

And the cat purred, "The bad omen of one is the good omen of another."

And the second slave said, "What if she should wake, and find her crown fallen! She would surely slay us."

And the cat purred, "Daily from your birth she has slain you and you know it not."

And the third slave said, "Yes, she would slay us and she would call it making sacrifice to the gods."

And the cat purred, "Only the weak are sacrificed to the gods."

And the fourth slave silenced the others, and softly he picked up the crown and replaced it, without waking her, on the old queen's head.

And the cat purred, "Only a slave restores a crown that has fallen."

And after a while the old queen woke, and she looked about her and yawned. Then she said, "Methought I dreamed, and I saw four caterpillars chased by a scorpion around the trunk of an ancient oaktree. I like not my dream."

Then she closed her eyes and went to sleep again. And she snored. And the four slaves went on fanning her.

And the cat purred, "Fan on, fan on, stupids. You fan but the fire that consumes you."

Tyranny

Thus sings the She-Dragon that guards the seven caves by the sea:

"My mate shall come riding on the waves. His thundering roar shall fill the earth with fear, and the flames of his nostrils shall set the sky afire. At the eclipse of the moon we shall be wedded, and at the eclipse of the sun I shall give birth to a Saint George, who shall slay me."

Thus sings the She-Dragon that guards the seven caves by the sea.

The Saint

In my youth I once visited a saint in his silent grove beyond the hills; and as we were conversing upon the nature of virtue a brigand came limping wearily up the ridge. When he reached the grove he knelt down before the saint and said, "O saint, I would be comforted! My sins are heavy upon me."

And the saint replied, "My sins, too, are heavy upon me."

And the brigand said, "But I am a thief and a plunderer."

And the saint replied, "I too am a thief and a plunderer."

And the brigand said, "But I am a murderer, and the blood of many men cries in my ears."

And the saint replied, "I too am a murderer, and in my ears cries the blood of many men."

And the brigand said, "I have committed countless crimes."

And the saint replied, "I too have committed crimes without number."

Then the brigand stood up and gazed at the saint, and there was a strange look in his eyes. And when he left us he went skipping down the hill.

And I turned to the saint and said, "Wherefore did you accuse yourself of uncommitted crimes? See you not that this man went away no longer believing in you?"

And the saint answered, "It is true he no longer believes in me. But he went away much comforted."

At that moment we heard the brigand singing in the distance, and the echo of his song filled the valley with gladness.

The Plutocrat

In my wanderings I once saw upon an island a man-headed, iron-hoofed monster who ate of the earth and drank of the sea incessantly. And for a long while I watched him. Then I approached him and said, "Have you never enough; is your hunger never satisfied and your thirst never quenched?"

And he answered saying, "Yes, I am satisfied, nay, I am weary of eating and drinking; but I am afraid that tomorrow there will be no more earth to eat and no more sea to drink."

The Greater Self

This came to pass. After the coronation of Nufsibaäl, King of Byblus, he retired to his bed chamber—the very room which the three hermit-magicians of the mountain had built for him. He took off his crown and his royal raiment, and stood in the centre of the room thinking of himself, now the all-powerful ruler of Byblus.

Suddenly he turned; and he saw stepping out of the silver mirror which his mother had given him, a naked man.

The king was startled, and he cried out to the man, "What would you?"

And the naked man answered, "Naught but this: Why have they crowned you king?"

And the king answered, "Because I am the noblest man in the land."

Then the naked man said, "If you were still more noble, you would not be king."

And the king said, "Because I am the mightiest man in the land they crowned me."

And the naked man said, "If you were mightier yet, you would not be king."

Then the king said, "Because I am the wisest man they crowned me king."

And the naked man said, "If you were still wiser you would not choose to be king."

Then the king fell to the floor and wept bitterly.

The naked man looked down upon him. Then he took up the crown and with tenderness replaced it upon the king's bent head.

And the naked man, gazing lovingly upon the king, entered into the mirror.

And the king roused, and straightway he looked into the mirror. And he saw there but himself crowned.

War and the Small Nations

Once, high above a pasture, where a sheep and a lamb were grazing, an eagle was circling and gazing hungrily down upon the lamb. And as he was about to descend and seize his prey, another eagle appeared and hovered above the sheep and her young with the same hungry intent. Then the two rivals began to fight filling the sky with their fierce cries.

The sheep looked up and was much astonished. She turned to the lamb and said,

"How strange, my child, that these two noble birds should attack one another. Is not the vast sky large enough for both of them? Pray, my little one, pray in your heart that God may make peace between your winged brothers."

And the lamb prayed in his heart.

Critics

One nightfall a man travelling on horseback toward the sea reached an inn by the roadside. He dismounted, and confident in man and night like all riders toward the sea, he tied his horse to a tree beside the door and entered into the inn.

At midnight, when all were asleep, a thief came and stole the traveller's horse.

In the morning the man awoke, and discovered that his horse was stolen. And he grieved for his horse, and that a man had found it in his heart to steal.

Then his fellow-lodgers came and stood around him and began to talk.

And the first man said, "How foolish of you to tie your horse outside the stable."

And the second said, "Still more foolish, without even hobbling the horse!"

And the third man said, "It is stupid at best to travel to the sea on horseback."

And the fourth said, "Only the indolent and the slow of foot own horses."

Then the traveller was much astonished. At last he cried, "My friends, because my horse is stolen, you have hastened one and all to tell me my faults and my shortcomings. But strange, not one word of reproach have you uttered about the man who stole my horse."

Poets

Four poets were sitting around a bowl of punch that stood on a table.

Said the first poet, "Methinks I see with my third eye the fragrance of this wine hovering in space like a cloud of birds in an enchanted forest."

The second poet raised his head and said, "With my inner ear I can hear those mist-birds singing. And the melody holds my heart as the white rose imprisons the bee within her petals."

The third poet closed his eyes and stretched his arm upward, and said, "I touch them with my hand. I feel their wings, like the breath of a sleeping fairy, brushing against my fingers."

Then the fourth poet rose and lifted up the bowl, and he said, "Alas, friends! I am too dull of sight and of hearing and of touch. I cannot see the fragrance of this wine, nor hear its song, nor feel the beating of its wings. I perceive but the wine itself. Now therefore must I drink it, that it may sharpen my senses and raise me to your blissful heights."

And putting the bowl to his lips, he drank the punch to the very last drop.

The three poets, with their mouths open, looked at him aghast, and there was a thirsty yet unlyrical hatred in their eyes.

The Weather-cock

Said the weather-cock to the wind, "How tedious and monotonous you are! Can you not blow any other way but in my face? You disturb my God-given stability."

And the wind did not answer. It only laughed in space.

The King of Aradus

Once the elders of the city of Aradus presented themselves before the king, and besought of him a decree to forbid to men all wine and all intoxicants within their city.

And the king turned his back upon them and went out from them laughing.

Then the elders departed in dismay.

At the door of the palace they met the lord chamberlain. And the lord chamberlain observed that they were troubled, and he understood their case.

Then he said, "Pity, my friends! Had you found the king drunk, surely he would have granted you your petition."

Out of My Deeper Heart

Out of my deeper heart a bird rose and flew skyward.

Higher and higher did it rise, yet larger and larger did it grow.

At first it was but like a swallow, then a lark, then an eagle, then as vast as a spring cloud, and then it filled the starry heavens.

Out of my heart a bird flew skyward. And it waxed larger as it flew. Yet it left not my heart.

* * *

O my faith, my untamed knowledge, how shall I fly to your height and see with you man's larger self pencilled upon the sky?

How shall I turn this sea within me into mist, and move with you in space immeasurable?

How can a prisoner within the temple behold its golden domes?

How shall the heart of a fruit be stretched to envelop the fruit also?

O my faith, I am in chains behind these bars of silver and ebony, and I cannot fly with you.

Yet out of my heart you rise skyward, and it is my heart that holds you, and I shall be content.

Dynasties

The Queen of Ishana was in travail of childbirth; and the King and the mighty men of his court were waiting in breathless anxiety in the great hall of the Winged Bulls.

At eventide there came suddenly a messenger in haste and prostrated himself before the King, and said, "I bring glad tidings unto my lord the King, and unto the kingdom and the slaves of the King. Mihrab the Cruel, thy life-long enemy, the King of Bethroun, is dead."

When the King and the mighty men heard this, they all rose and shouted for joy; for the powerful Mihrab, had he lived longer, had assuredly overcome Ishana and carried the inhabitants captive.

At this moment the court physician also entered the hall of Winged Bulls, and behind him came the royal midwives. And the physician prostrated himself before the king, and said, "My lord the King shall live for ever, and through countless generations shall he rule over the people of Ishana. For unto thee, O King, is born this very hour a son, who shall be thy heir."

Then indeed was the soul of the King intoxicated with joy, that in the same moment his foe was dead and the royal line was established.

Now in the City of Ishana lived a true prophet. And the prophet was young, and bold of spirit. And the King that very night ordered that the prophet should be brought before him. And when he was brought, the King said unto him, "Prophesy now, and foretell what shall be the future of my son who is this day born unto the kingdom."

And the prophet hesitated not, but said, "Hearken, O King, and I will indeed prophesy of the future of thy son, that is this day born. The soul of thy enemy, even of thy enemy King Mihrab, who died yestereve, lingered but a day upon the wind. Then it sought for itself a body to enter into. And that which it entered into was the body of thy son that, is born unto thee this hour."

Then the King was enraged, and with his sword he slew the prophet.

And from that day to this, the wise men of Ishana say one to another secretly, "Is it not known, and has it not been said from of old, that Ishana is ruled by an enemy."

Knowledge and Half-Knowledge

Four frogs sat upon a log that lay floating on the edge of a river. Suddenly the log was caught by the current and swept slowly down the stream. The frogs were delighted and absorbed, for never before had they sailed.

At length the first frog spoke, and said, "This is indeed a most marvellous log. It moves as if alive. No such log was ever known before."

Then the second frog spoke, and said, "Nay, my friend, the log is like other logs, and does not move. It is the river, that is walking to the sea, and carries us and the log with it."

And the third frog spoke, and said, "It is neither the log nor the river that moves. The moving is in our thinking. For without thought nothing moves."

And the three frogs began to wrangle about what was really moving. The quarrel grew hotter and louder, but they could not agree.

Then they turned to the fourth frog, who up to this time had been listening attentively but holding his peace, and they asked his opinion.

And the fourth frog said, "Each of you is right, and none of you is wrong. The moving is in the log and the water and our thinking also."

And the three frogs became very angry, for none of them was willing to admit that his was not the whole truth, and that the other two were not wholly wrong.

Then the strange thing happened. The three frogs got together and pushed the fourth frog off the log into the river.

"Said a Sheet of Snow-White Paper...."

Said a sheet of snow-white paper, "Pure was I created, and pure will I remain for ever. I would rather be burnt and turn to white ashes than suffer darkness to touch me or the unclean to come near me."

The ink-bottle heard what the paper was saying, and it laughed in its dark heart; but it never dared to approach her. And the multicoloured pencils heard her also, and they too never came near her.

And the snow-white sheet of paper did remain pure and chaste for ever—pure and chaste—and empty.

The Scholar and the Poet

Said the serpent to the lark, "Thou flyest, yet thou canst not visit the recesses of the earth where the sap of life moveth in perfect silence."

And the lark answered, "Aye, thou knowest over much, nay thou art wiser than all things wise—pity thou canst not fly."

And as if he did not hear, the serpent said, "Thou canst not see the secrets of the deep, nor move among the treasures of the hidden empire. It was but yesterday I lay in a cave of rubies. It is like the heart of a ripe pomegranate, and the faintest ray of light turns it into a flame-rose. Who but me can behold such marvels?"

And the lark said, "None, none but thee can lie among the crystal memories of the cycles: pity thou canst not sing."

And the serpent said, "I know a plant whose root descends to the bowels of the earth, and he who eats of that root becomes fairer than Ashtarte."

And the lark said, "No one, no one but thee could unveil the magic thought of the earth—pity thou canst not fly."

And the serpent said, "There is a purple stream that runneth under a mountain, and he who drinketh of it shall become immortal even as the gods. Surely no bird or beast can discover that purple stream."

And the lark answered, "If thou willest thou canst become deathless even as the gods—pity thou canst not sing."

And the serpent said, "I know a buried temple, which I visit once a moon: It was built by a forgotten race of giants, and upon its walls are graven the secrets of time and space, and he who reads them shall understand that which passeth all understanding."

And the lark said, "Verily, if thou so desirest thou canst encircle with thy pliant body all knowledge of time and space—pity thou canst not fly."

Then the serpent was disgusted, and as he turned and entered into his hole he muttered, "Empty headed songster!"

And the lark flew away singing, "Pity thou canst not sing. Pity, pity, my wise one, thou canst not fly."

Values

Once a man unearthed in his field a marble statue of great beauty. And he took it to a collector who loved all beautiful things and offered it to him for sale, and the collector bought it for a large price. And they parted.

And as the man walked home with his money he thought, and he said to himself, "How much life this money means! How can any one give all this for a dead carved stone buried and undreamed of in the earth for a thousand years?"

And now the collector was looking at his statue, and he was thinking, and he said to himself, "What beauty! What life! The dream of what a soul!—and fresh with the sweet sleep of a thousand years. How can any one give all this for money, dead and dreamless?"

Other Seas

A fish said to another fish, "Above this sea of ours there is another sea, with creatures swimming in it—and they live there even as we live here."

The fish replied, "Pure fancy! Pure fancy! When you know that everything that leaves our sea by even an inch, and stays out of it, dies. What proof have you of other lives in other seas?"

Repentance

On a moonless night a man entered into his neighbour's garden and stole the largest melon he could find and brought it home.

He opened it and found it still unripe.

Then behold a marvel!

The man's conscience woke and smote him with remorse; and he repented having stolen the melon.

The Dying Man and the Vulture

Wait, wait yet awhile, my eager friend.
I shall yield but too soon this wasted thing,
Whose agony overwrought and useless
Exhausts your patience.
I would not have your honest hunger
Wait upon these moments:
But this chain, though made of a breath,
Is hard to break.
And the will to die,
Stronger than all things strong,
Is stayed by a will to live
Feebler than all things feeble.
Forgive me comrade; I tarry too long.
It is memory that holds my spirit;
A procession of distant days,
A vision of youth spent in a dream,
A face that bids my eyelids not to sleep,
A voice that lingers in my ears,
A hand that touches my hand.
Forgive me that you have waited too long.
It is over now, and all is faded:—
The face, the voice, the hand and the mist
that brought them hither.
The knot is untied.
The cord is cleaved.
And that which is neither food nor drink is withdrawn.
Approach, my hungry comrade;
The board is made ready,
And the fare, frugal and spare,
Is given with love.

Come, and dig your beak here, into the left side,
And tear out of its cage this smaller bird,
Whose wings can beat no more:
I would have it soar with you into the sky.
Come now, my friend, I am your host tonight,
And you my welcome guest.

Beyond My Solitude

Beyond my solitude is another solitude, and to him who dwells therein my aloneness is a crowded market-place and my silence a confusion of sounds.

Too young am I and too restless to seek that above-solitude. The voices of yonder valley still hold my ears, and its shadows bar my way and I cannot go.

Beyond these hills is a grove of enchantment and to him who dwells therein my peace is but a whirlwind and my enchantment an illusion.

Too young am I and too riotous to seek that sacred grove. The taste of blood is clinging in my mouth, and the bow and the arrows of my fathers yet linger in my hand and I cannot go.

Beyond this burdened self lives my freer self; and to him my dreams are a battle fought in twilight and my desires the rattling of bones.

Too young am I and too outraged to be my freer self.

And how shall I become my freer self unless I slay my burdened selves, or unless all men become free?

How shall my leaves fly singing upon the wind unless my roots shall wither in the dark?

How shall the eagle in me soar against the sun until my fledglings leave the nest which I with my own beak have built for them?

The Last Watch

At the high-tide of night, when the first breath of dawn came upon the wind, the Forerunner, he who calls himself echo to a voice yet unheard, left his bed-chamber and ascended to the roof of his house. Long he stood and looked down upon the slumbering city. Then he raised his head, and even as if the sleepless spirits of all those asleep had gathered around him, he opened his lips and spoke, and he said:

"My friends and my neighbours and you who daily pass my gate, I would speak to you in your sleep, and in the valley of your dreams I would walk naked and unrestrained; far heedless are your waking hours and deaf are your sound-burdened ears.

"Long did I love you and overmuch.

"I love the one among you as though he were all, and all as if you were one. And in the spring of my heart I sang in your gardens, and in the summer of my heart I watched at your threshing-floors.

"Yea, I loved you all, the giant and the pigmy, the leper and the anointed, and him who gropes in the dark even as him who dances his days upon the mountains.

"You, the strong, have I loved, though the marks of your iron hoofs are yet upon my flesh; and you the weak, though you have drained my faith and wasted my patience.

"You the rich have I loved, while bitter was your honey to my mouth; and you the poor, though you knew my empty-handed shame.

"You the poet with the barrowed lute and blind fingers, you have I loved in self indulgence; and you the scholar, ever gathering rotted shrouds in potters' fields.

"You the priest I have loved, who sit in the silences of yesterday questioning the fate of my tomorrow; and you the worshippers of gods the images of your own desires.

"You the thirsting woman whose cup is ever full, I have loved you in understanding; and you the woman of restless nights, you too I have loved in pity.

"You the talkative have I loved, saying, 'Life hath much to say'; and you the dumb have I loved, whispering to myself, 'Says he not in silence that which I fain would hear in words?'

"And you the judge and the critic, I have loved also; yet when you have seen me crucified, you said, 'He bleeds rhythmically, and the pattern his blood makes upon his white skin is beautiful to behold.'

"Yea, I have loved you all, the young and the old, the trembling reed and the oak.

"But alas! it was the over-abundance of my heart that turned you from me. You would drink love from a cup, but not from a surging river. You would hear love's faint murmur, but when love shouts you would muffle your ears.

"And because I have loved you all you have said, 'Too soft and yielding is his heart, and too undiscerning is his path. It is the love of a needy one, who picks crumbs even as he sits at kingly feasts. And it is the love of a weakling, for the strong loves only the strong.'

"And because I have loved you overmuch you have said, 'It is but the love of a blind man who knows not the beauty of one nor the ugliness of another. And it is the love of the tasteless who drinks vinegar even as wine. And it is the love of the impertinent and the overweening, for what stranger could be our mother and father and sister and brother?'

"This you have said, and more. For often in the marketplace you pointed your fingers at me and said mockingly, 'There goes the ageless one, the man without seasons, who at the noon hour plays games with our children and at eventide sits with our elders and assumes wisdom and understanding.'

"And I said 'I will love them more. Aye, even more. I will hide my love with seeming to hate, and disguise my tenderness as bitterness. I will wear an iron mask, and only when armed and mailed shall I seek them.'

"Then I laid a heavy hand upon your bruises, and like a tempest in the night I thundered in your ears.

"From the housetop I proclaimed you hypocrites, pharisees, tricksters, false and empty earth-bubbles.

"The short-sighted among you I cursed for blind bats, and those too near the earth I likened to soulless moles.

"The eloquent I pronounced fork-tongued, the silent, stone-lipped, and the simple and artless I called the dead never weary of death.

"The seekers after world knowledge I condemned as offenders of the holy spirit and those who would naught but the spirit I branded as hunters of shadows who cast their nets in flat waters and catch but their own images.

"Thus with my lips have I denounced you, while my heart, bleeding within me, called you tender names.

"It was love lashed by its own self that spoke. It was pride half slain that fluttered in the dust. It was my hunger for your love that raged from the housetop, while my own love, kneeling in silence, prayed your forgiveness.

"But behold a miracle!

"It was my disguise that opened your eyes, and my seeming to hate that woke your hearts.

"And now you love me.

"You love the swords that strike you and the arrows that crave your breast. For it comforts you to be wounded and only when you drink of your own blood can you be intoxicated.

"Like moths that seek destruction in the flame you gather daily in my garden: and with faces uplifted and eyes enchanted you watch me tear the fabric of your days. And in whispers you say the one to the other, 'He sees with the light of God. He speaks like the prophets of old. He unveils our souls and unlocks our hearts, and like the eagle that knows the way of foxes he knows our ways.'

"Aye, in truth, I know your ways, but only as an eagle knows the ways of his fledglings. And I fain would disclose my secret. Yet in my need for your nearness I feign remoteness, and in fear of the ebbtide of your love I guard the floodgates of my love."

After saying these things the Forerunner covered his face with his hands and wept bitterly. For he knew in his heart that love humiliated in its nakedness is greater than love that seeks triumph in disguise; and he was ashamed.

But suddenly he raised his head, and like one waking from sleep he outstretched his arms and said, "Night is over, and we children of night must die when dawn comes leaping upon the hills; and out of our ashes a mightier love shall rise. And it shall laugh in the sun, and it shall be deathless."

SPIRITS REBELLIOUS

Madame Rose Hanie

Part One

Miserable is the man who loves a woman and takes her for a wife, pouring at her feet the sweat of his skin and the blood of his body and the life of his heart, and placing in her hands the fruit of his toil and the revenue of his diligence; for when he slowly wakes up, he finds that the heart, which he endeavoured to buy, is given freely and in sincerity to another man for the enjoyment of its hidden secrets and deepest love. Miserable is the woman who arises from the inattentiveness and restlessness of youth and finds herself in the home of a man showering her with his glittering gold and precious gifts and according her all the honours and grace of lavish entertainment but unable to satisfy her soul with the heavenly wine which God pours from the eyes of a man into the heart of a woman.

I knew Rashid Bey Namaan since I was a youngster; he was a Lebanese, born and reared in the City of Beyrouth. Being a member of an old and rich family which preserved the tradition and glory of his ancestry, Rashid was fond of citing incidents that dealt mainly with the nobility of his forefathers. In his routine life he followed their beliefs and customs which, at that time, prevailed in the Middle East.

Rashid Bey Namaan was generous and good-hearted, but like many of the Syrians, looked only at the superficial things instead of reality. He never hearkened to the dictates of his heart, but busied himself in obeying the voices of his environment. He amused himself with shimmering objects that blinded his eyes and heart to life's secrets; his soul was diverted away from an understanding of the law of nature, and to a temporary self-gratification. He was one of those men who hastened to confess their love or disgust to the people, then regretted their impulsiveness when it was too late for recall. And then shame and ridicule befell them, instead of pardon or sanction.

These are the characteristics that prompted Rashid Bey Namaan to marry Rose Hanie far before her soul embraced his soul in the shadow of the true love that makes union a paradise.

After a few years of absence, I returned to the City of Beyrouth. As I went to visit Rashid Bey Namaan, I found him pale and thin. On his face one could see the spectre of bitter disappointment; his sorrowful eyes bespoke his crushed heart and melancholy soul. I was curious to find the cause for his miserable plight; however, I did not hesitate to ask for explanation and said, "What became of you, Rashid? Where is the radiant smile and the happy countenance that accompanied you since childhood? H as death taken away from you a dear friend? Or have the black nights stolen from you the gold you have amassed during the white days? In the name of friendship, tell me what is causing this sadness of heart and weakness of body?"

He looked at me ruefully, as if I had revived to him some secluded images of beautiful days. With a distressed and faltering voice he responded, "When a person loses a friend, he consoles himself with the many other friends about him, and if he loses his gold, he meditates for a while and casts misfortune from his mind, especially when he finds himself healthy and still laden with ambition. But when a man loses the ease of his heart, where can he find comfort, and with what can he replace it? What mind can master it? When death strikes close by, you will suffer. But when the day and the night pass, you will feel the smooth touch of the soft fingers of Life; then you will smile and rejoice.

"Destiny comes suddenly, bringing concern; she stares at you with horrible eyes and clutches you at the throat with sharp fingers and hurls you to the ground and tramples upon you with ironclad feet; then she laughs and walks away, but later regrets her actions and asks you through good fortune to forgive her. She stretches her silky hand and lifts you high and sings to you the Song of Hope and causes you to lose your cares. She creates in you a new zest for confidence and ambition. If your lot in life is a beautiful bird that you love dearly, you gladly feed to him the seeds of your inner self, and make your heart his cage and your soul his nest. But while you are affectionately admiring him and looking upon him with the eyes of love, he escapes from your hands and flies very high; then he descends and enters into another cage and never comes back to you. What can you do? Where can you find patience and condolence? How can you revive your hopes and dreams? What power can still your turbulent heart?"

Having uttered these words with a choking voice and suffering spirit, Rashid Bey Namaan stood shaking like a reed between the north and south wind. He extended his hands as if to grasp something with his bent fingers and destroy it. His wrinkled face was livid, his eyes grew larger as he stared a few moments, and it seemed to him as if he saw a demon appearing from non-existence to take him away; then he fixed his eyes on mine and his appearance suddenly changed; his anger was converted into keen suffering and distress, and he cried out saying, "It is the woman whom I rescued from between the deathly paws of poverty; I opened my coffers to her and made her envied by all women for the beautiful raiment and precious gems and magnificent carriages drawn by spirited horses; the woman whom my heart has loved and at whose feet I poured affection; the woman, to whom I was a true friend, sincere companion and a faithful husband; The woman who betrayed me and departed me for another man to share with him destitution and partake his evil bread, kneaded with shame and mixed with disgrace. The woman I loved; the beautiful bird whom I fed, and to whom I made my heart a cage and my soul a nest, has escaped from my hands and entered into another cage; that pure an gel, who resided in the paradise of my affection and love, now appears to me as a horrible demon, descended into the darkness to suffer for her sin and cause me to suffer on earth for her crime."

He hid his face with his hands as if wanting to protect himself from himself, and became silent for a moment. Then he sighed and said, "This is all I can tell you; please do not ask anything further. Do not make a crying voice of my calamity, but le t it rather be mute misfortune; perhaps it will grow in silence and deaden me away so that I may rest at last with peace."

I rose with tears in my eyes and mercy in my heart, and silently bade him goodbye; my words had no power to console his wounded heart, and my knowledge had no torch to illuminate his gloomy self.

Part Two

A few days thereafter I met Madame Rose Hanie for the first time, in a poor hovel, surrounded by flowers and trees. She had heard of me through Rashid Bey Namaan, the man whose heart she had crushed and stamped upon and left under the terrible hoofs of Life. As I looked at her beautiful bright eyes, and heard her sincere voice, I said to myself, "Can this be the sordid woman? Can this clear face hide an ugly soul and a criminal heart? Is this the unfaithful wife? Is this the woman of whom I have spoken evil and imagined as a serpent disguised in the form of a beautiful bird?" Then I whispered again to myself saying, "Is it this beautiful face that made Rashid Bey Namaan miserable? Haven't we heard that obvious beauty is the cause of many hidden distresses and deep suffering? Is not the beautiful moon, that inspires the poets, the same moon that angers the silence of the sea with a terrible roar?"

As we seated ourselves, Madame Rose Hanie seemed to have heard and read my thoughts and wanted not to prolong my doubts. She leaned her beautiful head upon her hands and with a voice sweeter than the sound of the lyre, she said, "I have never met you, but I heard the echoes of your thoughts and dreams from the mouths of the people, and they convinced me that you are merciful and have understanding for the oppressed woman – the woman whose heart's secrets you have discovered and whose affections you have known. Allow me to reveal to you the full contents of my heart so you may know that Rose Hanie never was an unfaithful woman.

"I was scarcely eighteen years of age when fate led me to Rashid Bey Namaan, who was then forty years old. He fell in love with me, according to what the people say, and took me for a wife and put me in his magnificent home, placing at my disposal clothes and precious gems. He exhibited me as a strange rarity at the homes of his friends and family; he smiled with triumph when he saw his contemporaries looking at me with surprise and admiration; he lifted his chin high with pride when he heard the ladies speak of me with praise and affection. But never could he hear the whispers, 'Is this the wife of Rashid Bey Namaan, or his adopted daughter?' And another one commenting, 'If he had married at the proper age, his first born would have been older than Rose Hanie.'

"All that happened before my life had awakened from the deep swoon of youth, and before God inflamed my heart with the torch of love, and before the growth of the seeds of my affections. Yes, all this transpired during the time when I believed that real happiness came through beautiful clothes and magnificent mansions. When I woke up from the slumber of childhood, I felt the flames of sacred fire burning in my heart, and a spiritual hunger gnawing at my soul, making it suffer. When I opened my eyes, I found my wings moving to the right and left, trying to ascend into the spacious firmament of love, but shivering and dropping under the gusts of the shackles of laws that bound my body to a man before I knew the true meaning of that law. I felt all these things and knew that a woman's happiness does not come through man's glory and honour, nor through his generosity and affection, but through love that unites both of their hearts and affections, making them one member of life's body and one word upon the lips of God. When Truth showed herself to me, I found myself imprisoned by law in the mansion of Rashid Bey Namaan, like a thief stealing his bread and hiding in the dark and friendly corners of the night. I knew that every hour spent with him was a terrible lie written upon my forehead with letters of fire before heaven and earth. I could not give him my love and affection in reward for his generosity and sincerity. I tried in vain to love him, but love is a power that makes our hearts, yet our hearts cannot make that power. I prayed and prayed in the silence of the night before God to create in the depths of my heart a spiritual attachment that would carry me closer to the man who had been chosen for me as a companion through life.

"My prayers were not granted, because Love descends upon our souls by the will of God and not by the demand or the plea of the individual. Thus I remained for two years in the home of that man, envying the birds of the field their freedom while my friends envied me my painful chains of gold. I was like a woman who is torn from her only child; like a lamenting heart, existing without attachment; like an innocent victim of the severity of human law. I was close to death from spiritual thirst and hunger.

"One dark day, as I looked behind the heavy skies, I saw a gentle light pouring from the eyes of a man who was walking forlornly on the path of life; I closed my eyes to that light and said to myself, 'Oh, my soul, darkness of the grave is thy lot, do not be greedy for the light.' Then I heard a beautiful melody from heaven that revived my wounded heart with its purity, but I closed my ears and said, 'Oh, my soul, the cry of the abyss is thy lot, do not be greedy for heavenly songs.' I closed my eyes again so I could not see, and shut my ears so I could not hear, but my closed eyes still saw that gentle light, and my ears still heard that divine sound. I was frightened for the first time and felt like the beggar who found a precious jewel near the Emir's palace and could not pick it up on account of fear, or leave it because of poverty. I cried – a cry of a thirsty soul who sees a brook surrounded by wild beasts, and falls upon the ground waiting and watching fearfully."

Then she turned her eyes away from me as if she remembered the past that made her ashamed to face me, but she continued, "Those people who go to back to eternity before they taste the sweetness of real life are unable to understand the meaning of a woman's suffering. Especially when she devotes her soul to a man she loves by the will of God, and her body to another whom she caresses by the enforcement of earthly law. It is a tragedy written with the blood of the woman's blood and tears which the man reads with ridicule because he cannot understand it; yet, if he does understand, his laughter will turn into scorn and blasphemy that act like fire upon her heart. It is a drama enacted by the black nights upon the stage of a woman's soul, whose body is tied up into a man, known to her as husband, ere she perceives God's meaning of marriage. She finds her soul hovering about the man whom she adores by all agencies of pure and true love and beauty. It is a terrible agony that began with the existence of weakness in a woman and the commencement of strength in a man. It will not end unless the days of slavery and superiority of the strong over the weak are abolished. It is a horrible war between the corrupt law of humanity and the sacred affections and holy purpose of the heart. In such a battlefield I was lying yesterday, but I gathered the remnants of my strength, and unchained my irons of cowardice, and untied my wings from the swaddles of weakness and arose into the spacious sky of love and freedom.

"Today I am one with the man I love; he and I sprang out as one torch from the hand of God before the beginning of the world. There is no power under the sun that can take my happiness from me, because it emanated from two embraced spirits, engulfed by understanding, radiated by Love, and protected by heaven."

She looked at me as if she wanted to penetrate my heart with her eyes in order to discover the impression of her words upon me, and to hear the echo of her voice from within me; but I remained silent and she continued. Her voice was full of bitterness of memory and sweetness of sincerity and freedom when she said, "The people will tell you that Rose Hanie is an heretic and unfaithful woman who followed her desires by leaving the man who elated her into him and made her the elegance of his home. They will tell you that she is an adulteress and prostitute who destroyed with her filthy hands the wreath of a sacred marriage and replaced it with a besmirched union woven of the thorns of hell. She took off the garment of virtue and put on the cloak of sin and disgrace. They will tell you more than that, because the ghosts of their fathers are still living in their bodies. They are like the deserted caves of the mountains that echo voices whose meanings are not understood. They neither understand the law of God, nor comprehend the true intent of veritable religion, nor distinguish between a sinner and an innocent. They look only at the surface of objects without knowing their secrets. They pass their verdicts with ignorance, and judge with blindness, making the criminal and the innocent, the good and the bad, equal. Woe to those who prosecute and judge the people. . . .

"In God's eyes I was unfaithful and an adulteress only while at the home of Rashid Bey Namaan, because he made me his wife according to the customs and traditions and by the force of haste, before heaven had made him mine in conformity with the spiritual law of Love and Affection. I was a sinner in the eyes of God and myself when I ate his bread and offered him my body in reward for his generosity. Now I am pure and clean because the law of Love has freed me and made me honourable and faithful. I ceased selling my body for shelter and my days for clothes. Yes, I was an adulteress and a criminal when the people viewed me as the most honourable and faithful wife; today I am pure and noble in spirit, but in their opinion I am polluted, for they judge the soul by the outcome of the body and measure the spirit by the standard of matter."

Then she looked through the window and pointed out with her right hand toward the city as if she had seen the ghost of corruption and the shadow of shame among its magnificent buildings. She said pityingly, "Look at those majestic mansions and sublime palaces where hypocrisy resides; in those edifices and between their beautifully decorated walls resides Treason beside Putridity; under the ceiling painted with melted gold lives Falsehood beside Pretension. Notice those gorgeous homes that represent happiness, glory and domination; they are naught but caverns of misery and distress. They are plastered graves in which Treason of the weak woman hides behind her kohled eyes and crimsoned lips; in their corners selfishness exists, and the animality of man through his gold and silver rules supreme.

"If those high and impregnable buildings scented the door of hatred, deceit and corruption, they would have cracked and fallen. The poor villager looks upon those residences with tearful eyes, but when he finds that the hearts of the occupants are empty of that pure love that exists in the heart of his wife and fills its domain, he will smile and go back to his fields contented."

And then she took hold of my hand and led me to the side of the window and said, "Come, I will show you the unveiled secrets of those people whose path I refused to follow. Look at that palace with giant columns. IN it lives a rich man who inherited his gold from his father. After having led a life of filth and putrefaction, he married a woman about whom he knew nothing except that her father was one of the Sultan's dignitaries. As soon as the wedding trip was over he became disgusted and commenced associations with women who sell their bodies for pieces of silver. His wife was left alone in that palace like an empty bottle left by a drunkard. She cried and suffered for the first time; then she realized that her tears were more precious than her degenerate husband. Now she is busying herself in the love and devotion of a young man upon whom she showers her joyous hours, and into whose heart she pours her sincere love and affection.

"Let me take you now to that gorgeous home surrounded by beautiful gardens. It is the home of a man who comes from a noble family which ruled the country for many generations, but whose standards, wealth, and prestige have declined due to their indulgence in mad spending and slothfulness. A few years ago this man married an ugly but rich woman. After he acquired her fortune, he ignored her completely and commenced devoting himself to an attractive young woman. His wife today is devoting her time to curling her hair, painting her lips and perfuming her body. She wears the most expensive clothes and hopes that some young man will smile and come to visit her, but it is all in vain, for she cannot succeed except in receiving a smile from her ugly self in the mirror.

"Observe that big manor, encircled with the marble statuary; it is the home of a beautiful woman who possesses strange character. When her first husband died, she inherited all his money and estate; then she selected a man with a weak mind and feeble body and became his wife to protect herself from the evil tongues, and to use him as a shield for her abominations. She is now among her admirers like a bee that sucks the sweetest and most delicious flowers.

That beautiful home next to it was built by the greatest architect in the province; it belongs to a greedy and substantial man who devotes all of his time to amassing gold and grinding the faces of the poor. He has a wife of supernatural beauty, bodily and spiritually, but she is like the rest, a victim of early marriage. Her father committed a crime by giving her away to a man before she attained understanding age, placing on her neck the heavy yoke of corrupt marriage. She is thin and pale now, and cannot find an outlet for her imprisoned affection. She is sinking slowly and craving for death to free her from the mesh of slavery and deliver her from a man who spends his life gathering gold and cursing the hour he married a barren woman who could not bring him a child to carry on his name and inherit his money.

In that home among the orchards lives an ideal poet; he married an ignorant woman who ridicules his works because she cannot understand them, and laughs at his conduct because she cannot adjust herself to his sublime way of life. That poet found freedom from despair in his love for a married woman who appreciates his intelligence and inspires him by kindling in his heart the torch of affections, and revealing to him the most beautiful and eternal sayings by means of her charm and beauty."

Silence prevailed for a few moments, and Madame Hanie seated herself on a sofa by the window as if her soul were tired of roaming those quarters. Then she slowly continued, "These are the residences in which I refused to live; these are the graves in which I, too, was spiritually buried. These people from whom I have freed myself are the ones who become attracted by the body and repelled by the spirit, and who know naught of Love and Beauty. The only mediator between them and God is God's pity for their ignorance of the law of God. I cannot judge, for I was one of them, but I sympathize with all my heart. I do not hate them, but I hate their surrender to weakness and falsehood. I have said all these things to show you the reality of the people from whom I have escaped against their will. I was trying to explain to you the life of persons who speak every evil against me because I have lost their friendship and finally gained my own. I emerged from their dark dungeon and directed my eyes towards the light where sincerity, truth and justice prevail. They have exiled me now from their society and I am pleased, because humanity does not exile except the one whose noble spirit rebels against despotism and oppression. He who does not prefer exile to slavery is not free by any measure of freedom, truth and duty.

"Yesterday I was like a tray containing all kinds of palatable foods, and Rashid Bey Namaan never approached me unless he felt a need for that food; yet both of our souls remained far apart from us like two humble, dignified servants. I have tried to reconcile myself to what people call misfortune, but my spirit refused to spend all its life kneeling with me before a horrible idol erected by the dark ages and called LAW. I kept my chains until I heard Love calling me and saw my spirit preparing to embark. Then I broke them and walked out from Rashid Bey Namaan's home like a bird freed from his iron cage and leaving behind me all the gems, clothes and servants. I came to live with my beloved, for I knew that what I was doing was honest. Heaven does not want me to weep and suffer. Many times at night I prayed for dawn to come and when dawn came, I prayed for the day to be over. God does not want me to lead a miserable life, for He placed in the depths of my heart a desire for happiness; His glory rests in the happiness of my heart.

"This is my story and this is my protest before heaven and earth; this is what I sing and repeat while people are closing their ears for fear of hearing me and leading their spirits into rebellion that would crumble the foundation of their quavering society.

"This is the rough pathway I have carved until I reached the mountain peak of my happiness. Now if death comes to take me away, I will be more than willing to offer myself before the Supreme Throne of Heaven without fear or shame. I am ready for the day of judgment and my heart is white as the snow. I have obeyed the will of God in everything I have done and followed the call of my heart while listening to the angelic voice of heaven. This is my drama which the people of Beyrouth call 'A curse upon the lips of life,' and 'An ailment in the body of society.' But one day love will arouse their hearts like the sun rays that bring forth the flowers even from contaminated earth. One day the wayfarers will stop by my grave and greet the earth that enfolds my body and say, 'Here lies Rose Hanie who freed herself from the slavery of decayed human laws in order to comply with God's law of pure love. She turned her face toward the sun so she would not see the shadow of her body amongst the skulls and thorns.' "

The door opened and a man entered. His eyes were shining with magic rays and upon his lips appeared a wholesome smile. Madame Hanie rose, took the young man's arm and introduced him to me, then gave him my name with flattering words. I knew that he was the one for whose sake she denied the whole world and violated all earthly laws and customs.

As we sat down, silence controlled. Each one of us was engrossed in deep thought. One minute worthy of silence and respect had passed when I looked at the couple sitting side by side. I saw something I had never seen before, and realized instantly the meaning of Madame Hanie's story. I comprehended the secret of her protest against the society which persecutes those who rebel against confining laws and customs before determining the cause for the rebellion. I saw one heavenly spirit before me, composed of two beautiful and united persons, in the midst of which stood the god of Love stretching his wings over them to protect them from evil tongues. I found a complete understanding emanating from two smiling faces, illuminated by sincerity and surrounded by virtue. For the first time in my life I found the phantom of happiness standing between a man and a woman, cursed by religion and opposed by the law. I rose and bade them goodbye and left that poor hovel which Affection had erected as an altar to Love and Understanding. I walked past the buildings which Madame Hanie pointed out to me. As I reached the end of these quarters I remembered Rashid Bey Namaan and meditated his miserable plight and said to myself, "He is oppressed; will heaven ever listen to him if he complains about Madame Hanie? Had that woman done wrong when she left him and followed the freedom of her heart? Or did he commit a crime by subduing her heart into love? Which of the two is the oppressed and which is the oppressor? Who is the criminal and who is the innocent?"

Then I resumed talking to myself after a few moments of deep thinking. "Many times deception had tempted woman to leave her husband and follow wealth, because her love for riches and beautiful raiment blinds her and leads her into shame. Was Madame Hanie deceitful when she left her rich husband's palace for a poor man's hut? Many times ignorance kills a woman's honour and revives her passion; she grows tired and leaves her husband, prompted by her desires, and follows a man to whom she lowers herself. Was Madame Hanie an ignorant woman following her physical desires when she declared publicly her independence and joined her beloved young man? She could have satisfied herself secretly while at her husband's home, for many men were willing to be the slaves of her beauty and martyrs of her love. Madame Hanie was a miserable woman. She sought only happiness, found it, and embraced it. This is the very truth which society disrespects." Then I whispered through the ether and inquired of myself, "Is it permissible for a woman to buy her happiness with her husband's misery?" And my soul added, "Is it lawful for a man to enslave his wife's affection when he realizes he will never possess it?"

I continued walking and Madame Hanie's voice was still sounding in my ears when I reached the extreme end of the city. The sun was disappearing and silence ruled the fields and prairies while the birds commenced singing their evening prayers. I stood there meditating, and then I sighed and said, "Before the throne of Freedom, the trees rejoice with the frolicsome breeze and enjoy the rays of the sun and the beams of the moon. Through the ears of Freedom these birds whisper and around Freedom they flutter to the music of the brooks. Throughout the sky of Freedom these flowers breathe their fragrance and before Freedom's eyes they smile when day comes.

"Everything lives on earth according to the law of nature, and from that law emerges the glory and joy of liberty; but man is denied this fortune, because he set for the God-given soul a limited and earthly law of his own. He made for himself strict rules. Man built a narrow and painful prison in which he secluded his affections and desires. He dug out a deep grave in which he buried his heart and its purpose. If an individual, through the dictates of his soul, declares his withdrawal from society and violates the law, his fellowmen will say he is a rebel worthy of exile, or an infamous creature worthy only of execution. Will man remain a slave of self-confinement until the end of the world? Or will he be freed by the passing of time and live in the Spirit for the Spirit? Will man insist upon staring downward and backward at the earth? Or will he turn his eyes toward the sun so he will not see the shadow of his body amongst the skulls and thorns?"

The Cry of the Graves

Part One

The Emir walked into the court room and took the central chair while at his right and left sat the wise men of the country. The guards, armed with swords and spears, stood in attention, and the people who came to witness the trial rose and bowed ceremoniously to the Emir whose eyes emanated a power that revealed horror to their spirits and fear to their hearts. As the court came to order and the hour of judgment approached, the Emir raised his hand and shouted saying, "Bring forth the criminals singly and tell me what crimes they have committed." The prison door opened like the mouth of a ferocious yawning beast. In the obscure corners of the dungeon one could hear the echo of shackles rattling in unison with the moaning and lamentations of the prisoners. The spectators were eager to see the prey of Death emerging from the depths of that inferno. A few moments later, two soldiers came out leading a young man with his arms pinioned behind his back. His stern face bespoke nobility of spirit and strength of the heart. He was halted in the middle of the court room and the soldiers marched a few steps to the rear. The Emir stared at him steadily and said, "What crime has this man, who is proudly and triumphantly standing before me, committed?" One of the courtmen responded, "He is a murderer; yesterday he slew one of the Emir's officers who was on an important mission in the surrounding villages; he was still grasping the bloody sword when he was arrested." The Emir retorted with anger, "Return the man to the dark prison and tie him with heavy chains, and at dawn cut off his head with his own sword and throw his body in the woods so that the beasts may eat the flesh, and the air may carry its remindful door into the noses of his family and friends." The youth was returned to prison while the people looked upon him with sorrowful eyes, for he was a young man in the spring of life.

The soldiers returned back again from the prison leading a young woman of natural and frail beauty. She looked pale and upon her face appeared the signs of oppression and disappointment. Her eyes were soaked with tears and her head was bent under the burden of grief. After eyeing her thoroughly, the Emir exclaimed, "And this emaciated woman, who is standing before me like the shadow beside a corpse, what has she done?" One of the soldiers answered him, saying, "She is an adulteress; last night her husband discovered her in the arms of another. After her lover escaped, her husband turned her over to the law." The Emir looked at her while she raised her face without expression, and he ordered, "Take her back to the dark room and stretch her upon a bed of thorns so she may remember the resting place which she polluted with her fault; give her vinegar mixed with gall to drink so she may remember the taste of those sweet kisses. At dawn drag her naked body outside the city and stone her. Let the wolves enjoy the tender meat of her body and the worms pierce her bones." AS she walked back to the dark cell, the people looked upon her with sympathy and surprise. They were astonished with the Emir's justice and grieved over her fate. The soldiers reappeared, bringing with them a sad man with shaking knees and trembling like a tender sapling before the north wind. He looked powerless, sickly and frightened, and he was miserable and poor. The Emir stared at him loathfully and inquired, "And this filthy man, who is like dead amongst the living; what has he done?" One of the guards returned, "He is a thief who broke into the monastery and stole the sacred vases which the priests found under his garment when they arrested him."

As a hungry eagle who looks at a bird with broken wings, the Emir looked at him and said, "Take him back to the jail and chain him, and at dawn drag him into a lofty tree and hang him between heaven and earth so his sinful hands may perish and the members of his body may be turned into particles and scattered by the wind." As the thief stumbled back into the depths of the prison, the people commenced whispering one to another saying, "How dare such a weak and heretic man steal the sacred vases of the monastery?"

At this time the court adjourned and the Emir walked out accompanied by all his wise men, guarded by the soldiers, while the audience scattered and the place became empty except of the moaning and wailing of the prisoners. All this happened while I was standing there like a mirror before passing ghosts. I was meditating the laws, made by man for man, contemplating what the people call "justice," and engrossing myself with deep thoughts of the secrets of life. I tried to understand the meaning of the universe. I was dumbfounded in finding myself lost like a horizon that disappears beyond the cloud. As I left the place I said to myself, "The vegetable feeds upon the elements of the earth, the sheep eats the vegetable, the wolf preys upon the sheep, and the bull kills the wolf while the lion devours the bull; yet Death claims the lion. Is there any power that will overcome Death and make these brutalities an eternal justice? Is there a force that can convert all the ugly things into beautiful objects? Is there any might that can clutch with its hands all the elements of life and embrace them with joy as the sea joyfully engulfs all the brooks into its depths? Is there any power that can arrest the murdered and the murderer, the adulteress and the adulterer, the robber and the robbed, and bring them to a court loftier and more supreme than the court of the Emir?"

Part Two

The next day I left the city for the fields where silence reveals to the soul that which the spirit desires, and where the pure sky kills the germs of despair, nursed in the city by the narrow streets and obscured places. When I reached the valley, I saw a flock of crows and vultures soaring and descending, filling the sky with cawing, whistling and rustling of the wings. As I proceeded I saw before me a corpse of a man hanged high in a tree, the body of a dead naked woman in the midst of a heap of stones, and a carcass of a youth with his head cut off and soaked with blood mixed with earth. It was a horrible sight that blinded my eyes with a thick, dark veil of sorrows. I looked in every direction and saw naught except the spectre of Death standing by those ghastly remains. Nothing could be heard except the wailing of non-existence, mingled with the cawing of crows hovering about the victims of human laws. Three human beings, who yesterday were in the lap of Life, today fell as victims to Death because they broke the rules of human society. When a man kills another man, the people say he is a murderer, but when the Emir kills him, the Emir is just. When a man robs a monastery, they say he is a thief, but when the Emir robs him of his life, the Emir is honourable. When a woman betrays her husband, they say she is an adulteress, but when the Emir makes her walk naked in the streets and stones her later, the Emir is noble. Shedding of blood is forbidden, but who made it lawful for the Emir? Stealing one's money is a crime, but taking away one's life is a noble act. Betrayal of a husband may be an ugly deed, but stoning of living souls is a beautiful sight. Shall we meet evil with evil and say this is the Law? Shall we fight corruption with greater corruption and say this is the Rule? Shall we conquer crimes with more crimes and say this is Justice? Had not the Emir killed an enemy in his past life? Had he not robbed his weak subjects of money and property? Had he not committed adultery? Was he infallible when he killed the murderer and hanged the thief in the tree? Who are those who hanged the thief in the tree? Are they angels descended from heaven, or men looting and usurping? Who cut off the murderer's head? Are they divine prophets, or soldiers shedding blood wherever they go? Who stoned that adulteress? Were they virtuous hermits who came from their monasteries, or humans who loved to commit atrocities with glee, under the protection of ignorant Law? What is Law? Who saw it coming with the sun from the depths of heaven? What human saw the heart of God and found its will or purpose? In what century did the angels walk among the people and preach to them, saying, "Forbid the weak from enjoying life, and kill the outlaws with the sharp edge of the sword, and step upon the sinners with iron feet?"

As my mind suffered in this fashion, I heard a rustling of feet in the grass close by. I took heed and saw a young woman coming from behind the trees; she looked carefully in every direction before she approached the three carcasses that were there. As she glanced, she saw the youth's head that was cut off. She cried fearfully, knelt, and embraced it with her trembling arms; then she commenced shedding tears and touching the blood-matted, curly hair with her soft fingers, crying in a voice that came from the remnants of a shattered heart. She could bear the sight no longer. She dragged the body to a ditch and placed the head gently between the shoulders, covered the entire body with earth, and upon the grave she planted the sword with which the head of the young man had been cut off.

As she started to leave, I walked toward her. She trembled when she saw me, and her eyes were heavy with tears. She sighed and said, "Turn me over to the Emir if you wish. It is better for me to die and follow the one who saved my life from the grip of disgrace than to leave his corpse as food for the ferocious beasts." Then I responded, "Fear me not, poor girl, I have lamented the young man before you did. But tell me, how did he save you from the grip of disgrace?" She replied with a choking and fainting voice, "One of the Emir's officers came to our farm to collect the tax; when he saw me, he looked upon me as a wolf looks upon a lamb. He imposed on my father a heavy tax that even a rich man could not pay. He arrested me as a token to take to the Emir in ransom for the gold which my father was unable to give. I begged him to spare me, but he took no heed, for he had no mercy. Then I cried for help, and this young man, who is dead now, came for my help and saved me from a living death. The officer attempted to kill him, but this man took an old sword that was hanging on the wall of our home and stabbed him. He did not run away like a criminal, but stood by the dead officer until the law came and took him into custody." Having uttered these words which would make any human heart bleed with sorrow, she turned her face and walked away.

In a few moments I saw a youth coming and hiding his face with a cloak. As he approached the corpse of the adulteress, he took off the garment and placed it upon her naked body. Then he drew a dagger from under the cloak and dug a pit in which he placed the dead girl with tenderness and care, and covered her with earth upon which he poured his tears. When he finished his task, he plucked some flowers and placed them reverently upon the grave. As he started to leave, I halted him saying, "What kin are you to this adulteress? And what prompted you to endanger your life by coming here to protect her naked body from the ferocious beasts?"

When he stared at me, his sorrowful eyes bespoke his misery, and he said, "I am the unfortunate man for whose love she was stoned; I loved her and she loved me since childhood; we grew together; Love, whom we served and revered, was the lord of our hearts. Love joined both of us and embraced our souls. One day I absented myself from the city, and upon my return I discovered that her father obliged her to marry a man she did not love. My life became a perpetual struggle, and all my days were converted into one long and dark night. I tried to be at peace with my heart, but my heart would not be still. Finally I went to see her secretly and my sole purpose was to have a glimpse of her beautiful eyes and hear the sound of her serene voice. When I reached her house I found her lonely, lamenting her unfortunate self. I sat by her; silence was our important conversation and virtue our companion. One hour of understanding quiet passed, when her husband entered. I cautioned him to contain himself but he dragged her with both hands into the street and cried out saying, 'Come, come and see the adulteress and her lover!' All the neighbours rushed about and later the law came and took her to the Emir, but I was not touched by the soldiers. The ignorant Law and sodden customs punished the woman for her father's fault and pardoned the man."

Having thus spoken, the man turned toward the city while I remained pondering the corpse of the thief hanging in that lofty tree and moving slightly every time the wind shook the branches, waiting for someone to bring him down and stretch him upon the bosom of the earth beside the Defender of Honour and Martyr of Love. An hour later, a frail and wretched woman appeared, crying. She stood before the hanged man and prayed reverently. Then she struggled up into the tree and gnawed with her teeth on the linen rope until it broke and the dead fell on the ground like a huge wet cloth; whereupon she came down, dug a grave, and buried the thief by the side of the other two victims. After covering him with earth, she took two pieces of wood and fashioned a cross and placed it over the head. When she turned her face to the city and started to depart, I stopped her saying, "What incited you to come and bury this thief?" She looked at me miserably and said, "He is my faithful husband and merciful companion; he is the father of my children – five young ones starving to death; the oldest is eight years of age, and the youngest is still nursing. My husband was not a thief, but a farmer working in the monastery's land, making our living on what little food the priests and monks gave him when he returned home at eventide. He had been farming for them since he was young, and when he became weak, they dismissed him, advising him to go back home and send his children to take his place as soon as they grew older. He begged them in the name of Jesus and the angels of heaven to let him stay, but they took no heed of his plea. They had no mercy on him nor on his starving children who were helplessly crying for food. He went to the city seeking employment, but in vain, for the rich did not employ except the strong and the healthy. Then he sat on the dusty street stretching his hand toward all who passed, begging and repeating the sad song of his defeat in life, while suffering from hunger and humiliation, but the people refused to help him, saying that lazy people did not deserve alms. On night, hunger gnawed painfully at our children. especially the youngest, who tried hopelessly to nurse on my dry breast. My husband's expression changed and he left the house under the cover of the night. He entered the monastery's bin and carried out a bushel of wheat. As he emerged, the monks woke up from their slumber and arrested him after beating him mercilessly. At dawn they brought him to the Emir and complained that he came to the monastery to steal the golden vases of the altar. He was placed in prison and hanged the second day. He was trying to fill the stomachs of his little hungry one with the wheat he had raised by his own labour, but the Emir killed him and used his flesh as food to fill the stomachs of the birds and the beasts." Having spoken in this manner, she left me alone in a sorrowful plight and departed.

I stood there before the graves like a speaker suffering wordlessness while trying to recite a eulogy. I was speechless, but my falling tears substitute for my words and spoke for my soul. My spirit rebelled when I attempted to meditate a while, because the soul is like a flower that folds its petals when dark comes, and breathes not its fragrance into the phantoms of the night. I felt as if the earth that enfolded the victims of oppression in that lonely place were filling my ears with sorrowful tunes of suffering souls, and inspiring me to talk. I resorted to silence, but if the people understood what silence reveals to them, they would have been as close to God as the flowers of the valleys. If the flames of my sighing soul had touched the trees, they would have moved from their places and marched like a strong army to fight the Emir with their branches and tear down the monastery upon the heads of those priests and monks. I stood there watching, and felt that the sweet feeling of mercy and the bitterness of sorrow were pouring from my heart upon the newly dug graves – a grave of a young man who sacrificed his life in defending a weak maiden, whose life and honour he had saved from between the paws and teeth of a savage human; a youth whose head was cut off in reward for his bravery; and his sword was planted upon his grave by the one he saved, as a symbol of heroism before the face of the sun that shines upon an empire laden with stupidity and corruption. A grave of a young woman whose heart was inflamed with love before her body was taken by greed, usurped by lust, and stoned by tyranny.... She kept her faith until death; her lover placed flowers upon her grave to speak through their withering hours of those souls whom Love had selected and blessed among a people blinded by earthly substance and muted by ignorance. A grave of a miserable man, weakened by hard labour in the monastery's land, who asked for bread to feed his hungry little ones, and was refused. He resorted to begging, but the people took no heed. When his soul led him to restore a small part of the crop which he had raised and gathered, he was arrested and beaten to death. His poor widow erected a cross upon his head as a witness in the silence of the night before the stars of heaven to testify against those priests who converted the kind teaching of Christ into sharp swords by which they cut the people's necks and tore the bodies of the weak.

The sun disappeared behind the horizon as if tiring of the world's troubles and loathing the people's submission. At that moment the evening began to weave a delicate veil from the sinews of silence and spread it upon Nature's body. I stretched my hand toward the graves, pointing at their symbols, lifted my eyes toward heaven and cried out, "Oh, Bravery, this is your sword, buried now in the earth! Oh, Love, these are your flowers, scorched by fire! Oh, Lord Jesus, this is Thy cross, submerged in the obscurity of the night!"

Khalil the Heretic

Part One

Sheik Abbas was looked upon as a prince by the people of a solitary village in North Lebanon. His mansion stood in the midst of those poor villagers' huts like a healthy giant amidst the sickly dwarfs. He lived amid luxury while they pursued an existence of penury. They obeyed him and bowed reverently before him as he spoke to them. It seemed as though the power of mind had appointed him its official interpreter and spokesman. His anger would make them tremble and scatter like autumn leaves before a strong wind. If he were to slap one's face, it would be heresy on the individual's part to move or lift his head or make any attempt to discover why the blow had come. If he smiled at a man, the villagers would consider the person thus honoured as the most fortunate. The people's fear and surrender to Sheik Abbas were not due to weakness; however, their poverty and need of him had brought about this state of continual humiliation. Even the huts they lived in and the fields they cultivated were owned by Sheik Abbas who had inherited them from his ancestors.

The farming of the land and the sowing of the seeds and the gathering of wheat were all done under the supervision of the Sheik who, in reward for their toil, compensated them with a small portion of the crop which barely kept them from falling as victims of gnawing starvation.

Often many of them were in need of bread before the crop was reaped, and they came to Sheik Abbas and asked him with pouring tears to advance them a few piastres or a bushel of wheat and the Sheik gladly granted their request for he knew that they would pay their debts doubly when harvest time came. Thus those people remained obligated all their lives, left a legacy of debts to their children and were submissive to their master whose anger they had always feared and whose friendship and good will they had constantly but unsuccessfully endeavoured to win.

Part Two

Winter came and brought heavy snow and strong winds; the valleys and the fields became empty of all things except leafless trees which stood as spectres of death above the lifeless plains.

Having stored the products of the land in the Sheik's bins and filled his vases with the wine of the vineyards, the villagers retreated to their huts to spend a portion of their lives idling by the fireside and commemorating the glory of the past ages and relating to one another the tales of weary days and long nights.

The old year had just breathed its last into the grey sky. The night had arrived during which the New Year would be crowned and placed upon the throne of the Universe. The snow began to fall heavily and the whistling winds were racing from the lofty mountains down to the abyss and blowing the snow into heaps to be stored away in the valleys.

The trees were shaking under the heavy storms and the fields and knolls were covered with a white floor upon which Death was writing vague lines and effacing them. The mists stood as partitions between the scattered villages by the sides of the valleys. The lights that flickered through the windows of those wretched huts disappeared behind the thick veil of Nature's wrath.

Fear penetrated the fellahin's hearts and the animals stood by their mangers in the sheds, while the dogs were hiding in the corners. One could hear the voices of the screaming winds and thundering of the storms resounding from the depths of the valleys. It seemed as if Nature were enraged by the passing of the old year and trying to wrest revenge from those peaceful souls by fighting with weapons of cold and frost.

That night under the raging sky, a young man was attempting to walk the winding trail that connected Deir Kizhaya with Sheik Abbas' village. The youth's limbs were numbed with cold, while pain and hunger usurped him of his strength. The black raiment he wore was bleached with the falling snow, as if he were shrouded in death before the hour of his death had come. He was struggling against the wind. His progress was difficult, and he took but a few steps forward with each effort. He called for help and then stood silent, shivering in the cold night. He had slim hope, withering between great despair and deep sorrow. He was like a bird with a broken wing, who fell in a stream whose whirlpools carried him down to the depths.

The young man continued walking and falling until his blood stopped circulating and he collapsed. He uttered a terrible sound . . . the voice of a soul who encountered the hollow face of Death . . . a voice of dying youth, weakened by man and trapped by nature . . . a voice of the love of existence in the space of nothingness.

Part Three

On the north side of that village, in the midst of the wind-torn fields, stood the solitary home of a woman named Rachel, and her daughter Miriam who had not then attained the age of eighteen. Rachel was the widow of Samaan Ramy, who was found slain six years earlier, but the law of man did not find the murderer.

Like the rest of the Lebanese widows, Rachel sustained life through long, hard work. During the harvest season, she would look for ears of corn left behind by others in the field, and in Autumn she gathered the remnants of some forgotten fruits in the gardens. In Winter she spun wool and made raiment for which she received a few piastres or a bushel of grain. Miriam, her daughter, was a beautiful girl who shared with her mother the burden of toil.

That bitter night the two women were sitting by the fireplace whose warmth was weakened by the frost and whose firebrands were buried beneath the ashes. By their side was a flickering lamp that sent its yellow, dimmed rays into the heart of darkness like a prayer that sends phantoms of hope into the hearts of the sorrowful.

Midnight had come and they were listening to the wailing winds outside. Every now and then Miriam would get up, open the small transom and look toward the obscured sky, and then she would return to her chair worried and frightened by the raging elements. Suddenly Miriam started, as if she had awakened from a swoon of deep slumber. She looked anxiously toward her mother and said, "Did you hear that, Mother? Did you hear a voice calling for help?" The mother listened a moment and said, "I hear nothing but the crying wind, my daughter." Then Miriam exclaimed, "I heard a voice deeper than the thundering heaven and more sorrowful than the wailing of the tempest."

Having uttered these words. she stood up and opened the door and listened for a moment. Then she said, "I hear it again, Mother!" Rachel hurried toward the frail door and after a moment's hesitation she said, "And I hear it, too. Let us go and see."

She wrapped herself with a long robe, opened the door and walked out cautiously, while Miriam stood at the door, the wind blowing her long hair.

Having forced her way a short distance through the snow, Rachel stopped and shouted out, "Who is calling . . . where are you?" There was no answer; then she repeated the same words again and again, but she heard naught except thunder. Then she courageously advanced forward, looking in every direction. She had walked for some time, when she found some deep footprints upon the snow; she followed them fearfully and in a few moments found a human body lying before her on the snow, like a patch on a white dress. As she approached him and leaned his head over her knees, she felt his pulse that bespoke his slowing heart beats and his slim chance in life. She turned her face toward the hut and called, "Come, Miriam, come and help me, I have found him!" Miriam rushed out and followed her mother's footprints, while shivering with cold and trembling with fear. As she reached the place and saw the youth lying motionless, she cried with an aching voice. The mother put her hands under his armpits, calmed Miriam and said, "Fear not, for he is still living; hold the lower edge of his cloak and let us carry him home."

Confronted with the strong wind and heavy snow, the two women carried the youth and started toward the hut. As they reached the little haven, they laid him down by the fireplace. Rachel commenced rubbing his numbed hands and Miriam drying his hair with the end of her dress. The youth began to move after a few minutes. His eyelids quivered and he took a deep sigh – a sigh that brought the hope of his safety into the hearts of the merciful women. They removed his shoes and took off his black robe. Miriam looked at her mother and said, "Observe his raiment, Mother; these clothes are worn by the monks." After feeding the fire with a bundle of dry sticks, Rachel looked at her daughter with perplexity and said, "The monks do not leave their convent on such a terrible night." And Miriam inquired, "But he has no hair on his face; the monks wear beards." The mother gazed at him with eyes full of mercy and maternal love; then she turned to her daughter and said, "It makes no difference whether he is a monk or a criminal; dry his feet well, my daughter." Rachel opened a closet, took from it a jar of wine and poured some in an earthenware bowl. Miriam held his head while the mother gave him some of it to stimulate his heart. As he sipped the wine he opened his eyes for the first time and gave his rescuers a sorrowful look mingled with tears of gratitude – the look of a human who felt the smooth touch of life after having been gripped in the sharp claws of death – a look of great hope after hope had died. Then he bent his head, and his lips trembled when he uttered the words, "May God bless both of you." Rachel placed her hand upon his shoulder and said, "Be calm, brother. Do not tire yourself with talking until you gain strength." And Miriam added, "Rest your head on this pillow, brother, and we will place you closer to the fire." Rachel refilled the bowl with wine and gave it to him. She looked at her daughter and said, "Hang his robe by the fire so it will dry." Having executed her mother's command, she returned and commenced looking at him mercifully, as if she wanted to help him by pouring into his heart all the warmth of her soul. Rachel brought two loaves of bread with some preserves and dry fruits; she sat by him and began to feed him small morsels, as a mother feeds her little child. At this time he felt stronger and sat up on the hearth mat while the red flames of fire reflected upon his sad face. His eyes brightened and he shook his head slowly, saying, "Mercy and cruelty are both wrestling in the human heart like the mad elements in the sky of this terrible night, but mercy shall overcome cruelty because it is divine, and the terror alone, of this night, shall pass away when daylight comes." Silence prevailed for a minute and then he added with a whispering voice, "A human hand drove me into desperation and a human hand rescued me; how severe man is, and how merciful man is!" And Rachel inquired, "How ventured you, brother, to leave the convent on such a terrible night, when even the beasts do not venture forth?"

The youth shut his eyes as if he wanted to restore his tears back into the depths of his heart, whence they came, and he said, "The animals have their caves, and the birds of the sky their nests, but the son of man has not place to rest his head." Rachel retorted, "That is what Jesus said about himself." And the young man resumed, "This is the answer for every man who wants to follow the Spirit and the Truth in this age of falsehood, hypocrisy and corruption."

After a few moments of contemplation, Rachel said, "But there are many comfortable rooms in the convent, and the coffers are full of gold, and all kinds of provisions. The sheds of the convent are stocked with fat calves and sheep; what made you leave such haven in this deathly night?" The youth sighed deeply and said, "I left that place because I hated it." And Rachel rejoined, "A monk in a convent is like a soldier in the battlefield who is required to obey the orders of his leader regardless of their nature. I heard that a man could not become a monk unless he did away with his will, his thoughts, his desires, and all that pertains to the mind. But a good priest does not ask his monks to do unreasonable things. How could the head priest of Deir Kizhaya ask you to give up your life to the storms and snow?" And he remarked, "In the opinion of the head priest, a man cannot become a monk unless he is blind and ignorant, senseless and dumb. I left the convent because I am a sensible man who can see, feel, and hear."

Miriam and Rachel stared at him as if they had found in his face a hidden secret; after a moment of meditation the mother said, "Will a man who sees and hears go out on a night that blinds the eyes and deafens the ears?" And the youth sated quietly, "I was expelled from the convent." "Expelled!" exclaimed Rachel; and Miriam repeated the same word in unison with her mother.

He lifted his head, regretting his words, for he was afraid lest their love and sympathy be converted into hatred and disrespect; but when he looked at them and found the rays of mercy still emanating from their eyes, and their bodies vibrating with anxiety to learn further, his voice choked and he continued, "Yes, I was expelled form the convent because I could not dig my grave with my own hands, and my heart grew weary of lying and pilfering. I was expelled form the convent because my soul refused to enjoy the bounty of a people who surrendered themselves to ignorance. I was driven away because I could not find rest in the comfortable rooms, built with the money of the poor fellahin. My stomach could not hold bread baked with the tears of the orphans. My lips could not utter prayers sold for gold and food by the heads to the simple and faithful people. I was expelled from the convent like a filthy leper because I was repeating to the monks the rules that qualified them to their present position."

Silence prevailed while Rachel and Miriam were contemplating his words and gazing at him, when they asked, "Are your father and mother living?"

And he responded, "I have no father or mother now a place that is my home." Rachel drew a deep sigh and Miriam turned her face toward the wall to hide hr merciful and loving tears.

As a withering flower is brought back to life by dew drops that dawn pours into its begging petals, so the youth's anxious heart was enlivened by his benefactor's affection and kindness. He looked at them as a soldier looks upon his liberators who rescue him from the grip of the enemy, and he resumed, "I lost my parents before I reached the age of seven. The village priest took me to Deir Kizhaya and left me at the disposal of the monks who were happy to take me in and put me in charge of the cows and sheep, which I led each day to the pasture. When I attained the age of fifteen, they put on me this black robe and led me into the altar whereupon the head priest addressed me saying, 'Swear by the name of God and all saints, and make a vow to live a virtuous life of poverty and obedience.' I repeated the words before I realized their significance or comprehended his own interpretation of poverty, virtue and obedience.

"My name was Khalil, and since that time the monks addressed me as Brother Mobarak, but they never did treat me as a brother. They ate the most palatable foods and drank the finest wine, while I lived on dry vegetables and water, mixed with tears. They slumbered in soft beds while I slept on a stone slab in a dark and cold room by the shed. Oftentimes I asked myself, 'When will my heart stop craving for the food they eat and the wine they eat? When will I cease to tremble with fear before my superiors?' But all my hopes were in vain, for I was kept in the same state; and in addition to caring for the cattle, I was obliged to move heavy stones on my shoulders and to dig pits and ditches. I sustained life on a few morsels of bread given to me in reward for my toil. I knew of no other place to which I might go, and the clergymen at the convent had caused me to abhor everything they were doing. They had poisoned my mind until I commenced to think that the whole world was an ocean of sorrows and miseries and that the convent was the only port of salvation. But when I discovered the source of their food and gold, I was happy that I did not share it."

Khalil straightened himself and looked about with wonder, as if he had found something beautiful standing before him in that wretched hut. Rachel and Miriam remained silent and he proceeded, "God, who took my father and exiled me as an orphan to the convent, did not want me to spend all my life walking blindly toward a dangerous jungle; nor did He wish me to be a miserable slave for the rest of my life. God opened my eyes and ears and showed me the bright light and made me hear Truth when Truth was talking."

Rachel thought aloud, "Is there any light, other than the sun, that shines over all the people? Are human beings capable of understanding the Truth?" Khalil returned, "The true light is that which emanates from within man, and reveals the secrets of the heart to the soul, making it happy and contented with life. Truth is like the stars; it does not appear except from behind obscurity of the night. Truth is like all beautiful things in the world; it does not disclose its desirability except to those who first feel the influence of falsehood. Truth is a deep kindness that teaches us to be content in our everyday life and share with the people the same happiness."

Rachel rejoined, "Many are those who live according to their goodness, and many are those who believe that compassion to others is the shadow of the law of God to man; but still, they do not rejoice in life, for they remain miserable until death." Khalil replied, "Vain are the beliefs and teachings that make man miserable, and false is the goodness that leads him into sorrow and despair, for it is man's purpose to be happy on this earth and lead the way to felicity and preach its gospel wherever he goes. He who does not see the kingdom of heaven in this life will never see it in the coming life. We came not into this life by exile, but we came as innocent creatures of God, to learn how to worship the holy and eternal spirit and seek the hidden secrets within ourselves from the beauty of life. This is the truth which I have learned from the teachings of the Nazarene. This is the light that came from within me and showed me the dark corners of the convent that threatened my life. This is the deep secret which the beautiful valleys and fields revealed to me when I was hungry, sitting lonely and weeping under the shadow of the trees.

"This is the religion as the convent should impart it; as God wished it; as Jesus taught it. One day, as my soul became intoxicated with the heavenly intoxication of Truth's beauty, I stood bravely before the monks who were gathering in the garden, and criticized their wrong deeds saying, 'Why do you spend your days here and enjoy the bounty of the poor, whose bread you eat was made with the sweat of their bodies and the tears of their hearts? Why are you living in the shadow of parasitism, segregating yourselves from the people who are in need of knowledge? Why are you depriving the country your help? Jesus has sent you as lambs amongst the wolves; what has made you as wolves amongst the lambs? Why are you fleeing from mankind and from God who created you? If you are better than the people who walk in the procession of life, you should go to them and better their lives; but if you think they are better than you, you should desire to learn from them. How do you take an oath and vow to live in poverty, then forget what you have said and live in luxury? How do you swear an obedience to God and then revolt against all that religion means? How do you adopt virtue as your rule when your hearts are full of lusts? You pretend that you are killing your bodies, but in fact you are killing your souls. You feign to abhor the earthly things, but your hearts are swollen with greed. You have the people believe in you as religious teachers; truly speaking you are like busy cattle who divert themselves from knowledge by grazing in a green and beautiful pasture. Let us restore to the needy the vast land of the convent and give back to them the silver and gold we took from them. Let us disperse from our aloofness and serve the weak who made us strong, and cleanse the country in which we live. Let us teach this miserable nation to smile and rejoice with heaven's bounty and glory of life and freedom.

"The people's tears are more beautiful and God-joined than the ease and tranquillity to which you have accustomed yourselves in this place. The sympathy that touches the neighbour's heart is more supreme than the hidden virtue in the unseen corners of the convent. A word of compassion to the weak criminal or prostitute is nobler than the long prayer which we repeat emptily every day in the temple.'"

At this time Khalil took a deep breath. Then he lifted his eyes toward Rachel and Miriam saying, "I was saying all of these things to the monks and they were listening with an air of perplexity, as if they could not believe that a young man would dare stand before them and utter such bold words. When I finished, one of the monks approached me and angrily said to me, 'How dare you talk in such fashion in our presence?' And another one came laughing and added, 'Did you learn all this from the cows and pigs you tended in the fields?' And a third one stood up and threatened me saying, 'You shall be punished, heretic!' Then they dispersed as though running away from a leper. Some of them complained to the head priest who summoned me before him at eventide. The monks took delight in anticipation of my suffering, and there was glee on their faces when I was ordered to be scourged and put into prison for forty days and nights. They lad me into the dark cell where I spent the time lying on that grave without seeing the light. I could not tell the end of the night from the beginning of the day, and could feel nothing but crawling insects and the earth under me. I could hear naught save the tramping of their feet when my morsel of bread and dish of water mixed with vinegar were brought to me at great intervals.

"When I came out of the prison I was weak and frail, and the monks believed that they had cured me of thinking and that they had killed my soul's desire. They thought that hunger and thirst had choked the kindness which God placed in my heart. In my forty days of solitude I endeavoured to find a method by which I could help these monks to see the light and hear the true song of life, but all of my ponderings were in vain, for the thick veil which the long ages had woven around their eyes could not be torn away in a short time; and the mortar with which ignorance had cemented their ears was hardened and could not be removed by the touch of soft fingers."

Silence prevailed for a moment, and then Miriam looked at her mother as if asking permission to speak. She said, "You must have talked to the monks again, if they selected this terrible night in which to banish you from the convent. They should learn to be kind even to their enemies."

Khalil returned, "This evening, as the thunder storms and warring elements raged in the sky, I withdrew myself from the monks who were crouching about the fire, telling tales and humorous stories. When they saw me alone they commenced to place their wit at my expense. I was reading my Gospel and contemplating the beautiful sayings of Jesus that made me forget for the time the enraged nature and belligerent elements of the sky, when they approached me with a new spirit of ridicule. I ignored them by occupying myself and looking through the window, but they became furious because my silence dried the laughter of their hearts and the taunting of their lips. One of them said, 'What are you reading, Great Reformer?' In response to his inquiry, I opened my book and read aloud the following passage, 'But when he saw many of the Pharisees and Saducees come to his baptism, he said unto them, 'O generation of vipers, who hath warned you to flee from the wrath to come? Bring forth therefore fruits for repentance; And think not to say within yourselves, 'We have Abraham to our father;' for I say unto you, that God is able of these stones to raise the children unto Abraham. And now also the axe is laid unto the root of the trees; therefore every tree which bringeth not forth good fruit is hewn down, and cast into the fire.'

"As I read to them these words of John the Baptist, the monks became silent as if an invisible hand strangled their spirits, but they took false courage and commenced laughing. One of them said, 'We have read these words many times, and we are not in need of a cow grazier to repeat them to us.'"

"I protested, 'If you had read these words and comprehended their meaning, these poor villagers would not have frozen or starved to death.' When I said this, one of the monks slapped my face as if I had spoken evil of the priests; another kicked me and a third took the book from me and a fourth one called the head priest who hurried to the scene shaking with anger. He cried out, 'Arrest this rebel and drag him from this sacred place, and let the storm's fury teach him obedience. Take him away and let nature do unto him the will of God, and then wash your hands of the poisonous germs of heresy infesting his raiment. If he should return pleading for forgiveness, do not open the door for him, for the viper will not become a dove if placed in a cage, nor will the briar bear figs if planted in the vineyards.'

"In accordance with the command, I was dragged out by the laughing monks. Before they locked the door behind me, I heard one saying, 'Yesterday you were king of cows and pigs, and today you are dethroned, Oh Great Reformer; go now and be the king of wolves and teach them how to live in their lairs.' "

Khalil sighed deeply, then turned his face and looked toward the flaming fire. With a sweet and loving voice, and with a pained countenance he said, "Thus was I expelled from the convent, and thus did the monks deliver me over to the hands of Death. I fought through the night blindly; the heavy wind was tearing my robe and the piling snow was trapping me feet and pulling me down until I fell, crying desperately for help. I felt that no one heard me except Death, but a power which is all knowledge and mercy had heard my cry. That power did not want me to die before I had learned what is left of life's secrets. That power sent you both to me to save my life from the depth of the abyss and non-existence."

Rachel and Miriam felt as if their spirits understood the mystery of his soul, and they became his partners in feeling and understanding. Notwithstanding her will, Rachel stretched forth and touched his hand gently while tears coursed down from her eyes, and she said, "He who has been chosen by heaven as a defender of Truth will not perish by heaven's own storms and snow." And Miriam added, "The storms and snow may kill the flowers, but cannot deaden the seeds, for the snow keeps them warm from the killing frost."

Khalil's face brightened upon hearing those words of encouragement, and he said, "If you do not look upon me as a rebel and an heretic as the monks did, the persecution which I have sustained in the convent is the symbol of an oppressed nation that has not yet attained knowledge; and this night in which I was on the verge of death is like a revolution that precedes full justice. And from a sensitive woman's heart springs the happiness of mankind, and from the kindness of her noble spirit comes mankind's affection."

He closed his eyes and leaned down on the pillow; the two women did not bother him with further conversation for they knew that the weariness cause by long exposure had allured and captured his eyes. Khalil slept like a lost child who had finally found safety in his mother's arms.

Rachel and her daughter slowly walked to their bed and sat there watching him as if they had found in his trouble-torn face an attraction bringing their souls and hearts closer to him. And the mother whispered, saying, "There is a strange power in his closed eyes that speaks in silence and stimulates the soul's desires."

And Miriam rejoined, "His hands, Mother, are like those of Christ in the Church." The mother replied, "His face possesses at the same time a woman's tenderness and a man's boldness."

And the wings of slumber carried the two women's spirits into the world of dream, and the fire went down and turned into ashes, while the light of the oil lamp dimmed gradually and disappeared. The fierce tempest continued its roar, and the obscured sky spread layers of snow, and the strong wind scattered them to the right and the left.

Part Four

Five days passed, and the sky was still heavy with snow, burying the mountains and prairies relentlessly. Khalil made three attempts to resume his journey toward the plains, but Rachel restrained him each time, saying, "Do not give up your life to the blind elements, brother; remain here, for the bread that suffices two will also feed three, and the fire will still be burning after your departure as it was before your arrival. We are poor, brother, but like the rest of the people, we live our lives before the face of the sun and mankind, and God gives us our daily bread."

And Miriam was begging him with her kind glances, and pleading with her deep sighs, for since he entered the hut she felt the presence of a divine power in her soul sending forth life and light into her heart and awakening new affection in the Holy of Holies of her spirit. For the first time she experienced the feeling which made her heart like a white rose that sips the dew drops from the dawn and breathes its fragrance into the endless firmament.

There is no affection purer and more soothing to the spirit than the one hidden in the heart of a maiden who awakens suddenly and fills her own spirit with heavenly music that makes her days like poets' dreams and her nights prophetic. There is no secret in the mystery of life stronger and more beautiful than that attachment which converts the silence of a virgin's spirit into a perpetual awareness that makes a person forget the past, for it kindles fiercely in the heart the sweet and overwhelming hope of the coming future.

The Lebanese woman distinguishes herself from the woman of other nations by her simplicity. The manner in which she is trained restricts her progress educationally, and stands as a hindrance to her future. Yet for this reason, she finds herself inquiring of herself as to the inclination and mystery of her heart. The Lebanese young woman is like a spring that comes out from the heart of the earth and follows its course through the winding depressions, but since it cannot find an outlet to the sea, it turns into a calm lake that reflects upon its growing surface the glittering stars and the shining moon. Khalil felt the vibration of Miriam's heart twining steadily about his soul, and he knew that the divine torch that illuminated his heart had also touched her heart. He rejoiced for the first time, like a parched brook greeting the rain, but he blamed himself for his haste, believing that this spiritual understanding would pass like a cloud when he departed from the village. He often spoke to himself saying, "What is this mystery that plays so great a part in our lives? What is this Law that drives us into a rough road and stops us just before we reach the mountain top, smiling and glorying, then suddenly we are cast to the depths of the valley, weeping and suffering? What is this life that embraces us like a lover one day, and fights us like an enemy the second day? Was I not persecuted yesterday? Did I not survive hunger and thirst and suffering and mockery for the sake of the Truth which heaven had awakened in my heart? Did I not tell the monks that happiness through Truth is the will and the purpose of God in man? Then what is this fear? And why do I close my eyes to the light that emanates from that young woman's eyes? I am expelled and she is poor, but is it on bread only that man can live? Are we not, between famine and plenty, like trees between winter and summer? But what would Rachel say if she knew that my heart and her daughter's heart came to an understanding in silence, and approached close to each other and neared the circle of the Supreme Light? What would she say if she discovered that the young man whose life she saved longed to gaze upon her daughter? What would the simple villagers say if they knew that a young man, reared in the convent, came to their village by necessity and expulsion, and desired to live near a beautiful maiden? Will they listen to me if I tell them that he who leaves the convent to live amongst them is like a bird that flies from the bruising walls of the cage to the light of freedom? What will Sheik Abbas say if he hears my story? What will the priest of the village do if he learns of the cause of my expulsion?"

Khalil was talking to himself in this fashion while sitting by the fireplace, meditating the flames, symbol of his love; and Miriam was stealing a glance now and then at his face and reading his dreams through his eyes, and hearing the echo of his thoughts, and feeling the touch of his love, even though no word was uttered.

One night, as he stood by the small transom that faced the valleys where the trees and rocks were shrouded with white coverings, Miriam came and stood by him, looking at the sky. As their eyes turned and met, he drew a deep sigh and shut his eyes as if his soul were sailing in the spacious sky looking for a word. He found no word necessary, for the silence spoke for them. Miriam ventured, "Where will you go when the snow meets the stream and the paths are dry?" His eyes opened, looking beyond the horizon, and he explained, "I shall follow the path to wherever my destiny and my mission for truth shall take me." Miriam sighed sadly and offered, "Why will you not remain here and live close to us? Is it that you are obliged to go elsewhere?" He was moved by her kindness and sweet words, but protested, "The villagers here will not accept an expelled monk as their neighbour, and will not permit him to breathe the air they breathe because they believe that the enemy of the convent is an infidel, cursed by God and His saints." Miriam resorted to silence, for the Truth that pained her prevented further talk. Then Khalil turned aside and explained, "Miriam, these villagers are taught by those in authority to hate everyone who thinks freely; they are trained to remain afar from those whose minds soar aloft; God does not like to be worshipped by an ignorant man who imitates someone else; if I remained in this village and asked the people to worship as they please, they would say that I am an infidel disobeying the authority that was given to the priest by God. If I asked them to listen and hear the voices of their hearts and do according to the will of the spirit within, they would say I am an evil man who wants them to do away with the clergy that God placed between heaven and earth." Khalil looked straight into Miriam's eyes, and with a voice that bespoke the sound of silver strings said, "But, Miriam, there is a magic power in this village that possesses me and engulfs my soul; a power so divine that it causes me to forget my pain. In this village I met Death to his very face, and in this place my soul embraced God's spirit. In this village there is a beautiful flower grown over the lifeless grass; its beauty attracts my heart and it fragrance fills its domain. Shall I leave this important flower and go out preaching the ideas that caused my expulsion from the convent, or shall I remain by the side of that flower and dig a grave and bury my thoughts and truths among its neighbouring thorns? What shall I do, Miriam?" Upon hearing these words, she shivered like a lily before the frolicsome breeze of the dawn. Her heart glowed through her eyes when she faltered, "We are both in the hands of a mysterious ad merciful power. Let it do its will."

At that moment the two hearts joined and thereafter both spirits were one burning torch illuminating their lives.

Part Five

Since the beginning of the creation and up to our present time, certain clans, rich by inheritance, in co-operation with the clergy, had appointed themselves the administrators of the people. It is an old, gaping wound in the heart of society that cannot be removed except by intense removal of ignorance.

The man who acquires his wealth by inheritance builds his mansion with the weak poor's money. The clergyman erects his temple upon the graves and bones of the devoted worshippers. The prince grasps the fellah's arms while the priest empties his pocket; the ruler looks upon the sons of the fields with frowning face, and the bishop consoles them with his smile, and between the frown of the tiger and the smile of the wolf the flock is perished; the ruler claims himself as king of the law, and the priest as the representative of God, and between these two, the bodies are destroyed and the souls wither into nothing.

In Lebanon, that mountain rich in sunlight and poor in knowledge, the noble and the priest joined hands to exploit the farmer who ploughed the land and reaped the crop in order to protect himself from the sword of the ruler and the curse of the priest. The rich man in Lebanon stood proudly by his palace and shouted at the multitudes saying, "The Sultan had appointed me as your lord." And the priest stands before the altar saying, "God has delegated me as an executive of your souls." But the Lebanese resorted to silence, for the dead could not talk.

Sheik Abbas had friendship in his heart for the clergymen, because they were his allies in choking the people's knowledge and reviving the spirit of stern obedience among his workers.

That evening, when Khalil and Miriam were approaching the throne of Love, and Rachel was looking upon them with the eyes of affection, Father Elias informed Sheik Abbas that the head priest had expelled a rebellious young man from the convent and that he had taken refuge at the house of Rachel, the widow of Samaan Ramy. And the priest was not satisfied with the little information he gave the Sheik, but commented, "The demon they chased out of the convent cannot become an angel in this village, and the fig tree which is hewn and cast into the fire, does not bear fruit while burning. If we wish to clean this village of the filth of this beast, we must drive him away as the monks did." And the Sheik answered, "Are you certain that the young man will be a bad influence upon our people? Is it not better for us to keep him and make him a worker in our vineyards? We are in need of strong men."

The priest's face showed his disagreement. Combing his beard with his fingers, he said shrewdly, "If he were fit to work, he would not have been expelled from the convent. A student who works in the convent, and who happened to spend last night at my house, informed me that this young man had violated the rules of the head priest by preaching danger-ridden ideas among the monks, and he quoted him as saying, 'Restore the fields and the vineyards and the silver of the convent to the poor and scatter it in all directions; and help the people who are in need of knowledge; by thus doing, you will please your Father in Heaven.'"

On hearing these words, Sheik Abbas leaped to his feet, and like a tiger making ready to strike the victim, he walked to the door and called to the servants, ordering them to report immediately. Three men entered, and the Sheik commanded, "In the house of Rachel, the widow of Samaan Ramy, there is a young man wearing a monk's raiment. Tie him and bring him here. If that woman objects to his arrest, drag her out by her braided hair over the snow and bring her with him, for he who helps evil is evil himself." The men bowed obediently and hurried to Rachel's home while the priest and the Sheik discussed the type of punishment to be awarded to Khalil and Rachel.

Part Six

The day was over and the night had come spreading its shadow over those wretched huts, heavily laden with snow. The stars finally appeared in the sky, like hopes in the coming eternity after the suffering of death's agony. The doors and windows were closed and the lamps were lighted. The fellahin sat by the fireside, warming their bodies. Rachel, Miriam and Khalil were seated at a rough wooden table eating their evening meal when there was a knock at the door and three men entered. Rachel and Miriam were frightened, but Khalil remained calm, as if he awaited the coming of those men. One of the Sheik's servants walked toward Khalil, laid his hand upon his shoulder and asked, "Are you the one who was expelled from the convent?" And Khalil responded, "Yes, I am the one, what do you want?"

The man replied, "We are ordered to arrest you and take you with us to Sheik Abbas' home, and if you object we shall drag you out like a butchered sheep over the snow."

Rachel turned pale as she exclaimed, "What crime has he committed, and why do you want to tie him and drag him out?" The two women pleaded with tearful voices, saying, "He is one individual in the hands of three and it is cowardly of you to make him suffer." The men became enraged and shouted, "Is there any woman in this village who opposes the Sheik's order?" And he drew forth a rope and started to tie Khalil's hands. Khalil lifted his head proudly, and a sorrowful smile appeared on his lips when he said, "I feel sorry for you men, because you are a strong and blind instrument in the hands of a man who oppresses the weak with the strength of your arms. You are slaves of ignorance. Yesterday I was a man like you, but tomorrow you shall be free in mind as I am now. Between us there is a deep precipice that chokes my calling voice and hides my reality from you, and you cannot hear or see. Here I am, tie my hands and do as you please." The three men were moved by his talk and it seemed that his voice had awakened in them a new spirit, but the voice of Sheik Abbas still rang in their minds, warning them to complete the mission. They bound his hands and led him out silently with a heavy conscience. Rachel and Miriam followed them to the Sheik's home, like the daughters of Jerusalem who followed Christ to Mount Calvary.

Part Seven

Regardless of its import, news travels swiftly among the fellahin in the small villages, because their absence from the realm of society makes them anxious and busy in discussing the happenings of their limited environs. In winter, when the fields are slumbering under the quilts of snow, and when human life is taking refuge and warming itself by the fireside, the villagers become most inclined to learn of current news in order to occupy themselves.

It was not long after Khalil was arrested, when the story spread like a contagious disease amongst the villagers. They left their huts and hurried like an army from every direction into the home of Sheik Abbas. When Khalil's feet stepped into the Sheik's home, the residence was crowded with men, women and children who were endeavouring for a glance at the infidel who was expelled from the convent. They were also anxious to see Rachel and her daughter, who had helped Khalil in spreading the hellish disease if heresy in the pure sky of their village.

The Sheik took the seat of judgment and beside him sat Father Elias, while the throng was gazing at the pinioned youth who stood bravely before them. Rachel and Miriam were standing behind Khalil and trembling with fear. But what could fear do to the heart of a woman who found Truth and followed him? What could the scorn of the crowd do to the soul of a maiden who had been awakened by Love? Sheik Abbas looked at the young man, and with a thundering voice he interrogated him saying, "What is your name, man?" "Khalil is my name," answered the youth. The Sheik returned, "Who are your father and mother and relatives, and where were you born?" Khalil turned toward the fellahin, who looked upon him with hateful eyes, and said, "The oppressed poor are my clan and my relatives, and this vast country is my birthplace."

Sheik Abbas, with an air of ridicule, said, "Those people whom you claim as kin demand that you be punished, and the country you assert as your birthplace objects to your being a member of its people." Khalil replied, "The ignorant nations arrest their good men and turn them into their despots; and a country, ruled by a tyrant, persecutes those who try to free the people from the yoke of slavery. But will a good son leave his mother if she is ill? Will a merciful man deny his brother who is miserable? Those poor men who arrested me and brought me here today are the same ones who surrendered their lives to you yesterday. And this vast earth that disapproves my existence is the one that does not yawn and swallow the greedy despots."

The Sheik uttered a loud laugh, as if wanting to depress the young man's spirit and prevent him from influencing the audience. He turned to Khalil and said impressively, "You cattle grazier, do you think that we will show more mercy than did the monks, who expelled you from the convent? Do you think that we feel pity for a dangerous agitator?" Khalil responded, "It is true that I was a cattle grazier, but I am glad that I was not a butcher. I led my herds to the rich pastures and never grazed them on arid land. I led my animals to pure springs and kept them from contaminated marshes. At eventide I brought them safely to their shed and never left them in the valleys as prey for the wolves. Thus I have treated the animals; and if you had pursued my course and treated human beings as I treated my flock, these poor people would not live in wretched huts and suffer the pangs of poverty, while you are living like Nero in this gorgeous mansion."

The Sheik's forehead glittered with drops of perspiration, and his smirk turned into anger, but he tried to show only calm by pretending that he did not heed Khalil's talk, and he expostulated, pointing at Khalil with his finger, "You are a heretic, and we shall not listen to your ridiculous talk; we summoned you to be tried as a criminal, and you realize that you are in the presence of the Lord off this village who is empowered to represent his Excellency Emir Ameen Shehab. You are standing before Father Elias, the representative of the Holy Church whose teachings you have opposed. Now, defend yourself, or kneel down before these people and we will pardon you and make you a cattle grazier, as you were in the convent." Khalil calmly returned, "A criminal is not to be tried by another criminal, as an atheist will not defend himself before sinners." And Khalil looked at the audience and spoke to them saying, "My brethren, the man whom you call the Lord of your fields, and to whom you have yielded thus long, has brought me to be tried before you in this edifice which he built upon the graves of your forefathers. And the man who became a pastor of your church through your faith, has come to judge me and help to humiliate me and increase my sufferings. You have hurried to this place from every direction to see me suffer and hear me plead for mercy. You have left your huts in order to witness your pinioned son and brother. You have come to see the prey trembling between the paws of a ferocious beast. You came here tonight to view an infidel standing before the judges. I am the criminal and I am the heretic who has been expelled from the convent. The tempest brought me into your village. Listen to my protest, and do not be merciful, but be just, for mercy is bestowed upon the guilty criminal, while justice is all that an innocent man requires.

"I select you now as my jury, because the will of the people is the will of God. Awaken your hearts and listen carefully and then prosecute me according to the dictates of your conscience. You have been told that I am an infidel, but you have not been informed of what crime or sin I have committed. You have seen me tied like a thief, but you have not heard about my offences, for wrongdoings are not revealed in this court, while punishment comes out like thunder. My crime, dear fellowmen, is my understanding of your plight, for I felt the weight of the irons which have been placed upon your necks. My sin is my heartfelt sorrows for your women; it is my sympathy for your children who suck life from your breast mixed with the shadow of death. I am one of you, and my forefathers lived in these valleys and died under the same yolk which is bending your heads now. I believe in God who listens to the call of your suffering souls, and I believe in the Book that makes all of us brothers before the face of heaven. I believe in the teachings that make us all equal, and that render us unpinioned upon this earth, the steeping place of the careful feet of God.

"As I was grazing my cows at the convent, and contemplating the sorrowful condition you tolerate, I heard a desperate cry coming from your miserable homes – a cry of oppressed souls – a cry of broken hearts which are locked in your bodies as slaves to the lord of these fields. As I looked, I found me in the convent and you in the fields, and I saw you as a flock of lambs following a wolf to the lair; and as I stopped in the middle of the road to aid the lambs, I cried for help and the wolf snapped me with his sharp teeth.

"I have sustained imprisonment, thirst, and hunger for the sake of Truth that hurts only the body. I have undergone suffering beyond endurance because I turned your sad sighs into a crying voice that rang and echoed in every corner of the convent. I never felt fear, and my heart never tired, for your painful cry was injecting a new strength into me every day, and my heart was healthy. You may ask yourself now saying, 'When did we ever cry for help, and who dares open his lips?' But I say unto you, your souls are crying every day, and pleading for help every night, but you cannot hear them, for the dying man cannot hear his own heart rattling, while those who are standing by his bedside can surely hear. The slaughtered bird, in spite of his will, dances painfully and unknowingly, but those who witness the dance know what caused it. In what hour of the day do you sigh painfully? Is it in the morning, when love of existence cries at you and tears the veil of slumber off your eyes and leads you like slaves into the fields? Is it at noon, when you wish to sit under a tree to protect yourself from the burning sun? Or at eventide, when you return home hungry, wishing for sustaining food instead of a meagre morsel and impure water? Or at night when fatigue throws you upon your rough bed, and as soon as slumber closes your eyes, you sit up with open eyes, fearing that the Sheik's voice is ringing in your ears?

"In what season of the year do you not lament yourselves? Is it in Spring, when nature puts on her beautiful dress and you go to meet her with tattered raiment? Or in Summer, when you harvest the wheat and gather the sheaves of corn and fill the shelves of your master with the crop, and when the reckoning comes you receive naught but hay and tare? Is it in Autumn, when you pick the fruits and carry the grapes into the wine-press, and in reward for your toil you receive a jar of vinegar and a bushel of acorns? Or in Winter, when you are confined to your huts laden with snow, do you sit by the fire and tremble when the enraged sky urges you to escape from your weak minds?

"This is the life of the poor; this is the perpetual cry I hear. This is what makes my spirit revolt against the oppressors and despise their conduct. When I asked the monks to have mercy upon you, they thought that I was an atheist, and expulsion was my lot. Today I came here to share this miserable life with you, and to mix my tears with yours. Here I am now, in the grip of your worst enemy. Do you realize that this land you are working like slaves was taken from your fathers when the law was written on the sharp edge of the sword? The monks deceived your ancestors and took all their fields and vineyards when the religious rules were written on the lips of the priests. Which man or woman is not influenced by the lord of the fields to do according to the will of the priests? God said, 'With the sweat of thy brow, thou shall eat thy bread.' But Sheik Abbas is eating his bread baked in the years of your lives and drinking his wine mixed with your tears. Did God distinguish this man from the rest of you while in his mother's womb? Or is it your sin that made you his property? Jesus said, 'Gratis you have taken and gratis you shall give. . . . Do not possess gold, nor silver, neither copper.' Then what teachings allow the clergymen to sell their prayers for pieces of gold and silver? In the silence of the night you pray saying, 'Give us today our daily bread.' God has given you this land from which to draw your daily bread, but what authority has He given the monks to take his land and this bread away from you?

"You curse Judas because he sold his Master for a few pieces of silver, but you bless those who sell Him every day. Judas repented and hanged himself for his wrongdoing, but these priests walk proudly, dressed with beautiful robes, resplendent with shining crosses hanging over their chest. You teach your children to love Christ and at the same time you instruct them to obey those who oppose His teachings and violate His law.

"The apostles of Christ were stoned to death in order to revive in you the Holy Spirit, but the monks and the priests are killing that spirit in you so they may live on your pitiful bounty. What persuades you to live such a life in this universe, full of misery and oppression? What prompts you to kneel before that horrible idol which has been erected upon the bones of your fathers? What treasure are you reserving for your posterity?

"Your souls are in the grip of the priests, and your bodies are in the closing jaws of the rulers. What thing in life can you point at and say 'this is mine!' My fellowmen, do you know the priest you fear? He is a traitor who uses the Gospel as a threat to ransom your money. . . a hypocrite wearing a cross and using it as a sword to cut your veins. . . a wolf disguised in lambskin. . . a glutton who respects the tables more than the altars. . . a gold-hungry creature who follows the Denar to the farthest land. . . a cheat pilfering from widows and orphans. He is a queer being, with an eagle's beak, a tiger's clutches, a hyena's teeth and a viper's clothes. Take the Book away from him and tear his raiment off and pluck his beard and do whatever you wish unto him; then place in his hand one Denar, and he will forgive you smilingly.

"Slap his face and spit on him and step on his neck; then invite him to sit at your board. He will immediately forget and untie his belt and gladly fill his stomach with your food.

"Curse him and ridicule him; then send him a jar of wine or a basket of fruit. He will forgive you your sins. When he sees a woman, he turns his face, saying, 'Go from me, Oh, daughter of Babylon.' Then he whispers to himself saying, 'Marriage is better than coveting.' He sees the young men and women walking in the procession of Love, and he lifts his eyes toward heaven and says, 'Vanity of vanities, all is vanity.' And in his solitude he talks to himself saying, 'May the laws and traditions that deny me the joys of life, be abolished.'

"He preaches to the people saying, 'Judge not, lest ye be judged.' But he judges all those who abhor his deeds and sends them to hell before Death separates them from this life.

"When he talks he lifts his head toward heaven, but at the same time, his thoughts are crawling like snakes through your pockets.

"He addresses you as beloved children, but his heart is empty of paternal love, and his lips never smile at a child, nor does he carry an infant between his arms.

"He tells you, while shaking his head, 'Let us keep away from earthly things, for life passes like a cloud.' But if you look thoroughly at him, you will find that he is gripping on to life, lamenting the passing of yesterday, condemning the speed of today, and waiting fearfully for tomorrow.

"He asks you for charity when he has plenty to give; if you grant his request, he will bless you publicly, and if you refuse him, he will curse you secretly.

"In the temple he asks you to help the needy, and about his house the needy are begging for bread, but he cannot see or hear.

"He sells his prayers, and he who does not buy is an infidel, excommunicated from Paradise.

"This is the creature of whom you are afraid. This is the monk who sucks your blood. This is the priest who makes the sign of the Cross with the right hand, and clutches your throat with the left hand.

"This is the pastor whom you appoint as your servant, but he appoints himself as your master.

"This is the shadow that embraces your souls from birth until death.

"This is the man who came to judge me tonight because my spirit revolted against the enemies of Jesus the Nazarene Who loved all and called us brothers, and Who died on the Cross for us."

Khalil felt that there was understanding in the villagers' hearts; his voice brightened and he resumed his discourse saying, "Brethren, you know that Sheik Abbas has been appointed as Master of this village by Emir Shehab, the Sultan's representative and Governor of the Province, but I ask you if anyone has seen that power appoint the Sultan as the god of this country. That Power, my fellowmen, cannot be seen, nor can you hear it talk, but you can feel its existence in the depths of your hearts. It is that Power which you worship and pray for every day saying, 'Our Father which art in heaven.' Yes, your Father Who is in heaven is the one Who appoints Kings and princes, for He is powerful and above all. But do you think that your Father, Who loved you and showed you the right path through

His prophets, desires for you to be oppressed? Do you believe that God, Who brings forth the rain from heaven, and the wheat from the hidden seeds in the heart of the earth, desires for you to be hungry in order that but one man will enjoy His bounty? Do you believe that the Eternal Spirit Who reveals to you the wife's love, the children's pity and the neighbour's mercy, would have upon you a tyrant to enslave you through your life? Do you believe that the Eternal Law that made life beautiful, would send you a man to deny you of that happiness and lead you into the dark dungeon of painful Death? Do you believe that your physical strength, provided you by nature, belongs beyond your body to the rich?

"You cannot believe in all these things, because if you do you will be denying the justice of God who made us all equal, and the light of Truth that shines upon all people of the earth. What makes you struggle against yourselves, heart against body, and help those who enslave you while God has created you free on this earth?

"Are you doing yourselves justice when you lift your eyes towards Almighty God and call him Father, and then turn around, bow your heads before a man, and call him Master?

"Are you contented, as sons of God, with being slaves of man? Did not Christ call you brethren? Yet Sheik Abbas calls you servants. Did not Jesus make you free in Truth and Spirit? Yet the Emir made you slaves of shame and corruption. Did not Christ exalt you to heaven? Then why are you descending to hell? Did He not enlighten your hearts? Then why are you hiding your souls in darkness? God has placed a glowing torch in your hearts that glows in knowledge and beauty, and seeks the secrets of the days and nights; it is a sin to extinguish that torch and bury it in ashes. God has created your spirits with wings to fly in the spacious firmament of Love and Freedom; it is pitiful that you cut your wings with your own hands and suffer your spirits to crawl like insects upon the earth."

Sheik Abbas observed in dismay the attentiveness of the villagers, and attempted to interrupt, but Khalil, inspired, continued, "God has sown in your hearts the seeds of Happiness; it is a crime that you dig those seeds out and throw them wilfully on the rocks so the wind will scatter them and the birds will pick them. God has given you children to rear, to teach them the truth and fill their hearts with the most precious things of existence. He wants you to bequeath upon them the joy of Life and the bounty of Life;

why are they now strangers to their place of birth and cold creatures before the face of the Sun? A father who makes his son a slave is the father who gives his child a stone when he asks for bread. Have you not seen the birds of the sky training their young ones to fly? Why, then, do you teach your children to drag the shackles of slavery? Have you not seen the flowers of the valleys deposit their seeds in the sun-heated earth? Then why do you commit your children to the cold darkness?"

Silence prevailed for a moment, and it seemed as if Khalil's mind were crowded with pain. But now with a low and compelling voice he continued, "The words which I utter tonight are the same expressions that caused my expulsion from the convent. If the lord of your fields and the pastor of your church were to prey upon me and kill me tonight, I will die happy and in peace because I have fulfilled my mission and revealed to you the Truth which demons consider a crime. I have now completed the will of the Almighty God."

There had been a magic message in Khalil's voice that forced the villagers' interest. The women were moved by the sweetness of peace, and their eyes were rich with tears.

Sheik Abbas and Father Elias were shaking with anger. As Khalil finished, he walked a few steps and stopped near Rachel and Miriam. Silence dominated the courtroom, and it seemed as if Khalil's spirit hovered in that vast hall and diverted the souls of the multitude from fearing Sheik Abbas and Father Elias, who sat trembling in annoyance and guilt.

The Sheik stood suddenly and his face was pale. He looked toward the men who were standing about him as he said, "What has become of you, dogs? have your hearts been poisoned? Has you blood stopped running and weakened you so that you cannot leap upon this criminal and cut him to pieces? What awful thing has he done to you?" Having finished reprimanding the men, he raised a sword and started toward the fettered youth.

The Sheik trembled visibly and the sword fell from his hand. He addressed the man saying, "Will a weak servant oppose his Master and benefactor?" And the man responded, "The faithful servant does not share his Master in the committing of crimes; this young man has spoken naught but the truth." Another man stepped forward and assured, "This man is innocent and is worthy of honour and respect." And a woman raised her voice saying, "He did not swear at God or curse any saint; why do you call him heretic?" And Rachel asked, "What is his crime?" The Sheik shouted, "You are rebellious, you miserable widow; have you forgotten the fate of your husband who turned rebel six years ago?" Upon hearing these impulsive words, Rachel shivered with painful anger, for she had found the murderer of her husband. She choked her tears and looked upon the throng and cried out, "Here is the criminal you have been trying for six years to find; you hear him now confessing his guilt. He is the killer who has been hiding his crime. Look at him and read his face; study him well and observe his fright; he shivers like the last leaf on winter's tree. God has shown you that the Master whom you have always feared is a murderous criminal. He caused me to be a widow amongst these women, and my daughter an orphan amidst these children." Rachel's utterance fell like thunder upon the Sheik's head, and the uproar of men and exaltation of women fell like firebrands upon him.

The priest assisted the Sheik to his seat. Then he called the servants and ordered them saying, "Arrest this woman who has falsely accused your Master of killing her husband; drag her and this young man into a dark prison, and any who oppose you will be criminals, excommunicated as he was from the Holy Church." The servants gave no heed to his command, but remained motionless staring at Khalil who was still bound with rope. Rachel stood at his right and Miriam at his left like a pair of wings ready to soar aloft into the spacious sky of Freedom.

His beard shaking with anger, Father Elias said, "Are you denying your Master for the sake of an infidel criminal and a shameless adulteress?" And the oldest one of the servants answered him saying, "We have served Sheik Abbas long for bread and shelter, but we have never been his slaves." Having thus spoken, the servant took off his cloak and turban and threw them before the Sheik and added, "I shall no longer require this raiment, nor do I wish my soul to suffer in the narrow house of a criminal." And all the servants did likewise and joined the crowd whose faces radiated with joy, symbol of Freedom and Truth. Father Elias finally saw that his authority had declined, and left the place cursing the hour that brought Khalil to the village. A strong man strode to Khalil and untied his hands, looked at Sheik Abbas who fell like a corpse upon his seat, and boldly addressed him saying, "This fettered youth, whom you have brought here tonight to be tried as a criminal, has lifted our depressed spirits and enlightened our hearts with Truth and Knowledge. And this poor widow whom Father Elias referred to as a false accuser has revealed to us the crime you committed six years past. We came here tonight to witness the trial of an innocent youth and a noble soul. Now, heaven has opened our eyes and has shown us your atrocity; we shall leave you and ignore you and allow heaven to do its will."

Many voices were raised in that hall, and one could hear a certain man saying, "Let us leave this ill-famed residence for our homes." And another one remarking, "Let us follow this young man to Rachel's home and listen to his wise sayings and consoling wisdom." And a third one saying, "Let us seek his advice, for he knows our needs." And a fourth one calling out, "If we are seeking justice, let us complain to the Emir and tell him of Abbas' crime." And many were saying, "Let us petition the Emir to appoint Khalil as our Master and ruler, and tell the Bishop that Father Elias was a partner in these crimes." While the voices were rising and falling upon the Sheik's ears like sharp arrows, Khalil lifted his hands and calmed the villagers saying, "My brethren, do not seek haste, but rather listen and meditate. I ask you, in the name of my love and friendship for you, not to go to the Emir, for you will not find justice. Remember that a ferocious beast does not snap another one like him, neither should you go to the Bishop, for he knows well that the house cloven amid itself shall be ruined. Do not ask the Emir to appoint me as the Sheik in this village, for the faithful servant does not like to be an aid to the evil Master. If I deserve your kindness and love, let me live amongst you and share with you the happiness and sorrows of Life. Let me join hands and work with you at home and in the fields, for if I could not make myself one of you, I would be a hypocrite who does not live according to his sermon. And now, as the axe is laid unto the root of the tree, let us leave Sheik Abbas alone in the courtroom of his conscience and before the Supreme Court of God whose sun shines upon the innocent and the criminal."

Having thus spoken, he left the place, and the multitude followed him as if there were a divine power in him that attracted their hearts. The Sheik remained alone with the terrible silence, like a destroyed tower, suffering his defeat quietly like a surrendering commander. When the multitude reached the church yard and the moon was just showing from behind the cloud, Khalil looked at them with the eyes of love like a good shepherd watching over his herd. He was moved with sympathy upon these villagers who symbolized an oppressed nation; and he stood like a prophet who saw all the nations of the East walking in those valleys and dragging empty souls and heavy hearts.

He raised both hands toward heaven and said, "From the bottom of these depths we call thee, Oh, Liberty. Give heed to us! From behind the darkness we raise our hands to thee, Oh, Liberty. Look upon us! Upon the snow, we worship before thee, Oh, Liberty. Have mercy on us! Before thy great throne we stand, hanging on our bodies the blood-stained garments of our forefathers, covering our heads with the dust of the graves mixed with their remains, carrying the swords that stabbed their hearts, lifting the spears that pierced their bodies, dragging the chains that slowed their feet, uttering the cry that wounded their throats, lamenting and repeating the song of our failure that echoed throughout the prison, and repeating the prayers that came from the depths of our fathers' hearts. Listen to us, Oh, Liberty, and hear us. From the Nile to the Euphrates comes the wailing of the suffering souls, in unison with the cry of the abyss; and from the end of the East to the mountains of Lebanon, hands are stretched to you, trembling with the presence of Death. From the shores of the sea to the end of the desert, tear-flooded eyes look beseechingly toward you. Come, Oh Liberty, and save us.

"In the wretched huts standing in the shadow of poverty and oppression, they beat at their bosoms, soliciting thy mercy; watch us, Oh Liberty, and have mercy on us. In the pathways and in the houses miserable youth calls thee; in the churches and the mosques, the forgotten Book turns to thee; in the courts and in the palaces the neglected Law appeals to thee. Have mercy on us, Oh Liberty, and save us. In our narrow streets the merchant sells his days in order to make tribute to the exploiting thieves of the West, and none would give him advice. In the barren fields the fellah tills the soil and sows the seeds of his heart and nourishes them with his tears, but he reaps naught except thorns, and none would teach him the true path. In our arid plains the Bedouin roams barefoot and hungry, but none would have mercy upon him; speak, Oh Liberty, and teach us! Our sick lambs are grazing upon the grassless prairie, our calves are gnawing on the roots of the trees, and our horses are feeding on dry plants. Come, Oh Liberty, and help us. We have been living in darkness since the beginning, and like prisoners they take us from one prison to another, while time ridicules our plight. When will dawn come? Until when shall we bear the scorn of the ages? Many a stone have we been dragging, and many a yoke has been placed upon our necks. Until when shall we bear this human outrage? The Egyptian slavery, the Babylon exile, the tyranny of Persia, the despotism of the Romans, and the greed of Europe... all these things have we suffered. Where are we going now, and when shall we reach the sublime end of the rough roadway? From the clutches of Pharaoh to the paws of Nebuchadnezzar, to the iron hands of Alexander, to the swords of Herod, to the talons of Nero, and the sharp teeth of Demon... into whose hands are we now to fall, and when will Death come and take us, so we may rest at last?

"With the strength of our arms we lifted the columns of the temple, and upon our backs we carried the mortar to build the great walls and the impregnable pyramids for the sake of glory. Until when shall we continue building such magnificent palaces and living in wretched huts? Until when shall we continue filling the bins of the rich with provisions, while sustaining weak life on dry morsels? Until when shall we continue weaving silk and wool for our lords and masters while we wear naught except tattered swaddles?

"Through their wickedness we were divided amongst ourselves; and the better to keep their thrones and be at ease, they armed the Druze to fight the Arab, and stirred up the Shiite to attack the Sunnite, and encouraged the Kurdish to butcher the Bedouin, and cheered the Mohammedan to dispute with the Christian. Until when shall a brother continue killing his own brother upon his mother's bosom? Until when shall the Cross be kept apart from the Crescent before the eyes of God? Oh Liberty, hear us, and speak in behalf of but one individual, for a great fire is started with a small spark. Oh Liberty, awaken but one heart with the rustling of thy wings, for from one cloud alone comes the lightning which illuminates the pits of the valleys and the tops of the mountains. Disperse with thy power these black clouds and descend like thunder and destroy the thrones that were built upon the bones and skulls of our ancestors."

"Hear us, Oh Liberty; Bring mercy, Oh Daughter of Athens; Rescue us, Oh Sister of Rome; Advise us, Oh Companion of Moses; Help us, Oh Beloved of Mohammed; Teach us, Oh Bride of Jesus; Strengthen our hearts so we may live; Or harden our enemies so we may perish And live in peace eternally."

As Khalil was pouring forth his sentiment before heaven, the villagers were gazing at him in reverence, and their love was springing forth in unison with the song of his voice until they felt that he became part of their hearts. After a short silence, Khalil brought his eyes upon the multitude and quietly said, "Night has brought us to the house of Sheik Abbas in order to realize the daylight; oppression has arrested us before the cold Space, so we may understand one another and gather like chicks under the wings of the Eternal Spirit. Now let us go to our homes and sleep until we meet again tomorrow."

Having thus spoken, he walked away, following Rachel and Miriam to their poor hovel. The throng departed and each went to his home, contemplating what he had seen and heard this memorable night. They felt that a burning torch of a new spirit had scoured their inner selves and led them into the right path. In an hour all the lamps were extinguished and Silence engulfed the whole village while Slumber carried the fellahin's souls into the world of strong dreams; but Sheik Abbas found no sleep all night, as he watched the phantoms of darkness and the horrible ghosts of his crimes in procession.

Two months had already passed and Khalil was still preaching and pouring his sentiments in the villagers' hearts, reminding them of their usurped rights and showing them the greed and oppression of the rulers and the monks. They listened to him with care for he was a source of pleasure; his words fell upon their hearts like rain upon thirsty land. In their solitude, they repeated Khalil's sayings as they did their daily prayers. Father Elias commenced fawning upon them to regain their friendship; he became docile since the villagers found out that he was the Sheik's ally in crime, and the fellahin ignored him.

Sheik Abbas had a nervous suffering, and walked through his mansion like a caged tiger. He issued commands to his servants, but no one answered except the echo of his voice inside the marble walls. He shouted at his men, but no one came to his aid except his poor wife who suffered the pang of his cruelty as much as the villagers did. When Lent came and Heaven announced the coming of Spring, the days of the Sheik expired with the passing of Winter. He died after a long agony, and his soul was carried away on the carpet of his deeds to stand naked and shivering before that high Throne whose existence we feel, but cannot see. The fellahin heard various tales about the manner of Sheik Abbas' death; some of them related that the Sheik died insane, while others insisted that disappointment and despair drove him to death by his own hand. But the women who went to offer their sympathies to his wife reported that he died from fear, because the ghost of Samaan Ramy hunted him and drove him every midnight out to the place where Rachel's husband was found slain six years before.

The month of Nisan proclaimed to the villagers the love secrets of Khalil and Miriam. They rejoiced the good tidings which assured them that Khalil would thereby remain in their village. As the news reached all the inhabitants of the huts, they congratulated one another upon Khalil's becoming their beloved neighbour.

When harvest time came, the fellahin went to the fields and gathered the sheaves of corn and bundles of wheat to the threshing floor. Sheik Abbas was not there to take the crop and have it carried to his bins. Each fellah harvested his own crop; the villagers' huts were filled with good wine and corn; their vessels were replenished with good wine and oil. Khalil shared with them their toils and happiness; he helped them in gathering the crop, pressing the grapes and picking the fruits. He never distinguished himself from any one of them except by his excess of love and ambition. Since that year and up to our present time, each fellah in that village commenced to reap with joy the crop which he sowed with toil and labour. The land which the fellahin tilled and the vineyards they cultivated became their own property.

Now, half a century has passed since this incident, and the Lebanese have awakened.

On his way to the Holy Cedars of Lebanon, a traveller's attention is caught by the beauty of that village, standing like a bride at the side of the valley. The wretched huts are now comfortable and happy homes surrounded by fertile fields and blooming orchards. If you ask any one of the residents about Sheik Abbas' history, he will answer you, pointing with his finger to a heap of demolished stones and destroyed walls saying, "This is the Sheik's palace, and this is the history of his life." And if you inquire about Khalil, he will raise his hand toward heaven saying, "There resides our beloved Khalil, whose life's history was written by God with glittering letters upon the pages of our hearts, and they cannot be effaced by the ages."

www.ingramcontent.com/pod-product-compliance
Lightning Source LLC
LaVergne TN
LVHW091615070526
838199LV00044B/808